"Mapping"

Gifts from the Maps of Master Therapists

A
Course in the Theoretical
Foundation for Being an Eclectic
Practitioner

By
Wilton L. Hellams, Ph.D., LPC-S, NBCCH,
DAPA
&
Tobias S. Schreiber, M.A., LPC-S, CTS,
NBCCH, NCC

Published by Eclectic-Therapy Press
Moore, South Carolina

For information write to:
Eclectic-Therapy Press
274 Summerfield Road
Moore, South Carolina 29369

ISBN# 978-0-6151-4148-0

Editing and Typing by
Laine F. Schreiber and Roberta Hellams

Manuscript Review
N.C. Jacobs, LPC
Andrew Graham, M.A. LPC

Cover Art & Artistic Drawings
4 & 5: Laura Franklin, LPC-I

Cover Graphics
Rodney Wilson & Christina S. Wilson

Personal Acknowledgements

We, the authors, have many important people to thank, but most particularly our families for their love, support, and encouragement.

I, Wilton, want to extend to Dr. W. L. and Mrs. Beatrice Hellams my undying gratitude for the many personal and financial supports they offered in furthering my education and training, which certainly led to the development of this work, and especially to my mother, Beatrice, for her on-going support of my interest in research in hypnotic and trance phenomena, which started for me at seventeen years of age.

To my wife Roberta for the hours of support, operating as a sounding board, and lending her clerical skills to the production of this work.

To Laine Schreiber for the many hours of technical service and editing.

To my good friend and computer guru, Woody Dixon, for the many hours of discussion of philosophy and the relation to the nature of programming as it exists within a computer.

I would be more than remiss in not acknowledging the countless hours of clinical and professional supervision that I enjoyed from Dr. Linda Moore who served as my mentor and clinical supervisor for years.

To my late, great friend, Dr. Joseph Gilbert, who gave me many advantages from the initial training I received in Stekel's Ego Psychology, carrying me with him into his own version of Ericksonian hypnotherapy.

I am most appreciative of the numerous conversations, debates, and encouragements regarding the nature of ego that occurred in the summer of 1975 with English Morris. This certainly served as a beginning catalyst to challenge the concept of ego structure in my mind.

Profound personal gratitude to the technical readers, members of the focus group, and reviewers of the manuscript for this work for their kind support and encouragement of the continuance of writing and development.

Last, but certainly not least, to Drs. R. Bowersock, R. Deysach, F. O'Toole, and J. Joiner for the encouragement and educational experiences provided through and by them over the years.

I, Tobias, would like to acknowledge Herbert Schreiber, M.D. and Gladys Gaskin Schreiber who instilled in me a curiosity about life, a love for reading and learning, and a compassion for our existence. To Wilton and Roberta Hellams for their tireless efforts and friendship.

To my wife and life partner, Laine Schreiber, who has been an encouragement and inspiration during this challenging endeavor. She is able to have the patience to keep the writing and typing on track. She has challenged my thinking and helped me to achieve greater clarity.

To my children, Christina Schreiber Wilson, her husband, Rodney Wilson, Marie Schreiber, Joshua Tobias Schreiber, Brad Smothers, his wife, Angie, Joy Elaine Allen and her husband, David, and Chris Hankins and his wife, Donna, and of course our 13 grandchildren, Josh, Jacob, Nicholas, Jamie, Heather, Christa, Skyler, Tyler, Landon, Zoë, Callie,

Aeden and Owen, who inspire us to fight for freedom and wisdom for all people.

To all the individuals that have shared their stories and lives with me. They have pushed me to search for better means to assist others and myself to discover the pathless path of truth.

To Chrys Harris, Ph.D., LPC, LMFT for his efforts to encourage and lift the standards of counseling and trauma work in South Carolina and the world.

To Yvonne Dolan, M.A. for her compassion and courage to develop Ericksonian and solution focused therapies to a level that we all find a Path with a heart.

To R. Reid Wilson, you opened my eyes and mind to strategic psychotherapy, Ericksonian hypnosis and to the possibilities in my life.

To my brother, Stephen Wolinsky, Ph.D., who was able to bring me back to my essence in the search for myself. The discovery of his book "Trances People Live" began a marvelous journey through his writings, trainings, and personal conversations, which continue to be a daily inspiration.

To Sri Nisargadatta Maharaj, whose words find their mark, there are no words.

Professional Acknowledgments

There are many influences that shape our thoughts and that have gone into the writings in this book. These influences are of course our interpretation of these interactions and their meanings as will be the imagined meanings you will take from reading and utilizing these mappings. There are several professional colleagues to thank, R. Reid Wilson, Stephen Wolinsky, Yvonne Dolan, M.A., Ron Klein, CAAC, NBCCH. I greatly appreciate the influence of Sri Nisargadatta Maharaj through his teaching and the writings of his teaching and the teachings of those who have given interpretations of his teachings. Milton H. Erickson for his life, teachings, and the various interpretations of his teachings by those to seeking to emulate, interpret, and expand his work. We acknowledge Bandler and Grinder for their attempts to model and explain Milton Erickson, M.D., in addition, their subsequent development of Neuro-Linguistic Programming. We appreciate the foresight of Steve Andreas for his pioneering work in Gestalt therapy, his developments in NLP and Real People Press for publishing new works. We want to add thanks to several trainers: Norma and Philip Barretta, Bill O'Hanlan, Betty Alice Erickson, Francine Shapiro, Aaron Beck, M.D., David Burns, M.D. and Bruce Zahn. We also want to thank Linda Leech, Ph.D., LPC and John Holcomb, MRC, LPC for their courage and efforts to raise the standards for counselors. They are at The Medical University of South Carolina, in the Rehabilitation Counseling Program.

We would especially like to thank our focus group participants and our readers. They have been invaluable as far as their feedback and encouragement. The participants were as follows:

Dayle Allen, M.A., LPC
Sunil Bhatia, M.D.
Angela Brady, M.S., LPC
Jennette Brien, M.A., LPC-Intern
Joyce Callis, Ed.S, LMFT
Pete Camelo, M.S., LPC
Angie Carter, M.Ed., LPC-Intern, CACP
Marta F. Cothran, MSW, LMSW
Phyllis Cox, M. A., LPC
Daniel Craft, Ph.D., LPC
Jack Crawford, MS.S, LPC, Private Practice
David Dunbar, Ph.D., LPC, Private Practice
Susan Campbell-Duncan, M.D.
Debbie Durham, M.Ed. LPC
Patricia Edwards, M.A., LPC-Supervisor, LMSW
Kim Finucan, M.A., LPC
Laura Franklin, M.Ed., LPC-Intern
Linda Graddy, M.Ed., LPC-Intern
Andrew Graham, M.A., LPC
Michael Gravley, M.Ed., LPC-Intern
Amanda Hood, MSW, LISW-CP
Leslie Hull-Kimball, MSW, LISW-CP
Linda Hutton, MSW, LISW-CP-BCD
N. C. Jacobs, M.A., LPC
Shannon Johnson, MSW
Sabrina Sims-Kredich, MSW, LMSW
Deann McAtee, MSW, LISW-CP
William Mulkey, M.A., LPC-Intern
Kevin Pitts, M.Ed., LPC-Intern
Barbara Robinson, M.A., LPC- Intern
Victoria Tate, M.A., LPC
Shirley Thompson, M.Ed., LPC
Gwen Vinson, M.A., LPC-Intern, CACII
Shauna Galloway-Williams, M.Ed., LPC
Gregory Wright, M.A., LPC

Chapter Outline

Introduction

Your mission, should you choose to accept it, is to boldly go where no person has gone before. No, not to space, for space is not the final frontier, but seek the origin of space and time which is consciousness. In similar manner to Luke Skywalker when he was being trained by the Jedi Master Yoda, to be free, you must "unlearn that which you have learned," (Star Wars, 1980).

The writer John opined, "And ye shall know the truth, and the truth shall make you free" (John 8:32).

The rogue Indian saint Sri Nisargadatta Maharaj instructed, "Everything you know about yourself came from outside of you. Discard it." Abandon false ideas. That is all. There is no need of true ideas. There aren't any.

"Reality is not a concept, nor the manifestation of a concept. It has nothing to do with concepts. Concern yourself with your mind. Remove its distortions and impurities." The search for truth is the most dangerous of all for it will destroy the world in which you live.

"Memory of pleasure creates desire, while memory of pain creates fear; both make the mind restless." Sri Nisargadatta Maharaj (*I Am That*, 1973).

As *Eclectic* Therapists, we are urging you to be free from maps based on ignorance, illusions, and programming errors.

Learning to use the map is just a metaphor for the ability to become aware that your mappings are all stories and imaginings. Moving beyond the illusions allows you the freedom to be present, notice the sensory experience, and to become aware of the programming that alters your perceptions and reactions so that you can act rather than react. You become aware that you are not experiencing what is real. You are experiencing an abstracted version of what is and even worse, you experience it through the interpretations of others.

Therefore, as you begin your adventure as an *Eclectic* Therapist, we are sharing with you a guide to reading maps. *We have gleaned the information for this course from our years of working with and training therapists who saw themselves as Eclectic Practitioners.* At best, this is a map without the illusion that it is the "truth" or the "only" map. This is an encouragement to become aware. Be warned that as you absorb this way of thinking, it consumes all other ways of thinking. You may find yourself, your view of yourself, and your world changing. You may even find yourself experiencing physiological changes, as the body is a biological system, and changes in thinking equal changes in biology. Although most of us would like a linear map, this version, as with most accurate versions is non-linear. This map has come from trainings, therapy sessions, study groups, life experiences, readings, and many other sources. You will notice, as the blinders drop from your eyes, new vision requires an accommodation.

The Eclectic Therapist

The development of a theoretical foundation for the *Eclectic* Therapist came about from the interaction of three major efforts. 1. Tobias S. Schreiber was seeking to explain and define the continuum of sensory perception and its alterations or *trance* states within the sensory perceptive world of the individual. 2. Wilton Hellams was seeking to explain the mechanism behind cognitive *dissonance*. 3. Hellams and Schreiber were conducting a Meta Analysis of effective therapeutic methods by reviewing the works found in effective schools of therapy and isolating the most salient principles of change. These efforts led to the development of a unified system, giving a theoretical foundation for the E*clectic* Practitioner, as they sought to develop therapeutic interventions for the clients they were serving.

As a well-trained composer with a complete grasp of music and its theory creates a masterpiece for any occasion by selecting from the vast repertoire of musical traditions and schools, the *Eclectic* Therapist weaves the most effective treatment by selecting from a myriad of therapeutic approaches based upon an understanding of a unifying theoretical foundation for effective therapy. From this theoretical foundation, a creed developed which for the first time establishes guidelines and benchmarks for *Eclectic* Therapists to practice their art and join in a unified field of study.

Postulates for the Creed of the Eclectic Therapist

The following are postulates, which are interwoven into the *Eclectic* Therapist's mapping system, which are based on the best information available to the therapist now. As the *Eclectic* Therapist is always attempting alignment, with the territory and the mapping system of the client, the therapist's map remains open to updating. The therapist's map is subject to change as it is better informed by interaction with the territory and the client.

• We find for the most part that all forms of effective psychotherapy utilize certain common principles. These are true except when they are not. The map represents the territory, but it is not the territory. In other words, congruency and re-alignment is an ongoing process.

• All effective therapy is biological. Therefore, changes in thinking, feeling, believing, expressing, or behaving create biological change and results from biological change.

• Effective therapy involves a connection between one individual (the therapist) and some inner resources within the other individual (the client). Therapy is a biological interaction.

• Effective therapy involves interruption/deconstruction of territorially incongruent *sensory perceptive alteration* states (*trance*) and the construction or alignment and replacement of territorially congruent sensory states.

• Effective therapy, either directly or indirectly, involves the rearranging and updating of biologically encoded programming to bring about a change.

• Effective therapy addresses two phases of intervention, (1) acceptance by the organism of the intervention, and (2) change of the encoded programming once the intervention has been accepted.

• Effective therapists recognize a *homeostatic* function/status quo tendency of the organism. Every individual is attempting to stay in balance with the flow of energy in the river of life. Mapping directs the navigation and *homeostasis* is the gyroscope.

• Effective therapists are respectful of the *homeostatic* system of both the therapist and the client. This means there is respect for the *mapping system* of each. Maps are neither right nor wrong. They are attempts to assimilate sensory data (stimulation) within the individual's ability to sense, interpret, and integrate the flow within its existing mapping system.

• All therapies are maps to the territory of the client's world, but the effective therapist's map is recognized as a map and not the actual territory. Awareness allows an individual to recognize that maps are biological, abstract representations of the experiencing of life's movement.

• Effective therapists recognize the organism's need for closure to reduce or eliminate vacuums in the client's knowledge of the world. The Completion or *Gestalt closure error* is a naturally occurring attempt by the individual to locate him self within energy, mass, and space-time. Within the internal holographic representation of the experiential world, the individual attempts to know, predict, and control outcomes and thereby survive. Different scenarios are created, offered, and played out in the Nervous System's efforts to survive.

• Effective therapists recognize that the organism is one unit. Further, there is recognition that the establishment of the concept of mind and body are artificial contrivances, not a representation of the true nature of the client or the client's experience.

• Effective therapists are cognizant of the organism's resistance to change. The nervous system deals with change by filtering, modifying, and otherwise distorting incoming sensory data that is not consistent with the basic, pre-existing programming of the organism developed during the ongoing *socialization* period. Biological variance is dealt with by attempts to stay balanced. The map is also the biology's effort to represent its interaction and its changes within its appearance and disappearance.

• Effective therapists recognize that according to Quantum Physics being here and not here occurs approximately 14 times per second. The therapists recognize and respect the organism's response to the changing nature of reality. The organism resists the void by s*ensory perceptive mapping.*

• Effective therapists generally follow a principle of requisite variety. Greater flexibility generally means adaptation that is more effective.

• In effective therapists' maps, the organism and its environment are one and are represented in that way. The various aspects of the client's *sensory perceptive map* include all aspects of the client's world including the known and unknown parts.

• Effective therapists recognize that communication by the organism is biological and includes both verbal and nonverbal expressions from the organism's map.

• All effective *Eclectic* Therapists utilize best practice principles and stay within their areas of expertise and training.

Key Terms

1. Cognitive Programming:

Any information housed in the *neural information centers* and thus part of the *sensory perceptive holographic mapping, system.* This information can be accurate or inaccurate.

2. Cognitive Programming Errors:

Misinformation encoded into the *neural information centers* of the organism that is incongruent with the reality of the environment of the organism. This misinformation, consequently, leads to dysfunctional *SPA* (*trance*) states.

3. Congruent Cognitive Programming:

Programming that leads to congruent *SPA* states and therefore facilitates congruent interaction between the organism and the environment.

4. Descartes' Error:

Descartes' Error is dividing the mind/body into various parts as if it were separated into mind and body. This further leads to a division of thought and feelings, which then leads to the argument and debate over primacy, origination, and causation.

5.   Dissonance:

Dissonance is the state created when the accepted pool of programming stored in the biology is threatened by incoming information or shifts in information and thereby threatens a disturbance of the biology of the organism. Cognitive *dissonance* as it has been defined is a smaller subset of this larger action.

6.   Eclectic:

Being *eclectic* means to gather from or, to select from various doctrines or methods, choosing what appears to be the best from among the various doctrines, methods, or styles.   *Eclectic* is composed of elements drawn from various sources, also heterogeneous (*Merriam-Webster Online Dictionary*).

7.   Gestalt Closure Errors:

The tendency of the mapping system of the organism to seek closure where there is a deficit, incomplete stimulus, or information available to make a decision or render a judgment is called *Gestalt closure*.   This creates confabulatory errors, which are the merging of actual sensory stimuli with internally generated material.

8.   Homeostasis:

Homeostasis is a description of the ongoing mechanism that attempts to maintain sameness within the biological system. It does not involve a decision of right or wrong; good or bad, but simply is about maintaining the status quo. Thought as a biological process is part of the biological system.

9.   Neural Information Center:

This component is part programming, part electro-chemical, and involves both afferent and efferent pathways. In other words, this unit is a hybrid of the *neural information centers* mapping and biology that sends instruction and directs programming into the physiology of the organism, as well as receives feedback from the physiological responses of the organism and movement back into the center. The information within a particular *neural information center* and cluster of *neural information centers* is responsible for directing the various *SPA trance* experiences. It is therefore understood that these are the basic building blocks of the *sensory perceptive mapping system* of the organism.

10.   Persistent Patterns of Trance Clusters:

Persistent patterns which create the illusion of identity formed by the overlapping of *sensory perceptive alteration* states that are present and largely predictable, in a particular organism. These patterns are idiosyncratic in nature. These apparently predictable patterns are relatively stable but are impacted by variations in stimuli coming from within the biological organism and from the external environment.

11.   Semantic Reversal Mechanism:

This mechanism is part of the *homeostatic* system designed to protect the map. Its function is to neutralize incoming information that threatens *dissonance* to the organism. *Semantic reversal mechanisms* involve semantic alterations of the incoming stimuli, such as the addition of "not," inclusion of "yes, but" formulations, and pseudo-logical argumentations. Further, neutralization effects can be visual with images that attempt to counter the incoming threatening information.

12. Sensory Perceptive Holographic Mapping:

Mapping is a multi-sensorial, multi-dimensional, interactive, navigational system, which directs the organism's interactions with the environment both internally and externally. Contained within this mapping system is the flight/fight/freeze mechanism, as well as a completion mechanism. The mapping is balanced by *homeostasis*.

13. Socialization:

Socialization is an ongoing, interactive mapping process whereby the individual continues to adjust his programming in response to the programming of those in his environment. This obviously can influence pre-existing programming. As Alfred Korzybski reminds us, "The Map is not the territory." *Socialization* can lead to congruent or highly incongruent programming.

14. Trance:

Sensory perceptive alteration "SPA" is an integral function of *homeostasis* and dictated by the *sensory perceptive mapping* and the *neural information centers* that construct that map. *SPA* is a state (or series of states) that edits the sensory stimulus to be consistent with the *neural information center* programming already existing.

15. Trauma:

The state which occurs when information or stimuli entering the organism is not assimilated, accommodated, or synthesized into the *sensory mapping system*, thereby causing a response from the *homeostatic* defense mechanism. Attempts to contain the unassimilated, neural information can result in Post-traumatic Stress Disorder symptoms, such as flashbacks, intrusive memories, and emotional fluctuations.

The following is an example of a mental health counseling intern becoming oriented and being instructed in the methodology of this model. Through metaphor, the intern is introduced to the basic building blocks of: *dissonance, homeostasis, cognitive programming errors, sensory perceptive alteration* (hypnotic *trance* phenomena), *semantic reversal mechanism, sensory perceptive holographic mapping, Gestalt closure errors, and persistent patterns of trance clusters, trance deconstruction, and reconstruction.*

An Overview

*J*anice, you are here today with some questions about the theoretical model for being an *Eclectic* Therapist. In order to answer these questions fully, we need to give you a little bit of background and theoretical understanding. As a mental health-counseling intern, you have a great interest in human behavior and problem solving. I think you will find that our overall theoretical model fits together very well.

I would like you to imagine that there is a very benevolent king, and the people in his kingdom are very happy with him. The people in the kingdom like the way that he runs the kingdom. They like the way that he provides jobs, provides law and order, and dispenses justice. Overall, they are very "happy campers." The king sees over into another kingdom, and there he sees that there is another king on the throne who is not a bad person, but is a ruler who is misled and operates under many distortions. This misled king sees the world in a markedly different way, his consensus of reality being

1

different from that of most. In other words, his reality is skewed. His view of the world is awkward. As a result, the villagers he rules over also share a skewed and awkward reality, from the soldiers who defend the gates, down to the miller who grinds the grain. The distortions of the misled king have infected them all. The benevolent king knows through his scouts that the misled king is ultimately a threat to him. He can see that the neighboring kingdom is about ready to explode into civil unrest due to the distortions and warring within. He decides he will send his knights out to take a message of intervention and an offer of help in an attempt to form communication. The knights from the benevolent king arrive on horseback, and they approach the city gates. The people inside the walls see the knights are not like them. They dress differently. They ride different kinds of horses. They have different kinds of armor. They wear and carry different banners. The people quickly rally in defense and begin to hurl stones at the knights as they approach. They fail to listen to the cries and pleas of the knights, shouting, "We are friendly; we have come to help; we have come to assist." Their orders are to cause no harm, so the somewhat battered knights turn and leave. They go back and seek the audience of the benevolent king. The benevolent king is very, very frustrated. He realizes that in the kingdom there is civil unrest that soon may cook over and threaten his own kingdom. He worries he may have to use brute force to subdue the misled kingdom. He summons the wise man. The wise man comes. The wise man listens to what the knights, scouts, historian, and the king have to say. He listens also, to what the people in the kingdom say. They have learned from their interchanges over time with the distant kingdom that is threatened with unrest. He notes from his peoples' accounts that although stones immediately rebuffed the benevolent knights his people tell of a time when travelers were welcomed through the walls of the now conflicted kingdom to exchange goods and seek respite on long journeys. Sometimes they even settled in the kingdom.

"Umm," the wise man thinks. He goes to the king, and he says the following: "Oh King, this may take some time, but not as long as you might think. I can allow myself a long period or a short period, as such a period as necessary in order to be accepted into the other kingdom. Allow me to go with the knights dressed as I dictate they dress, knights acting as I direct that they act, carrying what I suggest that they carry, and with the knights fully under my orders and command to go with me to the kingdom."

The benevolent king who loves his knights, loves his wise man, and loves his people, looks in horror at the wise man and says, "They have thrown rocks at fully armed knights. They have thrown rocks at people who have been clearly identified as messengers. They have attacked us for no reason at all, just for approaching their gates. I fear what will happen if you lead knights to the walls of the castle to overtake it if they are not fully equipped and are without standard military garb and armor and are not following standard military strategies that have been proven effective." The wise man said, "Oh great King, trust me."

The king reluctantly grants the wise man his wishes. The wise man then summons the knights. The knights are instructed to dress exactly as the wise man dictates. The wise man and the knights dress according to the descriptions they have heard from travelers of how the people dress who are inside the walled city. Instead of riding on fine horses, they ride on pack animals that are more suitable to what the people in the village are accustomed to. In addition, instead of riding directly in a straight line from the kingdom from which they are from, they make a short detour to some nearby mountains and then form a straight line of approach, coming at a different angle to the castle than they would normally have come. The knights approach the castle, but instead of seeking entrance into the castle, they set up camp outside the walls. There they camp, they listen, and they form songs around their campfire like the songs they hear from inside the walled city. In order to be overheard, they very loudly tell jokes and discuss topics as though with great interest, based on what they have heard from travelers, and what they can hear through the walls that the people inside discuss.

Well, the king of the walled city-state gets news of these travelers and he sends spies to search them out.

They go back and they say, "Oh, King. They look like us. They act like us. They build fires like us. And they seem to share common concerns and topics with us."

The king can be heard to give a loud sigh and say, "I thought they were here to attack us. Please send out some of our soldiers and invite them to our banquet."

The large, thick, heavily defended gates of the city-state crack open. The soldiers go out. In the friendliest manner that can be mustered, they invite the "campers" into the city. There, the "campers" attend the banquet. There the "campers" are invited to stay. The "campers" begin to mirror, model, reflect and engage in the behaviors of the people, from the miller, to the advisors, to the king. The "campers" are so accepted, their new ideas are gradually and sometimes rather abruptly accepted because they are seen as no threat. They are simply accepted. They are seen as "part of the organism" of the city-state.

As the months roll by, they rise in power and importance to different levels of status within industry and commerce, becoming a most valuable part of the walled city-state. The wise man even rises in rank and becomes an advisor to the king, always asserting, and always being true to the assertion that he will respect and honor the king and the people who have invited him in. Eventually, given this new blood and this new influence, the kingdom begins to achieve a balance.

There is communication going on now that is flowing smoothly between the different parts, factions, and centers within this city-state. Overall unrest is almost non-existent. Oh, there is the occasional friction between this group that has not communicated well with that group. Yet with the facilitation of the "campers," their common needs and interests are met. After all, their over-riding interest is preserving the city-state.

Eventually, the wise men of the city, the advisors who were once campers, and the original residents who have now come to be more alike, invite the benevolent king from the distant kingdom to join with them in a massive celebration.

It is said that if you go to this part of the world today, you will find two kingdoms who almost act as one. They frequently understand each other. They agree to disagree. In addition, they work for the good of all.

Homeostasis

If you consider what goes on with us everyday, Janice, you know that if you go out on a brisk or even cold day like we sometimes experience in these damp parts, and you have not taken your sweater, you will begin to shiver. Moreover, you know that the reason you shiver is your muscles are beginning to move and your muscle fibers are beginning to operate in a way to produce and raise your body heat. Now it is not that your body and certainly not your muscles make a decision and say, "Hmm, I wonder if it's good to be this way, or that way." What happens is the force science calls *"homeostasis,"* whereby the organism notices and resists change is occurring. Change is seen as undesirable to the organism. The body seeks to neutralize, modify, or mitigate the change so that the organism can swing back to the way that it was. We know that this exists with all major life forms on this planet. In addition, we see this even with the single cell. Change the organism, and the organism will begin to change in order to mitigate the outside change and bring conditions back to the way they were.

Another mechanism of the body is rejection. Physical rejection in human body or any other complex organism occurs when the cells rally together to reject something that the body senses "is not suppose to be there." A splinter enters the skin, and immediately it is detected as a foreign object. It is not that the body makes a value judgment of whether it is a moral or immoral act. There is no weighing of value systems. What is weighed is if this thing is different from the existing pool of tissue called the human body. When this has been determined, then the body begins to react. There are certain physiological changes that occur, and there is an attempt to drive out/encapsulate/neutralize/mitigate/destroy/dissolve the invader. We know this process goes on and on many times a day. Individuals on this planet have been exposed numerous times to tuberculosis bacilli. However, very few people whose bodies are intact and whose health is not compromised, will contract this disease. The body recognizes that this small organism is alien to it. It begins to wall it off and attack it by the on-going immune system, and thereby keeps the body healthy.

There are, times, however, when this same system, this *homeostasis*, proves not to be beneficial. Suppose someone goes to his physician, and then is referred to a series of specialists where it is determined that the heart muscle is worn and diseased. In short, the coronary unit is soon to cease functioning, and thus is the life of the human who depends upon it. It is recommended that immediately a similar tissue match be searched for, and the individual receive a heart transplant. Eventually a suitable donor is found. The expertise of the surgical team is applied, and the new, healthy heart is installed. The old removed; however, we know that unless something happens to interrupt the *homeostasis* of this human body, although this is a beneficial change, the body will destroy the heart, not because the heart is bad, not because the heart is good, but just because the heart is different.

For years, as a therapist I would frequently use hypnotic applications, practicing more or less classical hypnosis. Sometimes the suggestions given would be taken and would work remarkably well. At other times, the suggestions offered would be rebuffed, and sometimes in a very dramatic fashion. I was working with a man who had lost several toes in a woodcutting accident and had come to me for pain control. He was reporting tremendous pain coming from the damaged area. However, in the opinion of the supervising healthcare team, the pain was inordinate in terms of the severity of the wound. It is also important to note that this individual, although he had been assured that there was a high probability he would receive disability, still held in doubt that he would receive compensation. I began to do a hypnotic set of inductions with him in which we would do glove anesthesia. We would create other feeling distortions, such as the whole body floating sensation. We would engage in dissociative phenomena in which the client very readily went into what was then termed a "deep state of *trance*" whereby he could observe himself from a distance. In this state, he would be very relaxed and would, report afterward absolutely no pain. We then worked with the individual using self-hypnosis, having the individual do self-suggesting, and self-programming. In this process, he achieved an experience in which for ten minutes (and at times, up to fifteen minutes), he would feel numbness in the injury site, but was able to move about with the assistance of a walker.

The client was elated with the experience of being able to induce up to a fifteen-minute state of total comfort, where before he had reported agonizing pain. He could, indeed, do multiple inductions for himself throughout the day and experience a fairly pain-free day, functioning, while successfully using self-hypnosis.

It was suggested that these periods of no pain could actually be lengthened. The client indicated that this would be wonderful. He readily welcomed this. Our work began to progress. However, when it was suggested in "deep *trance* state" that the client could gradually and progressively move to a place of experiencing relief for a period of up to two hours, the individual demonstrated a very dramatic and sudden transformation. A movement beginning in his lower extremities was noted. It was as though a wave was moving over him. This movement, a wave-like action of restlessness, moved up through his upper torso, rapidly through his neck, with nodding and shaking of his head. Opening his eyes, he exclaimed in a loud voice "What was that?" I explained that I was quite unsure as to what it was. As we discussed it, the client stated that he had awareness to some extent as he was drifting in and out of being very calm and very peaceful. Yet he only remembered the statement suggesting a lengthened period of being pain free. He reported at this point that it began to feel like "electricity shooting through my body. It was as though an electric current had surged through me." It was suggested to the client that, this might be a part of himself stating that he was not ready for this change. We again did the induction, but this time said to the individual that no changes in the length of pain-free states would occur that were not totally in harmony with all parts of the client. The client maintained a "very deep state" which continued until discharge from therapy. He was able to have extended and gradually increasing periods of comfort, but never any periods of comfort that exceeded three hours.

About Dissonance

Beside from hypnotic work, in my practice, I have engaged in a very classical form of Cognitive Behavior Therapy. This has been in the same vein of therapy as is taught by Ellis, Beck, and later on the form of therapy for depression that was developed by David Burns. However, in this practice of very traditional Cognitive Behavior Therapy, a therapy based on the idea that what a person tells himself or shows himself shapes his feelings, and his feelings then shape his behaviors, I repeatedly have encountered individuals who, when exposed to a new thought, a new image, or a new attempt at cognitive restructuring (where we replace the old schema of thought, or old collection of pictures, with new ones for a greater desired change in mood and behavior), experienced a widely accepted phenomena called *dissonance*. *Dissonance*, sometimes called resistance, is what an individual experiences in relation to a new idea. It is restlessness, sometimes described as an internal grinding, as though the new idea is butting heads, grinding, or interfacing in a combative way with the old idea, or old structure. Although no one I have encountered has doubted that *dissonance* exists, it certainly has not been developed as to origin in any formal writing on Cognitive Behavior Therapy, nor has its origin been spoken of in any personal training I have had with CBT. The actual mechanism behind *dissonance* was never even considered. *Dissonance* was explained as *dissonance*. When you asked about *dissonance*, practitioners or lecturers would just explain that *dissonance* was to be expected. There would then be a description in which *dissonance* would be identified as the state in which the new idea was being rebuffed by the old system. It was to be expected, and, indeed, the client was to be instructed to keep engaging in the thought replacement, maintaining the assertion of the new thought, or new interjection, despite the discomfort that they may initially experience, until, the client, accepted it. However, the explanation of *dissonance* became the description, and the description of the process of the individual rejecting the new message was simply relabeled as *dissonance* in a circular fashion.

In my earlier work and experience with more psycho-dynamically oriented therapies, (and certainly those forms which were more psychoanalytically influenced), roughly this same type of phenomena of offering a new way of being, a new perspective or observation that was met with resistance, protests, avoidance, or delays, was simply termed "resistance."

So if we look at "all our schools," the hypnotic example, Cognitive Behavior Therapy, psychodynamic, as well as biological, we find that the organism, whether it is tissue invading organism, thought invading thought, or programming invading programming or suggestion, there is an on-going tendency within the organism to reduce it, stop it, neutralize it, or at least mitigate it in some fashion to prevent change.

Thought is an electro-chemical process. To change thought is to change biology. When you learn to think a different way, you are learning to create new neural circuits. When you create new neural circuits, not only is there a change in electro-chemistry, it is also bringing about a change in more macro bodily functions, such as things that may have to deal with hormonal secretions, heart rate under certain circumstances, manufacture of protein, or disturbance of carbon dioxide and oxygen balance. All of these changes can occur with a change in thought. The overall system of a human is reacting to thought in the way that it would the splinter, the heart to be transplanted, or the bacillus. In other words, resistance, *dissonance*, and core "suggestibility" in hypnosis are all part of a very marvelous and protective function of the organism called *homeostasis*, a desire to keep change minimized for the on-going survival state of the organism. Therefore, we are always working from a biological model, whether we consider ourselves Cognitive Behavior Therapists, hypnotists, or sales people. We are all dealing with the idea that to change the way a person thinks, or sell a person on something, is ultimately reflected back into the biology.

Placebo Effect

If you go to your local pharmacy, you will see on the back of the containers or in the information leaflets that there are comparisons with placebo groups. The placebo effect is a very powerful one. The idea that thought input, a suggestion, or an idea can in and of itself produce a beneficial and physiological effect, is accepted and has become an on-going part of the process for testing the effectiveness of chemicals used to treat the human body. Again, this is a way in which we see the idea of thought, belief, or concept as, indeed, another tool for influencing biology. It is important to note, that we share a common trait with every other living organism on this planet. Those things that are not consistent with the pool of tissue structure processes within an organism will be rebuffed, and an attempt will be made to neutralize them in some way in order to prevent change. It is not a moral issue. It is not a value issue. It is a status quo non-change issue.

The Merging of Systems

In modern movie making, filmmakers are often able to cut through the compartmentalization we find in our field of specialization. An example of this can be seen in the film "Fearless," starring the martial artist Jet Li who portrays the Chinese Wushu master, Huo Yuanjia. In one scene, Huo is meeting with the Japanese master, Tanaka and they are discussing the grading of tea. Huo says, "The tea grows in nature and does not grade itself. We grade it."

Tanaka then asks, "Are all of the styles of Wushu equal."

Huo states, "They are all equal, and it is in the contest that we discover ourselves."

We also find that all styles of therapy are equal and have their unique usefulness. Each of us utilizes the styles that are most congruent with our particular mapping system. It is in this exploration that the *Eclectic* Therapist grows, discovering the strengths and weaknesses of each style of therapy as he assists the client. We the authors have merged many years of experience, study, and research, in arriving at this summation.

Dr. Hellams has been seeking ways to help individuals in solving their difficulties for over thirty years. He has studied a variety of therapeutic schools and has used Cognitive Behavioral Therapy, as well as classical hypnosis and Ericksonian style hypnosis. He has been trained in Gestalt, Behavioral Therapy, Eye Movement De-sensitization and Reprocessing (EMDR), Thought Field, Neuro-Linguistic Programming (NLP), and other modalities. Through his work with therapy, he became quite interested in *dissonance* and *homeostasis* in the organism. He repeatedly noticed how the organism is always seeking to achieve sameness or balance. He even considered a type of autoimmune system for mental as well as physical well being. He constantly observed how the system is always seeking ways to be congruent.

Mr. Schreiber, M.A. has also worked with trauma and its effect on the organism for over thirty years. He trained in Transactional Analysis, Gestalt, Cognitive Behavioral Therapy, traditional hypnosis, Ericksonian Hypnosis, Eye Movement De-sensitization and Reprocessing (EMDR), Quantum Psychology, Object Relations, Solution Focused, and a variety of therapeutic schools. He began to notice that what was called hypnosis was the ongoing state for the organism. The editing of sensory experience and the associated meanings attached to the experience were seen as incongruent with what was occurring in real time. [Mr. Schreiber recognizes that his training with R. Reid Wilson, who was training students in Strategic Psychotherapy and Ericksonian Hypnosis, influenced him. The following therapists also influenced him: Yvonne Dolan, M.A., Bill O'Hanolin, M.A., Stephen Gilligan, Earnest Rossi, Richard Landis, Michael Yapko, Norma & Phillip Barretta.] The next great leap came from a powerful teacher, Stephen Wolinsky, Ph.D. Wolinsky introduced Quantum Psychology and the influence of Sri Nisargadatta Maharaj as he introduced an integration and synthesis of Eastern, Western, and Middle-Eastern influences. Ron Klein, CAC, has also added to the development of this work with teachings in Eye Movement Integration and the work of NLP and Ericksonian pattern interruption.

Hellams and Schreiber have known each other since the 1980's and have shared an interest in Ericksonian Hypnosis and its influence over the field of therapy, to include solution focused, brief therapy, paradoxical methods, structural, and strategic methods of psychotherapy. As Hellams and Schreiber renewed their friendship at supervisory trainings, they both noticed the complimentary nature of their different theories. They began to explore ways to merge Cognitive Behavioral Therapy with Ericksonian style hypnotherapy and its understandings. The concept of *homeostasis* fits well with the concept of *sensory perceptive holographic mapping* and the editing of reality with *sensory perceptive alteration* or traditional *trance* phenomena. The addition of programming errors and *neural information centers* was a natural development of this powerful system. Soon the addition of s*emantic reversal mechanisms* and p*ersistent patterns of trance clusters* was linked to this growing theory. Hellams and Schreiber noticed some common elements of *homeostasis* and *trance*. This they labeled a "completion or a *Gestalt closure error*," which is the need for the organism to fill in the void of what is not known. Both *homeostasis* and *sensory perceptive mapping* employ confabulation as a key tool for completion.

Homeostasis as a function of the nervous system and with the mission of survival organizes the flow of energy through the organism in four ways:

1. Creating Structure by Organizing Chaos

2. Neutralizing Energy

3. Altering Sensory Data

4. Creating a congruent *sensory perceptive map*

Changing the sensory map requires pacing with the *homeostatic* System to allow entry into the mapping mechanism and disruption of the ongoing sensory alteration or *trance* state. Milton Erickson once stated that therapeutic *trance* is the "depotentiation of the conscious set." Since the organism is always in some state of abstraction or sensory experience, everything can be seen as some state of alteration. *Present time sensory alignment* is when the organism is present without the need for internal considering, explanations, or mediation.

What began as an attempt to merge two schools of therapy has ended in the development of a theoretical explanation for how therapeutic change is implemented, and how and why it does or does not work. This is being considered as the theoretical basis for being an *Eclectic* Therapist or counseling practitioner.

Chapter One

Chapter One

The Birth of a New Theoretical Model for the Eclectic Practitioner

"When you change thoughts, feelings, beliefs or behaviors you change biology."
Hellams &Schreiber 2006

"The mind-body is one organism."
Spinoza

On February 5, 2006, Hellams, and Schreiber, stepped in front of a group of therapists and began teaching them about a new theoretical model of therapy that unifies and enhances all other models of therapy. After nearly ten hours of interaction, one workshop participant excitedly voiced, "The world of therapy will be changed forever for me, and a new way of understanding client's problems and a new way of approaching solutions will be practiced by me as a participant in the training" (Workshop participant).

17

In this "mapping" model, therapeutic change, or change in general, is brought about by disrupting the ongoing *trance* or state of sensory alteration. All forms of therapy are methods of *trance* interruption. Whether it is altering programming errors, change of sequencing, change of location, or change in time, these alterations can be seen as a change in the state of the various internal representations, meanings, or associations. Therefore, therapy is an attempt to disrupt the ongoing, conscious set, an imposed, internal representation of the internal and external world that is experienced as a *sensory perceptive holographic mapping system* as if the person were in the reality. When the ongoing conscious set is interrupted, a neutral state reoccurs which allows for the possibility of the emergence of *present-time sensory awareness*, and a reconfiguration of the sensory mapping. This *sensory perceptive holographic mapping system* is fluid in that it is in a constant state of transmutation in its effort to maintain congruence and h*omeostasis* with the influx of divergent, sensory stimuli. The new theoretical model allows for a unified theoretical basis across all therapy schools.

The Sufis who are group of middle eastern wise men once told a story of the wise men who were asked to examine an elephant. In the story, each of the wise men had blinders or veils over their eyes. These blinders or veils can be considered to be like our various models of treatment and their imposed distortions of the organism. Each of the wise men in turn touched some part of the elephant and then gave some description of what he thought the elephant was like. The first grabbed the tail and stated that the elephant was like a rope in that it was coarse, round, and thin. The second wise man grabbed the elephant's ear and replied that the elephant was just like a plate in that it was flat and round. The third wise man touched the elephant's leg and proclaimed that the elephant was like a tree in that it was thick and circular. Each of the wise men was correct in his description of a part of the elephant, but each was incorrect in his description of the elephant. When the veils were removed, the men could see the elephant in its entirety, and each came to a clearer vision of the elephant as it was rather than his confabulated explanation.

"Meta Analysis"

Through the years as we (Hellams and Schreiber) have worked with many different individuals, seeking to help them solve their problems and cease their suffering, we have employed several strategies to attack the problems. Cognitive Behavioral Therapy, Gestalt, Transactional Analysis, Behavioral Methods, Ericksonian Hypnosis, Classical Hypnosis, Neuro-Linguistic Programming, Adlerian Methods, Eye Movement, Desensitization and Reprogramming, Emotional Freedom Therapy, Lowenian Psychotherapy, Focusing, Flow, Internal Family Systems Therapy, Solution Focused Brief Therapy, Hakomi and several other approaches to symptom identification and treatment have been utilized. Often we have found ourselves using a technique from one model along with a technique from another. Each of these techniques has some degree of effectiveness depending on the person and the particular problem. As we explored the similarities of these problems, the interventions, and the solutions, we discovered that all approaches merged in that they were attempts to alter and disrupt some ongoing *trance* or conscious or unconscious set. The *sensory perceptive holographic mapping system* of the organism is a way of describing the way the organism structures its organization of sensory flow. Stimuli move through the perceptive field of the organism and are altered, as well as their interpretive meanings to accommodate the pre-constructed, neural pool. Also affecting their meaning is the cognitive programming, the programming errors, *Gestalt closure errors,* and the fabric of the confabulatory map. The structure of the perceptive map is made of *neural information centers.* These centers contain representations of sensory stimuli, such as images, colors, shades, textures, tastes, smells and sounds. Further, they contain the referential, associative, and assumptive meanings collected by the organism. Kinesthetics are generated as the organism organizes and processes this sensory and associative data. These *neural information centers* link together to construct images, sensations, and experiences that form families and communities that grow, develop, and change by their association and interactions with the sensory world. Of course, what we are describing is an explanation and description of what may be occurring, for, at best, a map is only a metaphor.

Metaphor of Consciousness

The adjoining illustration is a metaphor demonstrating the unknown in the process of becoming the known. Imagine a cloud floating in the infinite unknown. As the unknown moves into the known, the senses digest, absorb, abstract, and interpret the stimuli. The human organism can only detect a minute amount of stimuli present in the unknown. Therefore, known is simply a term to suggest what has been detected and processed into the s*ensory perceptive mapping system* of the organism. Some call this the universe of human experience.

Conceptual Universe
of the Unknown

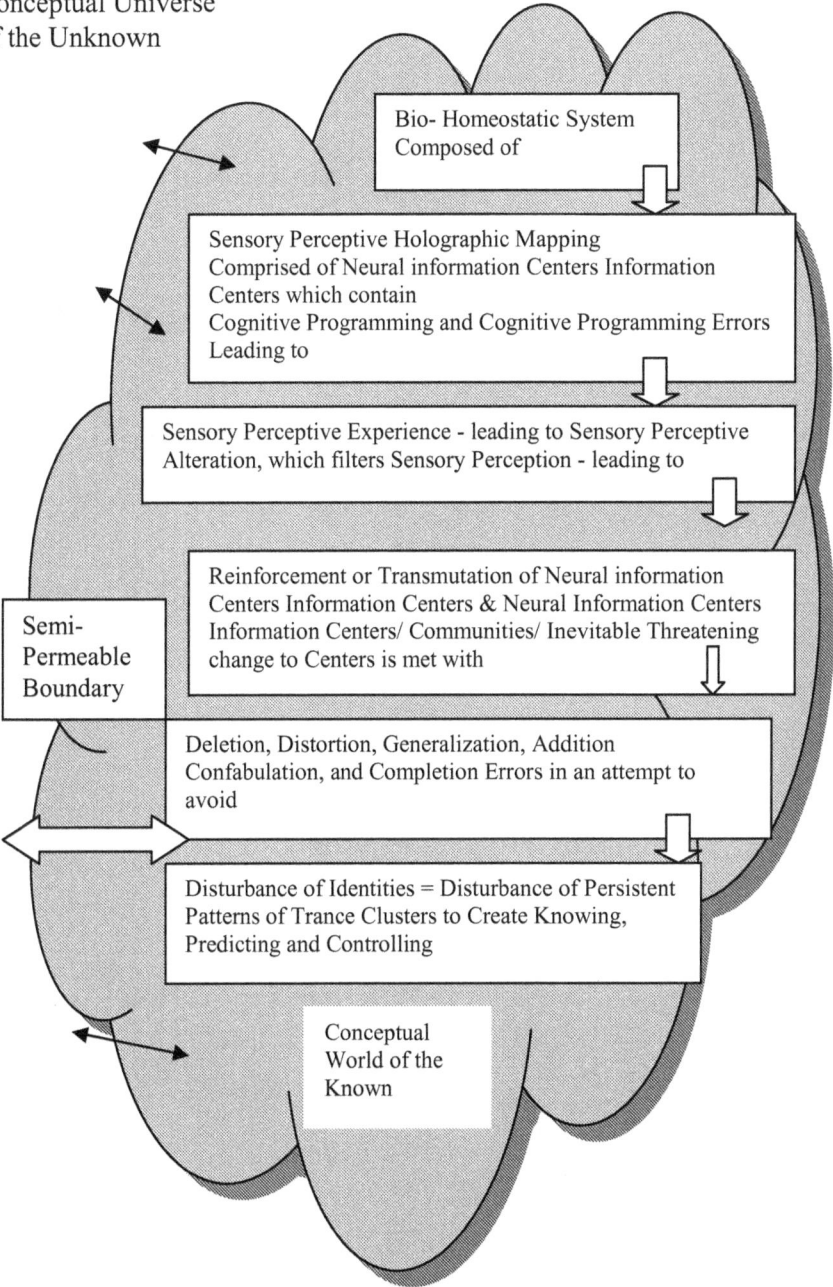

Bio- Homeostatic System
Composed of

Sensory Perceptive Holographic Mapping
Comprised of Neural information Centers Information
Centers which contain
Cognitive Programming and Cognitive Programming Errors
Leading to

Sensory Perceptive Experience - leading to Sensory Perceptive
Alteration, which filters Sensory Perception - leading to

Reinforcement or Transmutation of Neural information
Centers Information Centers & Neural Information Centers
Information Centers/ Communities/ Inevitable Threatening
change to Centers is met with

Semi-
Permeable
Boundary

Deletion, Distortion, Generalization, Addition
Confabulation, and Completion Errors in an attempt to
avoid

Disturbance of Identities = Disturbance of Persistent
Patterns of Trance Clusters to Create Knowing,
Predicting and Controlling

Conceptual
World of the
Known

Figure 1.

Chapter Two

Chapter Two

Socialization

"Here is a key point. Much of your ability to control will be based upon this principle: People, places and events are panic provoking only after we apply meaning to them. A store is just a store, a speech is just a speech, and a drive is just a drive, until the brain interprets them as "dangerous or threatening." To conquer panic you must intervene at the point of interpretation."
R. Reid Wilson, Ph.D, (Don't Panic, 1986, page 133)

"All exists in the mind, even the body is integration in the mind of a vast number of sensory perceptions, each perception also a mental state.
"Both mind and body are intermittent states. The sum total of these flashes creates the illusion of existence."
Sri Nisargadatta Maharaj (I Am That, 1973)

Socialization is the place of dynamic interaction where biology and the environment meet. The story is that each person is born into a unique reality, at a certain time, in a certain place, with unique biochemical properties that interact with the universe in their own particular ways. The mind/body develops and grows, meeting basic needs, eating, breathing, sleeping, voiding, learning, and merging. Depending on the particular structure of the physiology, the individual responds to the environmental stimuli as it interacts with the developing organism. Sight, sound, touch, pressure, heat, cold, and all manner of stimuli bombard the developing person. Some individuals are highly reactive to sight, sound, touch, smell, or taste, while others are less so, and the continuum of response is as varied as there are people. Whether the individual is in India, Africa, or the United States, in a rural or an urban setting, the person develops according to the interactive material of the surrounding environment. The neural information pool of the person is in part, the product of the environmental stimulus. The makeup of the family structure and its internal atmosphere further adds to the combinations and permutations of interactive information and experience available to the growing *neural information centers* within the bioenvironmental field. As the organism develops, the neural pathways are growing, proliferating, and then curbing back as needed, for all things work within the limits of *bio-homeostasis*, or perhaps that is just our description of how the system appears to organize itself. The nervous system is working to ensure survival and to organize the flow of energy through the form. Visual, auditory, tactile, olfactory, and gustatory senses are developing and achieving greater acuity. The depth, breath, and measurement of the organism's sensory ability is refining as greater levels of sensory experience are achieved. The development of kinesthetic awareness is coinciding with the sensory experience of the organism. Internal movement of the organism as it energetically moves toward or away from stimuli is the beginning of what will later be labeled and experienced as feelings, emotions, and motivations. Psychology will describe these phenomena as approach-approach, avoidance-avoidance, or approach-avoidance maneuvers.

Fight-flight-freeze is a variant of this type of internal organization, which is all directed to the survival of the organism. As we explore the nature of development of what Hellams and Schreiber have come to call *"neural information centers,"* let us keep in mind that these are descriptions and maps. Although they may approximate what may be occurring, they are not what is occurring. Some of the speculation on neural development comes from the work of Allan Schore, M.D., Joseph LeDeux, Ph.D., Antonio Damasio, and others. Approach and avoidance may be related to pleasure (need satiation), pain (tissue damage), or threat to the organism. These developments of stimulus-response behaviors are most likely organismic and have no associated meaning at that point. If we review the work of Piaget, he explored sensory-motor development. He further details assimilation, accommodation and synthesis, as well as concrete and abstract abilities in learning. (Piaget, 2000) This is a further explanation of neural development as seen in how the individual processes new and varying sensory information. It also demonstrates neural development at different stages of the organism's growth and maturation.

If we also review the observational works involved in object relations or characterological development involving defense positions associated with various places in the body (oral, genital, and other body armoring), we will notice that this may simply coincide with the neurological development of the organism as *neural information centers* develop in relation to physiological need and organismic awareness and interconnectedness. These particular studies come from various work but include Wilhelm Reich, M.D., Alexander Lowen, M.D., Margaret Mahler, Althea

Horner, Masterson, etc. The organism functions as a singular, biological unit that breathes, takes in fluid and food, digests, voids, rests, and navigates the bio environment. In a sensory way, the organism merges and detaches from environmental stimuli, incorporating more and more complexity in the linkages between and within *neural information centers.* Attachment, "separation interaction," and inter-stimulation are part of the organisms developing, experiential world. Attachment, connectedness, separation, and detachment are parts of the intricate dance of neural stimulation, association, and sensory development as the organism develops tactile, visual, olfactory, auditory, and gustatory refinement and acuity in relation to itself and the interactive environment.

Further, growth and development lead to the observation that the organism begins to go through phases described as symbiosis, separation, and differentiation as he appears to develop the ability to function with some degree of dependence, counter dependence, independence, and interdependence. In further explanations of neural development, and how the organism functions, some studies have led to theories about how the hippocampus region of the brain, as well as the amygdale, and the limbic system are affected by trauma, and different types of stimulation as the individual interacts with the environment.

Let us remember that we are speculating about the development of the organism as if it were made up of separate parts that work in concert. On the other hand, could it be that there is one organism, and we are subdividing it into various areas because we have a tendency to compartmentalize things in an attempt to understand and comprehend them? We employ deductive and/or inductive reasoning in an attempt to explain things as if they have or need explanation. One of the thought errors we list is a *completing error* or a *"knowledge error,"* which is the belief that things have meaning and are knowable, therefore predictable, and ultimately controllable. This particular thought error portends that if we have knowledge, then things, events, and life become knowable, predictable and, therefore controllable. Remember that everything we tell you is simply an explanation and a description of the territory, but like all maps may not be an exact replica of the territory. As the neurobiological development continues the organism gains greater and greater differentiation in the ability to engage and negotiate an ever more complex and complete relationship with the immediate environment. If we pause momentarily to think, it becomes increasingly evident that the organism and the environment are one. Consider that the organism exchanges oxygen, carbon dioxide, carbon monoxide, as well as other chemical structures. Nourishment from the environment and with environment is a complex exchange of chemical structures, each required to be in balance with the whole. The electro-chemical exchange within the biosphere further demonstrates the connectedness of the organism with the extended environment. To revisit our discussion of attachment, we need to notice that the organism's experience of need satiation in relation to caregivers may contribute to the particular biochemical disposition of the organism as to security, safety, and tolerance of ambiguous stimuli. Anxiety and depression are often linked to this developmental phase. Health, or atrophy of cellular growth in portions of the brain, is linked to abuse, neglect, or impoverishment of stimuli during this developmental timeframe.

Stimulation of cellular growth has also been attributed to interaction during this time. As the organism develops, it possesses the ability to be increasingly mobile in the environment through its ability to move the body and utilize fingers, thumbs, mouth, feet, tongue and limbs to navigate and interact with the environment. Motor movement is developed, strengthened, and refined over time by repetitious, arduous movement and practice. This movement begins with apparent unknowingness but becomes ever more directed and purposeful. Thus, the turning, rocking, crawling, walking, running, skipping, jumping, and other simple and complex movements are used by the organism as it ventures into an ever-widening area of the environment. Throughout this development, there are various degrees of interaction with caregiver(s), and encouragement or inhibition may be the interactive style. Depending on the organism's particular biological makeup, the interaction can be perceived as appropriate, intrusive, or abandoning. Various interactions by the organism with the caregiver(s) may be approach or avoidant in nature. Overlays of multiple variations in response sets are experienced over time. This has been explained as the "good mother = good me" or "angry mother = "bad me." As language begins to develop over time and with multiple repetitions and approximations, the organism begins developing symbolic representations of the world. Objectification begins to take place. This is the onset of differentiation, discrimination, compartmentalization and the fragmentation of the organism and the environment. Now the organism begins to have different experiences and begin to create the meaning of those experiences. Previously the environment and organism were in harmony but now they begin to be in conflict. The learning of judgments, preferences, and significances also enter into his world. *Socialization* is the mechanism whereby the organism learns how to interact and get his needs met from others who are in control. Now begins the interruption of meeting needs, feeling and behavioral interactions. The organism is told what he feels, how to act, when to meet needs, and what are the approved feelings and actions to express. Peeing in public is not acceptable, nor is burping, farting or touching one' self. If a child states that he "hates John," he may be told that such a comment is improper and will not be tolerated. Such language may put him in danger of "Hell's fire" or some other undesirable consequence. It may be during this time that programming or thought errors may enter the system. It is during *socialization* that there is a loss of connection to the biology and to the environment. Separation of mind, body, thoughts, feelings, and actions begins to solidify, as the rituals of the family group are imparted. Disconnection to the organism increases as demands from the group are put in place. "Self-Betrayal" is the first loss as the organism gives up connection to the biology in order to get needs met as prescribed by the group. Remember, "The map is not the territory and the map is only useful, if it has some similarity of structure or map language to what it measures," (Science and Sanity, Korzybski, 1993). Therefore the incongruence between what the organism needs and the information within the map it is given causes the organism to alter its sensory experience to match the map and thus loses connection to itself and the environment as it exists. Korzybski also said, "A map that misplaces the cities or misnames them or gives incorrect dimensions is worse than useless in that it misleads and misinforms," (Science and Sanity, Korzybski, 1993). The organism experiences greater degrees of incongruence as it attempts to navigate the environment with an incorrect map.

Chapter Three

Chapter Three

Homeostasis and Dissonance

"Homeostasis is about Balance or Sameness it is not about Truth or Reality."
Hellams & Schreiber 2006

"Neurotic or self-defeating behavior is not very hard to recognize intuitively especially in others. When it comes to spotting our own irrationalities, however, most of us are at least partially blind."
Albert Ellis, (A Guide to Rational Living, 1997, page 53)

Dissonance occurs when the accepted pool of programming stored in the biology is threatened by incoming information and thereby threatens a disturbance of the biology of the organism.

Cognitive Programming

*S*o what is it that this *"Psycho-Homeostatic Mechanism"* is attempting to keep from being disturbed? Very much like a computer, you can liken the way we function to software working through hardware in the computer, extending out through connections to drive the robotics of a factory. The mind, which is made up of the software of ideas, thoughts, pictures, and images, moves the electro-chemical circuitry, and is part of the electro-chemical circuitry of the brain. The brain in the neurological system (the hardware) then generates impulses or changes that direct the functioning of the body and its reactions to the world around it. Blood pressure, heart rate, changes in circulatory patterns, secretions of hormones and metabolic rates, all come under the influence of the hardware directed by the software of the mind. For convenience, we are terming the ideas that are both an electro-chemical reality and a philosophical abstraction as "programming." There is no difference between the idea of "giving a suggestion" in a hypnotic state and offering an alternative self-statement or different description of the world through cognitive restructuring. To change the programming, this thought, this body of suggestions, or however one would term it from a previously established view of the world, is to directly change and significantly alter the physiology of you and the way he sees and perceives the world. In other words, to think in a certain pattern generates a *sensory perceptive alteration*, and that alteration freezes an individual into a perception of the world whereby he tunes into certain elements while filtering out other elements. An example of this can be seen in individuals who have a preponderance of cognitive distortions, (as termed by many cognitive therapists,) and rarely see good things about the world. They overlook the laughing child eating the ice cream cone to see the car wreck two blocks ahead.

Émile Coué, who was a French pharmacist, is in many ways heralded as one of the early Hypnotherapists. It was said in "Waking State Hypnosis" that he would suggest that his clients repeat the following: "In every day and in every way, I am feeling better and better." It is said that Coué by the application of these self-affirmations, guided individuals in bringing about changes in their overall health status, or at least in the way that they perceived their health. It is very easy to look at Émile Coué as a hypnotist, a Behavior Therapist, a reframer of reality, but at his core, he is certainly a programmer.

One's programming dictates whom he will approach and his feelings when he approaches them. It dictates what he will see as he enters a room versus what he will not see. It may control his tolerance to pain, pressure, or discomfort. Overall, this programming is the basis of what we begin to call "us." In other words, by significantly changing the programming, we significantly change the way we are and even who we are.

Programming that is congruent and that is reality-based is programming that leads one to healthy perceptions and therefore healthy interactions with the world. Programming that is highly incongruent with the surrounding world leads one to reactions and perceptions that generate very dysfunctional responses to the world and dysfunctional patterns of behavior.

It is important here to begin to understand that the next level of organization from this collection of programming becomes something that we call _trance_. Unfortunately, _trance_ has been seen in a very isolated slice. It has been seen as the type of phenomena only demonstrated by a stage hypnotist or seen after some hypnotic ritual has been performed by a clinical hypnotherapist to bring about a change, such as smoking cessation. However, it is important to know that *trance*, in the way that we are terming it and viewing it, is a *sensory perceptive alteration*. The *sensory perceptive alteration* is directed by, guided by, and formed by the programming within the organism. To develop this further, if we look at the world, we find that there are certain programming elements that are clustered together which create *trances*. The *trances* are endless. There are, for example, certain beliefs that function together that produce for one perhaps a "mommy" *trance*. The programming that tells a person what a good mother does and does not do may lead a mother to screen out the traffic noise at night from a nearby street, yet be highly attuned to the soft whimpering and crying of a child.

There is a "surgeon" *trance*. The pager goes off. The surgeon responds by looking down, reading the number, and by shifting from being the engaged golfer to rapidly moving into a *trance* state in which he is the coach of the operating theater, and he is in command. Automatically and quickly, he begins to screen out extraneous elements in the environment as he focuses on only those essential elements at hand to deliver the patient care that is necessary. While he/she is engaged in a very lengthy operation, the surgeon is drawing on experiences stored in memory banks and meshing them with a current synthesis of the signs and indicators, he is receiving both from the patient's body directly and the secondary indicators and monitors that are monitoring the physiology of the patient. Hands move automatically. Eyes transmit certain key elements while discarding others. Noises in other parts of the theater are dismissed as the surgeon brings himself totally to bear in this process of the operation. The operation ends. It has taken eight hours. It is over. It seems like only an hour or two have passed. The *trance* then shifts from "surgeon" *trance* "daddy" *trance* as the surgeon moves into the afternoon or evening, assisting his child with homework. At this point, drawing back on memories, he operates within the programming that is consistent with the way that he has seen people tutor, parents assist and help, and perhaps as he has experienced himself.

The *trances* go on endlessly. It is interesting that for a very lengthy time, there has been an attempt to physiologically isolate what was called the hypnotic state to actually discern when a person was in *trance* from when a person was not in *trance*. There are certain phenomena and tests that can be applied to determine when a subject is in a hypnotic state. The professionals witnessing this would all agree that, "Yes, this person is in a hypnotic state." Certain physiological changes can be measured, such as slowing of the heartbeat, speeding up of the heartbeat, and other changes in bodily functions. However, despite this, no distinct state of *trance* could be distinguished from any other state of the person's life simply based on physiological markers. In other words, *trance* always exists. It is only a matter of which state that we find ourselves in. It is like going into a thick forest and trying to find a tree by taking samples of everything else around one tree to do a comparison. The sampling would simply lead one to believe that either the specific tree did not exist because of the lack of difference in comparing this tree with the rest of the forest, or the more logical assumption that trees are what make up the forest.

So if we are considering how this practically applies, let's look at what we have established so far. There is this thing called the *homeostatic mechanism* that resists change. Pertinent to our discussion, it resists change in thought, which is what we tell ourselves, or what we show ourselves. What we tell ourselves or what we show ourselves, is in a process of producing different *sensory perceptive alteration*s, or *trance*. We are never out of *trance*. We are simply changing from one *trance* state into another. In fact, we pay very good money, sometimes large sums, for developing certain types of *trances*. Driver education is about developing driver *trance* in that one learns to focus on certain elements when he is the driver that he doesn't focus on when he is the passenger. He notices certain signs, draws on memory banks, and automatically observes certain speed limits. The surgeon, the nurse, the engineer, all in his other role, learns to go into certain professional roles/*trances*. In these states, automatically a set of *sensory perceptive alteration*s occur that are based on underlying, encoded suggestions, structures or programs.

Incongruent programming statements and images, or, stated differently, images and programming self-statements (statements about the world that are not consistent with reality), produce dysfunctional *trances*. For instance, the individual who believes the incongruent statement, "Nobody likes me," might overlook the child who is waiting eagerly for his interaction in order to look at the person in the hallway that never speaks when he passes. The person who believes he is not physically attractive and no one would be interested in him," focuses on the rejected dates, but does not focus on the past experiences in which he was successful in having a dinner, an encounter, an activity, or a date because these are not consistent with the dysfunctional belief. Dysfunctional programming breeds dysfunctional *trances*, which promote dysfunctional programming, a vicious cycle. All attempts to disturb any type of programming and ultimately any type of state will be met with a counter-attack, a neutralization effort by the guardians of the castle/city state who seek to prevent change.

Frequently we are asked when presenting this, "Well, what about the *trances* that people do exhibit on stage or with the clinical hypnotist that are widely accepted as *trance*?" These *trance* states are the simplest form of *trance*. The most complex states that weave the fabric of our lives are so much closer to the other parts and like the other trees in the forest, we don't even recognize them. In other words, it is hard to see them in our complexity.

Since there is this on-going *trance* state, or more accurately, this on-going roll over of *trance* states that is dictated by our *cognitive programming*, responding to stimuli in the environment much as we are responding to some type of post-hypnotic suggestion, we come to develop actual sets of these *trances*. In other words, when we encounter our work place, we have developed certain *trance* state elements of our work in reaction to certain people, in reaction to certain tasks, in reaction to certain phone calls. This overall collection of *trances* is what people see, perceive, and call us. For convenience, we have referred to this collection of *trances* as persistent patterns of *trance* clusters. Simply all this means is that any human being in the course of his or her day has developed habits. The habits of thinking dictate habits of sub-*trances*, known collectively as the person. We are all acquainted with people saying, "Joe is not himself today." Well, obviously by this, we do not mean that we think that something has occurred on a scale of "Invasion of the Body Snatchers." However, what we really are saying about this is that as we look at this individual today, the perceptions are different. The response is different. In other words, there is something different in the *trance cluster* that we are observing with this person. Joe arrives the next day. The programming has shifted back to the usual firings and habituated ways of thinking leading to the usual pattern of *trance* and *trance clusters*, and we say, "Huh, Joe is back to himself."

Chapter Four

Chapter Four

Neural Information Centers

"The Map is not The Territory"
Alfred Korzybski (Science and Sanity1993)

*I*n our model, *cognitive programming*/suggestions/ information are housed within a ranging set of circuitry within the mind/brain termed *"neural information centers."* These are the same information centers that have linked such complex processes together as hearing a word or phrase, such as "write the letter *A,"* having accessed this memory, and then making the intricacies necessary in order to commit this formation and transmitted signals to the correct muscles so that an *A* is produced on a child's paper. However, the actions become much more complicated than this. Our everyday work of driving, carrying on conversations, engaging in complex tasks such as crafting objects, surgical procedures, writing texts, etc. are all based upon the integral connections of neural information circuits. For years, practitioners of classical hypnosis have referred to this in various ways. One very standard technique was to basically ask the individual "in *trance*" to get in touch with a part or segment of himself, to visualize this image, and to have this part that was the driver in charge of a certain behavior or habit to go and get in touch with other members. Some practicing hypnotists used the concept of encouraging the part to find other parts and have board meetings. Out of these board meetings, a resolution or set of resolutions would emerge, and this would be a suitable replacement that the part that was initially contacted or engaged could now use and invest its energy in rather than the habit/action/behavior that the client was seeking to beneficially replace. If we look at the concept of Dissociative Identity Disorder/Multiple Personality Disorder, it becomes readily apparent that the complexities of these *neural information centers* and communities and clusters of community information centers can be witnessed. The annals are replete with the range of so-called sub-personalities or multiple personalities that range in compartmentalized abilities, information, emotions, and skills. The DSM III-R cites differences in reactions to prescriptions, the need for glasses or not, differing IQ scores, etc. [Diagnostic and Statistical Manual of Mental Disorders, Third Edition Revised, American Psychiatric Association, 1987 page 270]. Of course, harkening back an early documented case of this phenomena, "Miss Beauchamps" by Morton Prince, we can see that following a trauma, the so-called personalities emerged. (James P. Bloch, Assessment and Treatment of Multiple Personality and Dissociative Disorders, 1991, page 2). Further, dramatic shifts in "personality" are also noted and accepted as part of the continuum of behavior found in the modern archives of neurology, with individuals experiencing different forms of brain trauma, particularly frontal lobe injuries.

It has been the bread and butter of stage hypnotists, and a very common plot in the sitcoms of the early 60's and 70's, that a visiting hypnotist would deliver a post-hypnotic suggestion. Then when the telephone rings or some other environmental stimulus, the person would begin to transform himself into some other personage, animal, or projected character and do so in a *"trance"* state. This phenomenon has been widely accepted and studied. It is further convincing of the link between hypnotically-induced changes in "personality" and "multiple personalities" in that cases of individuals with Dissociative Identity Disorder (DID) and Multiple Personality Disorder (MPD) have been seen as virtuosos as "deep *trance*" hypnotic subjects. It has frequently been viewed as the therapy of choice, to utilize some range of classical hypnosis to treat DID/MPD by the application of hypnotic techniques and *"trance"* phenomena.

Anyone who has ever participated in a play or drama knows the importance of rehearsing the script to the point where the lines become automatic. However, for the thespian, there is another important factor. That is, that the rehearsal of the script move to a point that the person stays "in role" and begins to live this part in response to certain cues (lines) emitted by other actors in the play. This, again, takes the format of post hypnotic suggestions, and self-induced *trance*. The *trances* themselves become quite complex throughout the movement of the play.

In the examples discussed above, whether it is MPD, an actor on a stage, a cop on the beat, a surgeon in the operating room, or a professor in the classroom, we are all seeing the *trance* and multiple *trance* states that are directed by a set of suggestions, programming or scripts.

In our working metaphor, neuro-information centers can be very simple or very complex. The *neuro information center* unit can simply carry a collected memory of places that are very cold or the *neuro information center* can carry a memory that is quite complex of a rape or other brutal victimization. Further, in order to generate the necessary *trance* for the organism, the *neural information centers* organize, and in these temporary and even more permanent communities, carry out even more complex actions through their collected directions of *sensory perceptive alteration*s.

In short, the mind is the software. The components and units of the software are the *neural information centers* with various loading bytes within them. The collection of this software into the hardware of the brain where these units are actually stored in an electro-chemical base determines the *trance* state that will actually occur to the organism based on internal and external cues, stimuli, or post-hypnotic suggestions. The more complex the *trance*, the more complex the *neural information centers* and their communities will be. Further, dysfunctional *cognitive programming* or cognitive errors yield dysfunctional *trances*. Dysfunctional *trances* are those *trances* simply that do not effectively work for the health of the organism. They are incongruent with the reality. Reality is the outside environment in which the organism as a biological being is seeking to survive.

Neural information centers can be addressed directly or indirectly. Borrowing from the legacy of classical hypnotic therapy, Neuro-linguistic Programming, Gestalt Therapy, psychoanalytically based approaches to DID and MPD, as well as Gendlin's Focus Therapy ("felt sense concept,") we have developed a series of specific techniques to interact and engage the *neural information centers* directly.

More indirectly, *Neural Information Centers* can be altered by utilizing an educational and an awareness approach until the client becomes increasingly attuned to the underlying programming of what he is telling himself and what he is showing himself. This obviously is very much the technique utilized in more classical approaches of Cognitive Behavior Therapy.

"Mapping"

It is fundamental to this work to understand that the *neural information centers* and their communities orchestrate a holographic map of the world. If this map is based on *cognitive programming errors* (errors that lead the organism and its developed *trances* not to be functional or congruent with the environment), then it means the organism/individual navigates through the world generating ineffective (at best) and highly dysfunctional and destructive (at worst) *trances* in response to the environmental stimuli and demands. To quote Korzybski, "The map is not the territory." However, like the guidance system of a high-tech missile/smart bomb, the organism will respond with its *sensory perceptive alteration*s and behaviors based on the information as though the map were entirely accurate. It is a widespread programming error that others must or should see the world the way the individual does. The holding of such error leads to the protection of the internal map, which is not examined or even recognized as a complex entity.

The changing of c*ognitive programming errors* leads to an alteration and reconfiguration of the map. Further disrupting the *trance* states or states of *sensory perceptive alteration* in and of themselves create fluxes within the map thus leading to change. Fundamental to this work is simply becoming aware of the concept of a map and beginning to update or own *neural information centers* that are within one's map. Acknowledgement that a map exists frequently brings about greater congruency of the map to the world. In other words, when the individual becomes aware of the map, he is aware of the distinction of this thing called a "map" from other individuals' maps. Given this insight, he can then move toward a greater congruency in reacting to and with the other organisms on the planet.

It is to be understood that perceived violations or changes to the map result in tremendous *dissonance* as a reaction from the h*omeostatic mechanism* to reduce change. Remember that to violate the integrity of the map, sends ripples throughout the map itself, and this creates much upheaval within the organism unless the changes are brought about with a respect of and a pacing with the *homeostatic* system. In other words, using our earlier metaphor of the city/state take over, if we launch a head-on assault of the map, as often occurs in classical Cognitive Behavior Therapy by direct, logical argumentation, the h*omeostatic* mechanism is very much aware, assaults the perceived attacker, and creates much fight or flight response within the organism. However, to begin to work within the organism for a balance, using such methods as will later be introduced as the H*omeostatic System Check*, we find much less *dissonance*, ripples, and disruption, and a greater opportunity for beneficial assimilation.

"Defenses"

Building on the metaphor already laid for our system, it is to be understood that any change to the components of this system invites attack. If the system perceives this change to be coming from an outside source and intrusive, the defense and rebuffing will be much greater than if it is seen by the organism as an internally evolved change.

For example, John comes to the therapist and explains that two years prior, he was in an automobile accident, and since then, he has been horribly disfigured. This is largely based on the programming that he developed due to the remarks of nursing staff and his own images of what he perceived in the mirror immediately following his first surgery before any reconstructive or cosmetic procedures were engaged. Despite what others consider as highly successful cosmetic surgery, and despite input from others that the scars are faint and barely noticeable, the client persists in seeing himself as "disfigured." After John presents his plight, the therapist begins a very direct form of logical argumentation based on facts. John moves around in his chair, becomes very restless, begins to issue a number of very audible "Yes, but" statements. It is obvious to any observer that great energy is being directed in defense of the map. It is not a case of the information being weighed as being good or bad or even factual. On this level, the assault comes from new input challenging change. Change meaning biological change, and thus the organism resists in an attempt to rock itself back to where it has accustomed itself to be. However, the organism does not engage in this effort without revealing definite strategies. The organism generates what are called in this system *semantic reversal mechanisms*. These are frequently as simple as adding the word "no" or "not" to the statements of the intruding information. A disguised form of this is the "yes, but" statement whereby the organism seems to agree with the "attacker" and then generates a "not" statement. In this case, John might think, "Yes, I did have reconstructive surgery, but it was a failure," or actually, more precisely, "No, it did not change my appearance." Other forms of *semantic reversal mechanisms* are the addition of statements and deletions of statements whereby the individual simply hears or does not hear things in the incoming information in order to prevent disturbance to the map. can become quite complex in their arguments, such as the thought being generated, "He's paid to tell you that," or later after John leaves the office, "Sure, you felt better in there, but now you are in the real world. You are just wasting your time." *Semantic reversal mechanisms* can also be quite visual, as the new information is being generated or presented to John, in the case of a here and now look in the mirror with a narrative by the therapist, countering images flash through John's mind of the witnessed disfigurement immediately following the first surgery. *Semantic reversal mechanisms* are a part of the *homeostatic* system that is designed to protect the map. As with the overall *homeostatic* system, there is no weighing by the organism initially regarding whether this is a good thing or bad a thing. It is simply a reaction that "You are trying to change my map, and I'm going to neutralize you." We have likened this in our work with *semantic reversal mechanisms* to the scene from Arthur Clark's "2001, A Space Odyssey" in which the astronaut finds himself in dialogue and a hostage to a high-tech computer in space. The computer is invested in only one thing, maintaining its autonomy and maintaining the status quo of its programming. Even though the overall safety of the mission and the computer itself is threatened unless changes are made, the computer insists on viciously defending the status quo, for to change the programming is a direct threat, in its interpretation, to the life of the computer.

Beyond the *semantic reversal mechanisms*, there are other mechanisms overlapping in a continuum as they extend from the same organism and process, *homeostasis* as it defends, may create extreme discomfort in the organism, generating a fight or flight response. The positive and negative hallucinations that are generated may move to a point of absolute defiance of reality. This is best seen in the extremes of psychotic behavior. The *homeostatic* system can create severe forms of negative hallucinations in which things are actually not seen and are filtered in the *trance* the person is in. The system can further generate defenses, such as extreme physiological changes and perceptual extremes, as are witnessed in psycho-physiological disorders and conversion reactions.

Defenses can also be as primitive as physically assaulting the perceived bearer of the information that is creating a map distortion and thereby threatening change. Examples of this in history are numerous, from Socrates and Copernicus, to the initial proponents of the germ theory.

A special type of defense is created when the map is presented with puzzles or questions for which it has no answers. The map perceives itself as being complete. Therefore, when new information is presented that challenges the completeness of the map, a Gestalt closure error occurs. That is, the map confabulates information to essentially "plug the holes." In other words, in the absence of sufficient data to close the gap in the map, the map will simply create what it needs in order to fill the void from the existing information in the map. The following personal example is given. While conducting some fieldwork in a small town, I, Hellams, decided to take a break to visit the local barbershop. Upon entering the shop, I immediately notice that the men inside were very distressed. In observing them and listening to their interactions, the following was found to have occurred. Earlier in the day, a car carrying two young people (who were actually distantly related to many of those in the barbershop) had rolled onto a train track maintained the position on the track until the car was virtually demolished by the train. It was obvious that the people in the shop were in search of some reason or some way to close the gap. One of the participants in the discussion ventured, "The other day a young person outside my store had his car radio so loud with one of those booster systems that it hurt my ears and almost shook the car." Another visitor to the shop added that he was quite sure the young driver of demolished vehicle had previously installed some boosters and amplification equipment for a new sound system. The guesses and assumptions continued largely based on fantasy and very little fact until the following emerged. It was decided that the young people had a very powerful amplifier in their car. It was further decided that it was so loud that it was deafening to them. Therefore, being almost entranced by the music and deafened by the volume of it, they moved onto the railroad track in front of a moving train because they could not hear or adequately think due to the very loud music. It was at this point that the writer observed an almost tranquility coming over the group. They paused, becoming almost still, and at this point, their discussion changed to other topics. It was as if the answer had been found. The quest had been satisfied. The search was over. We have termed the process of plugging the hole as confabulation. It is seen in many instances of human behavior, and its biologically related origins are well represented in the annals of neurology with confabulation being noted in individuals suffering brain injuries and in the peculiar and specific case of Korsakoff's psychosis. The Gestalt closure error is an on-going self-statement of the organism that notes at any given time, "I recognize a void in the map. The map must be complete. Therefore data must be provided to close the map." This, of course, is to be found in on-going, assumptions, as well as in on-going positive hallucinations in which the organism sees those things in the outside world, which are nothing more than projections of the assumptions or confabulations within the map. In an attempt of the system to avoid a sense of incompleteness or recognition of incompleteness in the map, the organism may further engage in negative hallucinations (i.e. not seeing or experiencing things that are actually there) in order to make the confabulations fit.

Chapter Five

Chapter Five

Neural Information Centers and the Representation of Reality

"A weak mind cannot control its projections. Be aware, therefore, of your mind and its projections. You cannot control what you do not know. On the other hand, knowledge gives power. In practice, it is simple. To control yourself-know yourself."
Sri Nisargadatta Maharaj, I Am That, 1973)

$\mathcal{T}$ he *neural information centers* refer to the metaphorical apparatus that contains or represents the sensory data as it flows through the organism. This involves the neuro-biology of how sensory information is contained in the biology. We are not telling you exactly how the neurobiology functions; but rather, we are using a map or metaphor for how it appears to operate. Further, it is the attempt to explain how the colors, images, textures, sounds, tastes and other sensory stimuli are represented in or by the neuro-peptides and neuro transmitters. Also linked to this are sensory stimuli, their detection, their representation, their singular state, their contextual meaning, and their synthesis to the operation of the organism and its biology to these units.

Neural Information Centers

A most important segment of our metaphor is the component called *neural information centers*. When we use this term, we are envisioning a component that is part programming and part electro-chemical and involving both afferent and efferent pathways. In other words, we see these units being hybrids of mind and biology that both send instruction and direct programming into the physiology of the organism, as well as receive feedback from the physiological responses of the organism and movement back into the center. Further, we see the *neural information centers* organized into clusters, and, indeed, it is from the *neural information centers* that simple to more complex states called "*trances*" emerge.

When we speak of *persistent patterns of trance clusters*, at the same time we are speaking of persistent patterns of communities of *neural information centers* that are behind these *trance* states. Further, we offer that such units as executive n*eural information centers* exist, which make decisions about which centers, will be in control, and under what circumstances, and what programming they will operate.

This can be seen in classical demonstrations of hypnosis in which a person is aged regressed and begins to speak as a child, write, or print as a child, and to have access to childhood memories while seemingly having walled off adult learning.

In our metaphor, such terms as "child state," "child ego state," "inner child," and "inner wounded child" all reflect the coalescing or clustering of *neural information centers* under an executive control.

Trauma states reflect a freezing of *neural information centers* into a type of circuitry whose firing is triggered when the programming demands of an executive center is met. From the very simple to the very complex *trances* all owe their origins to the shaping forces of the *neural information center* or clusters and communities of such centers.

If a client is asked to engage in a common Gestalt intervention titled the "empty chair," the *trance*, which develops allowing the client to project father, brother, sister, emotion, etc. into the empty chair for a therapeutic dialogue, comes from the operation of these *neural information centers*.

Cognitive restructuring, as practiced by Cognitive Behavior Therapists, is reworking the programming "housed" within the centers in order to bring about a deconstruction of one type of *sensory perceptive alteration* (*trance*) and a reconstruction of another.

The frequently touted phrase, "Think outside of the box." is really saying. "Access other *neural information centers* to address the problem or issue allowing the construction of a new, more functional, open, and less selective *trance* while deconstructing the old *trance* which has locked in perception and made creative problem solving difficult."

When the client is halted in carrying out a new action plan due to the deficits of better skills, it is these *neural information centers* and associations of them that are being updated and trained develop a functional trance, which employs the new skill.

It has been recognized for some time that within the trappings of classical hypnosis individuals attained those earmark behaviors that were labeled as "hypnotic *trance*" much more readily if shown a demonstration of an individual entering "a hypnotic *trance*," either in vivo or by film. In other words, feeding the *neural information centers* the definitions, images, blueprints, or templates desired will produce the *trance* that is desired.

It is important to understand that *neural information centers* do not operate in the world of real time unless it is established for them. This means that by simply dialoguing with the *neural information centers*, it is possible for an individual to experience existing in the past or the future. The wall calendar may read 2006, but the n*eural information centers* may be operating in 1994 or 2010. This can be accomplished without the stylized or ritualistic maneuvers of classical hypnosis.

The Case of Frances B.

Frances was seen for a clinical consultation due to severe tension and migraine headaches. The headaches, however, only occurred when Frances felt the need to assert herself. They became so disabling that they prevented Frances from voicing her opinion. In dialoguing with the Neural Information Center driving this behavior, Frances and the therapist were made aware that this behavior and center's function began when Frances was eight years old. This was a time before her mother left her alcoholic father. It seemed that during this time, the mother, other siblings, and the then eight-year-old Frances would face physical harm if any whimper or protest were given to the father's obstreperous behavior when on a binge. Frances would become angry while witnessing the maltreatment of her mother, but the center prevented her from protesting and thus endangering her life. Upon disclosure from the *neural information center* regarding this particular type of *trance*, the therapist was able to establish rapport with the center, an executive center. Through this executive center, other *neural information centers* were contacted (as evidenced by ideo-motor signaling) which effectively assisted in the updating of this old center and thereby deconstructing its dysfunctional, outdated *trance* while developing new n*eural information center* linkages to provide updated programming with an accompanying functional and congruent *trance*. With this, the incapacitating headaches ceased. Frances would frequently remind herself, "I'm an adult, not a child. I had no power then, but I have power now. I am in charge."

The work with *neural information centers* in addressing psycho-physiological disorders is endless. In our metaphor, the *neural information center* and the programming upon which it operates is at the heart of this psycho-physiological disorder. For this reason, it is the most fundamental level at which this disorder needs to be addressed.

Tyler's Concerns

Habit formation is a function of the training of *neural information centers* and established circuits of these centers. A client named Tyler was referred for treatment due to self-abuse in the form of nail and cuticle biting. This had become so severe that infections had developed requiring repeated medical intervention. Despite the use of noxious stimuli (in the form of coatings placed on the nails and cuticles), the habit persisted, and the client grew discouraged. Through ideo-motor signaling and the development of an internal dialogue with the *neural information center clusters* that were driving these behaviors, other centers were contacted. A replacement behavior was developed. A *Homeostatic System Check* was conducted within the *neural information centers* (*Homeostatic System Check*," page 266), and a congruent replacement behavior was installed. The *neural information centers*, in working with the former driving *neural Information centers*, arrived at a date and time that this new congruent behavior would occur. Upon the arrival of the established date and time, this once persisting and abusive behavior stopped to be replaced by the new behaviors that the *neural information centers* had negotiated within themselves.

All of the work, whether psychoanalytically based, neuro-linguistically oriented, or hypno-analytically founded, is a function of negotiating, departmentalizing, merging, and updating *neural information centers*, *neural information executive centers*, and associated clusters. This is beautifully illustrated in the so-called "splitting" in which an individual identified with MPD or DID seek a therapeutic intervention. The therapist expresses fascination by the existing number of "personalities" and ventures with enthusiasm and expectancy that there may, indeed, be more. The client becomes aware of others who have been reported by book and film as having various types and numbers of personalities and thus, the numbers, variety, and dramatic presentations multiply by the person and intensify these so-called "personalities." In our model, this is simply testimony to the great complexity that *neural information centers* and their communities and clusters can provide when the programming/suggestion is offered to them that this is desirable.

All phenomena witnessed through the rituals of classical hypnosis are directly the result of *neural information centers* and their clusters. Further, please understand that these clusters are always operating, whether there is a stylized ritual offered or not. For this reason, the so-called "classically occurring hypnotic phenomena" is constantly an on-going function of everyday life.

For instance, a stylized ritual is developed with the important pacing, which allows us entry into the walled city. We do not engage the *homeostatic* defense to fight against us, but instead it accepts us. After gaining access, the hypnotist suggests that the hand of the individual is becoming light, almost detached, as a cloud is detached from the bonds of earth. It is further suggested that while other facets of the client enjoy a wonderful trip to a beautiful place, that there are certain parts of the client that would like to convey information through the means of this detached hand. Without developing this further, this is probably obvious to the reader as a set of suggestions or programming which we call automatic writing suggestions. This phenomena of automatic writing can occur, without these specific suggestions, and in a very "naturalistic state." It is frequently witnessed that someone is writing a letter to one friend, somehow becomes distracted and begins to use another friend's name, even including fragments that he actually wishes to convey to the other friend. This, of course, is an extension of what has been called "Freudian slips."

These same phenomena can be produced by simply appealing directly to the *neural information centers* and patiently working with them minus any stylized ritual.

The scope and complexity of *neural information centers* and their associated phenomena is the scope and complexity of human behavior. From the very simplistic to the very complex behaviors/*trances*, they are all dictated by *neural information centers* that encapsulate specific suggestions or programming.

Before leaving our discussion of *neural information centers*, one might raise the question, "How do *neural information centers* play a part in this on-going map concept that has been presented earlier?" It is probably easiest to conceptualize this relationship through again another metaphor. Imagine that you have a puzzle. Each individual piece of this mosaic is a *neural information center*. Some pieces are merging together with their colors and their shapes. Other pieces form quite distinct barriers in their printed designs and color markings with other pieces in the puzzle. However, all the parts of this mosaic come together to form a map of the territory. The frame that holds the puzzle or map together is the *homeostatic* system. Any attempts to remove pieces are met by a tightening of the frame. Any attempts to jar the puzzle and its mosaics are responded to by cushioning and resistance by the frame. The individual pieces, the puzzle, and the frame together form a unified work of art. The framed work of art does not question whether it reflects the territory. It only seeks to maintain itself within the territory.

Figure 2. This is a representation of the body and the sensory perceptive organism. The exterioceptive system involves the eyes, the ears, the nose, the mouth, the skin and the internal sensory organs. The sense organs are a conduit for the organism to interact, represent and respond to stimuli within the extended biosphere.

Chapter Six

Chapter Six

Sensory Perceptive Holographic Mapping

"A map is only of some use if it bears some similarity to what it measures."
Korzybski (*Science and Sanity*, 1993)

*S*ensory perceptive mapping involves not only a sensory apparatus of the body, such as an eye, ear, nose, tongue, skin, or sensory tissue of the internal organism, but also involves the mind/body's detection, reception, interpretation, alteration, assimilation, and synthesis of sensation into a sensory map of the living experience. All of the sense organs are receptors of various sensations. These perceptions lead to actions, either excitatory or inhibitory. Perception has been defined in several ways.

1. Perception is the transmitting impulses from sense organs to nerve centers – afferent in nature, which means bearing or conducting inward. They are also efferent carrying impulses from the central nervous

system to an effector; an effector being a nerve ending that carries impulses to a muscle, a gland or an organ and activates muscle contraction or glandular secretion.

2. A molecular action (as an inducer, a corepressor, or an enzyme) that activates, controls, or inactivates a process or action (as protein synthesis or the release of a second messenger.) (Merriam Webster Online Dictionary)

Further perception is:

1. Having an ability to perceive; keen in discernment.

2. Perception is the organism being responsive to sensory stimulus.

3. Perception is marked by discernment, understanding, and being sensitive.

It must be remembered that senses are limited to the ability of the sense organ to detect the sensation and the nerve center to identify and respond to the sensation. We have only some awareness of the infinite number of sensations outside of our ability to detect and/or identify them. Therefore, we are limited to an abstracted limited world or life map with which to navigate these actual life experiences. As stimuli or energies are detected by the mind/body, they are transmuted into images, sounds, smells, tastes, thoughts, feelings, emotions, and behaviors. All of this is a description of the nervous system and its ability to vary its detection, reception, categorization, and response to stimuli.

The evolving map is holographic in nature, which indicates it is multi-dimensional, incorporating sensory data, associative data, meanings, sensations, and emotions.

Richard Bandler and John Grinder the creators of Neurolinquistic Programming referred to intense searches of the biological map. as Transderivational Search, (TDS). Those searches may be cued by words, tones, or gestures (Patterns of the Hypnotic Techniques of Milton H. Erickson, M.D. Volume I and II, 1996). We refer to TDS as *referential, assumptive, and associative searches*, and suggest it can be initiated by any stimulus the system detects at the threshold of sensory arousal. Psychology previously referred to this as "the just noticeable difference."

Mapping by the central nervous system is primarily concerned with the survival of the organism and the maintenance of *homeostasis*. *Homeostasis* has four guiding mechanisms that we are aware of:

1. A completing or Gestalting Principle

2. Sensory Alteration Principle

3. A congruence or Balancing Principle, and

4. A Neutralizing Principle

Given these factors, understand that any input, which challenges the pool of existing, accepted, and incorporated information, will create a *trance* shift of the existing *trance* (deconstruction). Input, which requires intense searches of the map (TDS), results in such deconstructions that a various simplistic, primitive *trance* changes commonly accepted as "hypnotic *trance.*"

A major point to be aware of is that there are billions of bits of information flowing through the form (organism), and the organism can only process a few thousand bits per moment. Therefore, this means most of the stimuli are not assimilated or digested, and therefore the *sensory perceptive holographic mapping* is made up of a limited amount of sensory data. The map is at best a confabulatory interweaving of stimuli with made up information. It is an abstraction.

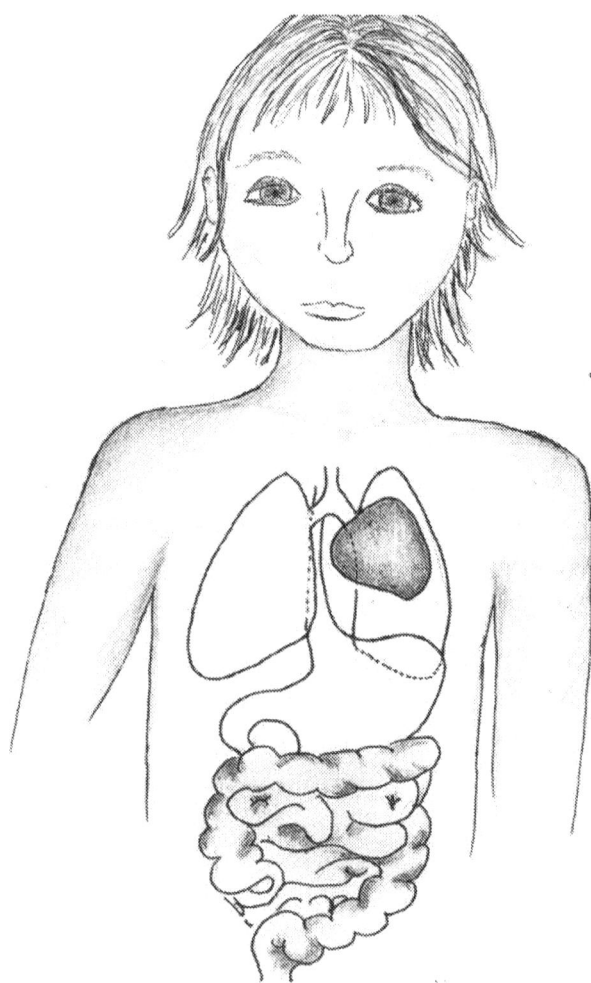

Figure 3: This artistic rendering of an organism is to indicate that the sensory organism is the entire cellular being. As the organism digests sensory stimuli, the organism is not an empty box. This includes proprioception and vestibular functions. The kinesthetics are the ways that the organism organizes in response to external stimuli. What we call emotions or feelings are the electro-biochemical, muscular changes in response to stimuli and the organism's perception of the stimuli. The organism responds by freezing, and moving toward or away from the stimuli. The heartbeat increases or slows. Pupils dilate. Digestion stops. Respiration shifts from diaphragmatic to upper respiratory. Muscles elongate or contract as the organism prepares to act, then it passes. The organism senses then it associates the sensed stimuli with past-labeled experiences if they exist in the organism's map. The final product is a feeling.

Experiences with Mapping

The following narrative is a further description of the application of theory in real life.

It is an unusually beautiful evening. The sky is very dark. Two individuals living in the same town and spaced only several miles apart look into the sky and see from roughly the same angle and visual context an event in the sky. The event is a very bright object glowing with a long, trailing light behind it. The trajectory of the object is a downward one. The object appears to be rapidly accelerating toward the earth.

Rosa looks into the sky. Her heart begins to race. Her palms sweat. The muscles in her neck begin to tighten. Her eyes begin to tear, and she begins to wail loudly as she moves her arms and hands to her face, attempting to momentarily disrupt her transfixed view of the night sky as if to provide some temporary relief from her agony.

Jim views the sky, also transfixed. His mouth widens into a very large smile and his heart races. He begins to move toward his vehicle, scrambling with his car keys to gain entry as quickly as possible.

Rosa gains some composure. She runs screaming into her house. She makes her way frantically to her telephone and begins to cry and scream as she attempts to dial 911.

Jim hastily speeds across town, thumping on the steering wheel, almost laughing at this point, heading steadily in the direction of the downward, traveling object.

Rosa can hardly speak the words "airline crash" as she screams into the telephone, breaking into sobs.

Jim is now on his cell phone to his colleague, prompting him to hurry, explaining that what they long have been waiting for is occurring. He gives his colleague rough coordinates and urges him to hurry to the site.

Rosa is having flashes of sounds and pictures from a near-fatal air crash she was involved in ten years prior. She begins to engage in verbal descriptions of what must be going on in the cockpit and passenger area of the airliner and intermingles this with her previous experience in the air crash.

Jim thinks back to all the videos he has seen and the samples he has examined from museums of meteorite collisions. He smiles and chuckles as he thinks back to one account of a meteorite landing in an individual's yard and the comical fallout that occurred between the homeowner, the fire department, and the local University over who owned it.

Rosa is now on her knees. She can barely hear the 911 operator as the phone has fallen to the floor. She feels weak, so very weak, and nauseated. She begins to think, "I'm having a heart attack." She then references the time that she witnessed her father having a heart attack, how his chest became tight, his shortness of breath, and his lips becoming cyanotic. She begins to predict and then recognizes these signs occurring with her.

Jim, as he steadily heads toward his projection of the collision site, sees himself in the morning paper as claiming the meteorite find, speculating on its value, beginning with a negotiation of the landowner for rights to recover samples and investigate by chemical and structural analysis this visitor from the galaxy. His mood is very upbeat. This is truly a high point in his life.

Rosa's older children have now come into the room. They are attempting to comfort their mother who is giving signs of a coronary event. They request an ambulance to respond to their home.

Jim is just about to the crash site. He can see some brush that has been set ablaze, but realizes this is nothing significant and will soon burn itself out. He begins to trudge rapidly up the sloped woodland to the object of his desire. He is asking himself where his colleague is and begins to project into the future of their meeting at the collision site with much joy and almost childish play.

The ambulance has now come to Rosa's house. Rosa is told that she is not giving the signs of a heart attack by any of the measures taken, but, indeed, is exhibiting the classic signs of a severe panic attack. As she is loaded into the ambulance, her son says, "Mom, don't be so upset. It's been all over the television and the radio that the streak of light was a meteor that landed in some nearby woods, and not a disaster of any kind."
Jim's colleague has now arrived. They are taking measurements, laughing. Jim has realized a dream that he has had since he was a boy of ten.

An examination of Rosa takes place in the nearby emergency room. Enzyme studies confirm no heart attack. The physician explains that Rosa, by her excitement over what she felt was an airline disaster, had created dramatic changes in her breathing, circulation, muscle tension, and therefore disturbances in the chemistry of the blood, thereby simulating a heart attack, with the actual experience of an anxiety or panic attack.

The preceding accounts illustrate how every day and in every moment of the day, there is a very powerful interconnection between our internal programming (what we tell ourselves/what we show ourselves) and our on-going mood and physical and physiological states. To visualize a show down with the boss two weeks from now is to create mood states and physiological changes consistent with those mood states each time the visualization is "run." The "show down" which may never occur can be relived hundreds of times without ever occurring as a real-life event.

In a summer job while conducting my assigned duties of replacing overhead light bulbs, I engaged in labeling behavior. I labeled myself as 'awkward'. I projected into the future images of myself falling. I regressed into the past and retrieved images of accidents I have had. Of course, in this process, I filtered out the numerous times I had successfully navigated objects, steps, and ladders in the past. In this process of my self-programmed running, I experienced a mood of fear. My biological self began to experience tension, rigidity, and stiffness. My hands began to sweat. I dropped my tool. I then stated, "There, you see, I am awkward. I am clumsy. I have no business on a ladder. I'm going to fall." A few minutes later, I began to become dizzy. I clutched the ladder, backing slowly down it. I walked into the office, resigned as of that moment and that day, and assumed that no one could ever understand the experience I just had experienced "since I believed that I was the only one who had been through such an experience."

It is almost impossible to over-estimate the power of self-programming. In our world, the cycle of telling ourselves/showing ourselves messages about external events, experiencing feelings which are created by this programming of what we are telling and showing ourselves, having these feeling then call up repertoires of behavioral choices and then other cognitive rules, and making a decision at this point about what the action should be is repeated thousands of times a day for every individual. When we fail to recognize and acknowledge this cycle, we find ourselves believing that we are literally at the mercy of our moods, with our moods making things happen, our moods "running" the show, and we are left with little choice or few alternatives because we are stuck in some type of mold, status, or position by this villainized mood.

Let us look at the following diagram.

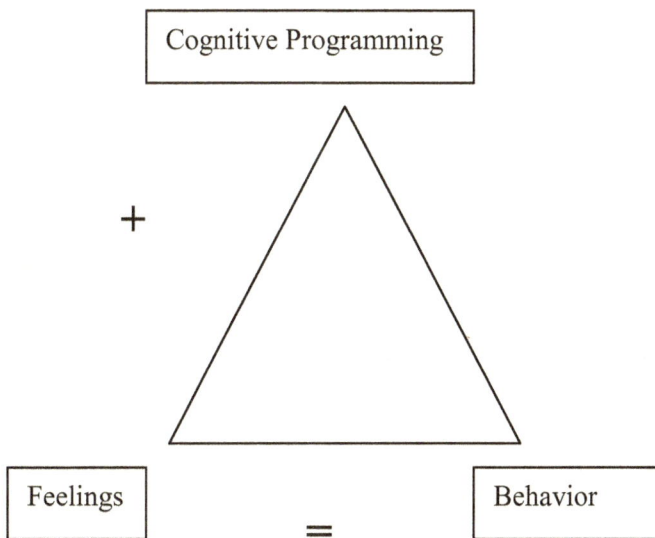

```
        ┌─────────────────────────┐
        │  Cognitive Programming  │
        └─────────────────────────┘
                   /\
                  /  \
    +            /    \
                /      \
               /        \
              /          \
             /            \
            /──────────────\
  ┌──────────────┐    ┌──────────────┐
  │   Feelings   │    │   Behavior   │
  └──────────────┘    └──────────────┘
              =
```

At the top, we see *cognitive programming* comprised of
what we tell ourselves and/or what we show ourselves.
This yields certain feelings (anger, happiness, sadness,
disappointment, frustration, etc.).   These feelings
trigger a call-up or repertoire of behavioral responses.
Given cognitive rules that are in place from previous
learning, a behavior is chosen and becomes a reality.

To understand this process better, we will utilize a real-
world scenario against the backdrop of this paradigm.
John is a freshman now eight weeks into the college

experience. He is invited to a group get-together on Friday at a local bar and grill. John is strongly attracted to the idea of attending a get-together in order to network, make friends, and hopefully make inroads toward establishing a dating relationship. However, almost immediately his self-programming begins. He begins to review experiences he has had in the past in which he experienced very severe anxiety and its accompanying physical punishments. He sees himself as becoming reticent and reserved as he imagines the upcoming gathering. In the running of his self-programming, he further sees others scrutinizing his behavior and therefore almost immediately notices his awkwardness. He then tells himself, "Nobody likes me. I'm unattractive. I have absolutely no skills, and I'm a social loser." This self-programming then leads into feelings of intense anxiety, a punishing physiological state of increased bodily tension, digestive disturbance, accelerated heart rate, disturbance in respiration, and re-routing of blood flow (blood being shunted more into internal organs than into the extremities). An overall punishing state of emotion and biological reality (a fight or flight response) is established. Out of these feelings, a repertoire of possible behaviors is drawn based on previous experiences the individual has observed, vicariously or directly experienced, and in other means had modeled for him. Based on a previous set of rules that are based largely on direct or modeled experiences, he chooses a behavior. In this case, the client can see and talk to himself about several possibilities: (1) He has read in a magazine that when you are afraid of something, to engage it rather than run; or (2) In his previous experiences when he has avoided social engagements by canceling or making excuses, he has experienced an almost immediate reduction in tension. Thus, option two becomes a very attractive choice. The individual elects to avoid, make an excuse, and declines the invitation. Upon declining, he begins to generate more self-programming that states, "I am a loser. This is just one more time when things did not work out for me. I am a victim of my anxiety. Things will never get better." This results in the student experiencing marked levels of sadness and disappointment. This state triggers a range of behavioral options consistent with this emotion and the person's life experiences. In this case, the range involves (1) yelling and screaming, (2) blaming others, (3) increased withdrawing and avoiding, and (4) journaling about what a negative and disgusting person he is.

Using the same paradigm, let's compare this with Frank's feeling and behavioral responses. Frank is also eight weeks into his semester of the college experience. Frank is invited by a friend to a group gathering at a local bar and grill on Friday evening. Frank thinks back to other pleasant experiences he has had with individuals. He thinks back to experiences in high school that he enjoyed very much, and how these experiences led to the development of intimate friendships and dating relationships. As he visually revisits these and even hears the sound track from some of these successful scenarios in the past, he begins to also self-talk about himself as a social person, getting along well with others, ascribing the phrase, "usually liked by others" to himself. In general, he begins to experience a very upbeat and positive mood. He begins to tell himself that Friday is something to really look forward to. He begins to project into the future and to see very positive visualizations of being accepted, meeting perhaps a female who is attracted to him as he is attracted to her, and experiences fantasies of a possible long-term dating relationship. His mood begins to climb. He readily accepts the invitation. He finds the upcoming gathering to prove to be a motivator as he engages in some less than exciting paper work. Friday comes. He is not disappointed. He engages with the new individuals he meets. He finds several people that he thinks, "I can really relate to them," and arranges a date with an attractive young lady. His mood as he leaves the gathering is very upbeat, and in his programming, he begins to tell himself, "I will seek out more of these opportunities in the future. I really get along with other individuals well. This is one more time that proves that I have a natural gift in relating to others."

It becomes increasingly obvious, as we look at people's *cognitive programming*, that very dramatic change in mood and behavior not only can occur, but will occur, if the programming, itself, changes. In the above examples, the programming makes all the difference in not only the mood states of the individuals, but also in the manifesting of successful and productive behaviors, or behaviors that lead to isolation and limitation.

Chapter Seven

Chapter Seven

Cognitive Programming Errors

"You can always say more about what you have already said."
Korzybski (Science and Sanity, 1993)

*C*ognitive programming errors interrupt the biological process and are instrumental in the birth of neurosis and compartmentalization. (These programming errors are the way the dysfunctional teachings, instructions, directives, and cultural beliefs from family, community, ethnic group, region, country, and religion are imparted and absorbed by the organism. When programming leads to dysfunction, we call the programming, programming errors.) These c*ognitive programming errors* are the cognitive distortions and archetypical errors that represent the distortions of thinking that come as the organism attempts to know, predict, and control the flow of energy through its corporeal existence. These pieces of information act as post-hypnotic suggestions and are activated during the organism's living in the environment. Keep in mind that the organism interprets these statements based on its own state of existence.

Some programming errors seem to be a part of the hardwiring of the organism, such as the "completion error," the "referencing error," and positive and negative hallucinatory command errors. These types of (distortions are ways) that the organism maintains *homeostasis*, keeping the information pool the same, and maintaining the congruence of the *sensory perceptive holographic mapping system*. Confabulatory creation within the *mapping system* is the standard where there is a mixture of incoming stimuli with associational, assumptive, and referential meanings (as well as billions of stimuli filtered out and not ever integrated into the perceptive mapping system). In order for any of the *cognitive programming errors* to exist and persist, there will be the accompanying "*trance* phenomena" or *sensory perceptive alteration*s. In addition, there will be *persistent patterns of trance clusters* that the organism and others perceive as the person. The "personality illusion" appears to be a product of the programming and programming errors as they begin to interrupt the biology and fragmentation and compartmentalization of the organism occur.

Frequently Found Cognitive Programming Errors

This list is not intended to be used as an exhaustive one. Its purpose is to serve as a catalyst to promote a personal search for programming errors

1. *(CT) Comparative Thinking Errors:*

Comparing self to the following:

    A.   Existing others (brothers, sisters, parents, friends, associates)

    B.   Implied others (everybody else, them, others.)

    C.   Unarticulated comparison or unspoken comparative object ("It is just not good enough;" "It can be done better;" "I am an imposter.")

Examples:
(1)

_____

_____

(2)

_____

_____

2. *(PT) Polarized Thinking Errors:*

Life exists at poles or extremist thinking (success – failure, awkward – athletic, failing – A's, bad – good, totally imperfect versus perfect – poor quality vs. excellent)

Examples:
(1)

_____

_____

(2)

_____

_____

3. *(DC) Discounting Errors:*

Subtracting from or reducing the actual positive contribution or input, you have made in defiance of objective reality ("You got an A on the test." "Yes, but the professor was very easy.")

Examples:
(1)

_____

_____

(2)

_____

_____

4. *(RT) Regressed Thinking Errors*:

RT is seeing current events interwoven with past events. ("Every time I come into this office now, I feel sad. I remember the day Jim was fired.")

Examples:
(1)

_____

_____

(2)

_____

_____

5. *(FP) Future Projection Errors:*

FP is to negate segments of the present with statements or visualizations about a possible future. ("I can't enjoy my vacation for picturing the board meeting next week.")

Examples:
(1)

_____

_____

(2)

_____

_____

6. *(NHCE) Negative Hallucinatory Command Errors:*

NHCE are self-programming leading to perceptual deletions in defiance of reality. ("There is nothing good about Frank." – Speaker deletes witnessed acts of kindness to friends and his children.)

Examples:
(1)

_____

_____

(2)

_____

_____

7. *(PHCE) Positive Hallucinatory Command Errors*:

PHCE is self-programming leading to perceptual additions that are of a visual, auditory, and even tactile or propriorceptive nature in defiance of reality. ("Lillian stared at me." vs. "Lillian looked in my direction." "They were laughing at me." vs. "Joe and Jim were in the corner of the room laughing about something.")

Examples:
(1)

_____

_____

(2)

_____

_____

8. (ECE): External Control Errors:

ECE is self programming which states that our feelings are externally created, controlled, and sustained rather than a product of ourselves ("They make me so angry.")

Examples:
(1)

_____

_____

(2)

_____

_____

9. (ATE): Assumptive Thinking Errors:

ATE is assuming that you know what someone else is thinking or meaning without clear communications from them concerning what their intent or meaning is to you.

Examples:
(1)

_____

_____

(2)

_____

_____

10. (MTE): Magical Thinking Errors:

Magical thinking errors is telling oneself that something is going to produce a certain outcome without a clear, logical chain of events moving toward that end. ("Even though I am not studying, somehow I will pass the test," or "No matter what I do, I cannot succeed. I'm cursed.")

Examples:
(1)

_____

_____

(2)

_____

_____

11. (OOE) Only One Errors:

Self-programming which indicates you are alone in your experience – ("No one else has ever done this, felt this, and had this experience.")

Examples:
(1)

_____

_____

(2)

_____

_____

12. *(NLE) Negative Label Errors:*

Although labels are a useful part of language, to label something is also to limit. For instance, once an object is labeled as a fruit it automatically excludes any uses of it as a hand tool, vehicle, book, etc. Applications of negative labels serve the same limiting function. To label oneself as a "loser" automatically limits his perception of the time that he has succeeded or won. Once the limit is established, it limits opportunities that are not consistent with the label. (i.e. "I do not apply for promotions. I do not enter contests.") Please note this programming error frequently operates in tandem with negative hallucinatory command errors and/or discounting errors.

Examples:
(1)

_____

_____

(2)

_____

_____

13. *(NCE) No Choice Errors:*

Self-programming which endorses that the individual had no choice or no alternatives, and therefore is not responsible for the consequences of his actions or is a victim.

Examples:
(1)

_____

_____

(2)

_____

_____

14. *(TPE) Trapped by the Past Errors*:

Self-programming whose message is "I cannot move to a different future course because I am stuck with or within the past. I am trapped by history in a set mold."

Examples:
(1)

_____

_____

(2)

_____

_____

15. *(GE) Best Not Good Enough Errors*:

Despite objective evidence that the individual exerted maximal effort, he tells himself that he should have done better.

Examples:
(1)

_____

_____

(2)

_____

_____

16. *(SOE) Should/Ought Errors:*

Should have (should have not statements) which imply
the existence of all necessary factors to cause an action.
(An apple, given appropriate levels of moisture and
temperature, should fall from a tree, and it does. Mary
is angry with Jim because she tells herself that Jim
should see things the way she does, but he obviously
does not.)

Examples:
(1)

_____

_____

(2)

_____

_____

17.   *(RE) Reference Errors:*

Self-programming that leads the individual to think that everything is about him/her. That the actions of others are in reference to him. Carl states, "Just like the Christmas party, they cancelled the dance to keep me from socializing with them."

Examples:
(1)

_____

_____

(2)

_____

_____

18.   *(CE/GE) Completion Errors/Gestalt Closure Errors:*

When there is insufficient information or no information to render a judgment, the individual fills in the blanks. Your friend has not shown up for lunch, you have no information as to why, so you begin to tell yourself what might have happened and believe it to be true. This type of error may involve associational, assumptive or referential searches to fill in the information. Frequently (CE/GE) errors will present in the form of two subtypes a) Extrapolative (Ext) and b) Interpolation (Int).(Ext) errors involve projections into the future based on inadequate sampling for such projections.(Int) errors involve filling in the blank as in the above example. A classic form of an (Ext) error would be, "I was turned down by the first college I applied to, therefore any college in the future I apply to will turn me down."

Examples:
(1)

_____

_____

(2)

_____

_____

19. *(EE) Expectation Errors/Contractual Thinking Errors*

Self-programming where the individual tells himself that certain things will occur because of something he has done. ("If I am nice to others, they will be nice to me.") This is often the source of confusion and resentment.

Examples:
(1)

_____

_____

(2)

_____

_____

20. *(KE) Knowledge Errors*:

This is the type of error that influences an individual to believe that there is special knowledge about existence, the world, and about things in it the world and if a person has, the correct knowledge then he will always make the perfect decision. (Helen reports, "If only my father had lived to advise me, I would not be in this bad marriage.")

Examples:
(1)

_____

_____

(2)

_____

_____

21. *(OA) Overly Attributive:*

Programming that exaggerates the accomplishments, power, and even magnitude of others or task at hand. (Client, "My father was a great man. He completed college and worked forty hours a week to accomplish this feat." (Therapist) "So did you, Bob. Can you see your accomplishments?"

"Or I feel so depressed. When I look at the sink, the dishes are like mountains."

"Or whenever I must confront the people at the car dealership, they look like giants to me."

Examples:
(1)

_____

_____

(2)

_____

_____

22. *(DE) Descartes' Error:*

This error occurs when one separates the mind/body and speaks as if it were two different things. Along with this error is the error of dividing a person into thoughts versus feelings. The compartmentalization of the various aspects of experience into separate areas of the body subdivides the person and his experience. This dividing of the organism leads to the debate, over which is primary, most important, or has origination, and is therefore causative.

Examples:
(1)

_____

_____

(2)

_____

_____

"He Saw Beyond His Death"

(Excerpt from a Cognitive Programming Workshop
Conducted Spring of 2000)

There is a man from whom I have learned much about the inner workings of psyche and flesh. His name is R. W. Rose. R. W. was born in a time period when America was transitioning from blacksmith to mechanic, from horse-drawn conveyances to motor cars and trucks, and dirt roads were largely succumbing to pavers and asphalt in the rural areas of the South Carolina countryside.

R. W. had learned that by hard work and ingenuity, it was possible to attain largely all of what you needed and a good bit of what you wanted. A most attractive job in his part of the country in terms of steady pay and higher pay involved construction and maintenance of railroad lines. Following a fire in which his parent's farmhouse burned, during which he rescued the family, R. W. left his formal education experience after the tenth grade and entered the workforce on a construction gang with a national railroad line. He soon distinguished himself for his ability to "see" how things came together and how designs and plans could readily be translated into concrete structures, rising rapidly up the ranks within this construction group.

The story I would like to unfold for you occurred when R. W. was around thirty-seven years of age. He was the major breadwinner in a household with a wife and five children. He also assisted in the support of other extended family.

Following almost a year of on-going bowel complaints and medical checkups, R. W. began to have increasing pain and problems with bowel functioning. As a last diagnostic effort, R. W. submitted to exploratory surgery. The surgery was performed. As R. W. lay in recovery, his wife was informed of the following: "I'm sorry, Mrs. Rose, but the prognosis is not very good for your husband. We excised a large tumor that was obstructing his intestine. It has been confirmed that it is malignant, and it appears to have spread within the intestine. He will never be able to work again." (Later he learned that his physician had noted in his medical chart a probable life expectancy of six months.) Mrs. Rose replied, "Doctor, thank you for your efforts. We are people of faith. We have received bad news before and have chosen not to believe it. We do not accept this, and R. W. will not die."

Later as R. W. emerged from recovery, his wife shared with him the news to which he responded, "I've got too much to do to die. I'm not going to die." Later that day the physician followed up with R. W., giving the same pronouncement of death to which R. W. again replied, "Doctor, I thank you for your efforts. However, I'm not ready to die. I have too much to do to die. I will not die. I will outlive you."

Against medical advice, in the next ensuing hours R. W. was making his way from the bed, pulling his I-V pole around with him, asserting the need to be discharged as soon as possible, and in general, in good spirits to the staff and those around him.

Against medical recommendations, R. W. was discharged from the hospital early. He was instructed to "go home and take it easy." He promptly returned home and refused the medical advice.

R. W., who was noted as a gifted mechanic, invited the neighbors to bring small projects to his home to include small tasks with their automobiles, such as replacing headlights, etc. He had decided on his own course of therapy. This, of course, was (1) he was going to act as though he was well again, and (2) he was going to actively refuse to see himself being sick or entertain any notion of himself being sick. Despite pain and discomfort, R. W. persisted with his plans. He fixed appliances and small projects on automobiles. He forced himself to move and walk, and put himself on a steady diet of visualization. He would see himself building large projects, such as rebuilding construction projects that he had previously been involved in with the railroad or taking apart pieces of farm equipment and vehicle engines, step-by-step, piece-by-piece, bolt by bolt, within his mind.

He utilized this extraordinary gift of visualization to minimize and eradicate pain. He also used this as a means to motivate and propel himself onward.

Now at eighty years of age, Robert is still working. He successfully retired from the railroad. He continued in farming and mechanical pursuits to today's current presentation. Currently he is managing his own wrecker service.

There is much to be learned from this remarkable man with whom I have spent countless hours. Robert, at every point, refused to see his death. He committed only to see his life. He would run snapshots, video footage of himself in the future, not only surviving, but doing quite well. As a pain management tool, he taught himself through the powers of visualization to translate himself through space and time, operating in the future as a healthy and dynamic individual. The response to this visual programming was the body healed itself. At every point, he relied on his faith, which was supported by his visualization that it was "not my time to die."

Frequently in conversations with this gifted man, I would see him engage in problem solving by looking off, being distracted to some type of internal stimulus, and obviously as gauged by his eye movements, engaging in complex visual patterning. Upon emerging back into conversation, he would have a response, frequently a response that would be highly technical and very accurate in nature.

On one very long ride with R. W., I was astounded as he drove and unfolded for me bit by bit how he had diagnosed the ills of a piece of farm equipment that he was yet to see. Further, he was dismantling the piece of farm equipment through his visualization, giving estimates of cost and time, of what would be necessary in order to fix the yet unseen but reported malfunctioning equipment. In the following weeks, I learned that his visual modeling had been right on target, even down to the hours that it took to fix what had been the distantly diagnosed equipment.

Other episodes I have noted with this individual included times when he would reduce his own blood flow by calming himself through visualization until he could receive medical aid. On one occasion, he as an older gentleman had his great toe amputated through his shoe by an accident. He controlled the blood flow, and managed his pain through visualization and self-talks, while driving himself to the hospital.

Other than the fact that this man provides a very interesting account of the powers of faith and visualization, I present this at this workshop for another great reason. Although I was practicing in the mental health field when I first met R. W., I had largely abandoned my early training in self-hypnosis and hypnosis for more classical behavioral work. My exposure to this very remarkable individual began to set the course for me to engage not only myself, but others, in the remarkable powers of visual programming.

When I was first introduced to Cognitive Behavior Therapy, it was taught as a matter of self-talk versus self-picturing. The focus was on what you tell yourself as opposed to what you show yourself.

The early and on-going experiences that R. W. Rose provided for me served as catalysts to incorporate and explore visualization as something far beyond the realm of classical hypnosis or simple mental rehearsals, but to see it as an integral part of the programming, which formed the software of the mind.

Testing for Programming Errors

1. *Is this thing I'm telling myself or showing myself something that I would teach to a child to enhance his life?*
2. *Would I recommend to my best friend that he incorporate this programming into his daily thoughts?*
3. *Are these programming thoughts/beliefs based on fact/evidence that I would present in court?*

Failing any one of these tests, suggest you may be entertaining a programming error.

Failing all three tests signifies a programming error.

Hellams/Schreiber 2003

*Please note: Programming errors are often seen in tandem such as (DC) Discounting Errors and (OA) Overly Attributive Errors. In addition, note the linkage between *cognitive programming errors* listed previously and the *sensory perceptive alteration* (*Trance* Phenomena) discussed in the chapter on *sensory perceptive alteration.*

Chapter Eight

Sensory Perceptive Alteration
(Hypnotic Trance Phenomena)

"Feelings are interactive perceptions."
Antonio Damasio

One of the primary ways bio-psycho-h*omeostasis* is maintained is through the mechanism of *sensory perceptive alteration (SPA)*. This phenomenon is involved in the realignment and construction of the sensorial mapping world. It is one of the mechanisms in the editing of the experiential world. The human organism has the ability to alter sensory data so that it will conform to the preexisting neural information pool contained in the *sensory perceptive holographic mapping.* Several elements appear common to s*ensory perceptive alteration*:

> A.   There appears to be a narrowing, shrinking, or fixating of attention. This change in attention is experienced as happening to the person.

B.   There is a spontaneous emergence of other *sensory perceptive alteration*s (<u>Trances People Live</u>, Wolinsky, Stephen 1991).   The interweaving of altered, Sensory Perceptive data is one of the keys to the confabulatory nature of the *sensory perceptive holographic mapping.*

C.   The alterations influence the experience of energy, space, mass, and time.

D.   The effect of *sensory perceptive alteration* is the editing of sensory data by deletions, distortions,   generalizations,   additions, confabulations, and changes within associational meaning.

E.   There is a beginning, middle, and end of the phenomena, although the *trance* continuum never ends.

F.   There is an appearance of a "conscious" and other conscious split.   Frequently there is the sense of a split between reality and *trance.*

There is always ongoing, *sensory perceptive alteration* for the nervous system continuously organizes the sensory flow and creates the experience of a knowable, predictable world.   Often when a sensory alteration occurs, it is accompanied by other alterations of sensory perception or interpretation.   The following are the different types of *sensory perceptive alteration*s that have been observed and named:

1. *Age Regression:*

Age regression is a distinct feeling in which the person feels younger than his chronological age or experiences being at an earlier time in his life. Auditory, visual, kinesthetic, or other types of hallucinations, as well as sensory or time distortion often accompany this *sensory perceptive alteration.*

Examples:
A. Bill remembers a time he was called into his boss's office, and before he ever arrived there, he had begun to imagine what kind of trouble he might be in. As the pictures and images flashed in front of him, he heard his boss's voice, and it sounded like his father's voice the time he was grounded in the 4th grade. The voice sounded deep and booming, and he felt small and childlike, like he did when he was younger. He stated that he often feels like this when he is being confronted about difficulties, even if he has done nothing wrong

B. Susan, now in her fifties, described feeling as giddy as a high schooler while on a beach trip with her friends, as they laughed and talked about memories of beach trips they had shared when they were in high school.

Examples from your experience:
(1)

(2)

---

2. *Age Progression or Pseudo Orientation in Time*:

Age progression or pseudo orientation in time is often used to designate future thoughts and images but could also refer to neutral or undesignated points in time.

Examples:

A. Robert stated that as the meeting for his promotion approached, he became concerned and began to anticipate the results. He could see images of himself and the committee as they inform him of the reasons he was not going to receive an upgrade, even though he knew he had worked hard and had earned the promotion.

B. Julie, thinking about her wedding day, which is only two months away, describes hearing herself saying her vows to Tom, and hearing Tom saying his vows to her. Her thoughts feel so real, she sometimes cries tears of joy.

C. Andrew meditates for peace and stress relief. He states that one of the benefits of this focused relaxation is a sense of there being the absence of time.

Examples from your experience:
(1)

_____

_____

(2)

_____

_____

3. *Dissociation:*

Dissociation is a blocking of the ability to experience internal feelings or sensations, external body parts or external events or things.

Examples:
A: Joe and Elizabeth have pet names for their sexual organs and talk about her "monkey" and his "banana."   As in this illustration, names are given to body parts as if they are separate from the person.

B: Jerry states that he feels angry most of the time, but does not ever remember a feeling of sadness. He says these types of feelings were not expressed in his family, and he does not remember his father ever expressing sadness. In fact, his father said, "the Williams men never show sadness, and it is a sign of weakness if you do."

C: Angie remembers her mother saying that her father had a problem with alcohol; however, she has no memory of her father's drunken rages or the abuse he acted out on the family.

Examples from your experience:
(1)

_____

_____

(2)

_____

_____

4. *Post-Hypnotic Suggestion:*

Interpersonal communication or interaction that is internalized and becomes an intrapersonal communication self to self in the form of introjects or auditory dialogues.

Examples:
A. Rodney is very successful at his job as a computer-programming consultant. He can still hear his father telling him that you have to get up early and work hard to be a success. He finds it difficult to relax and slow down, even though there is no concern about his business being successful.

B. Kelly has difficulty being assertive, even though she is a trained counselor. She remembers her mother's words that polite people and ladies don't talk back, but they do what they're told.

C. In the movie "What the Bleep, Do We Know" the Native Americans were unable to see the explorers' ships until given the programming by the Shaman of whom they implicitly trusted. (What the Bleep, Do We Know, 2004)

Examples from your experience:
(1)

<hr>

<hr>

(2)

<hr>

<hr>

5. *Amnesia, Denial, Hypermnesia:*

The continuum of remembering and forgetting, that is critical to the creation and maintenance of the *sensory perceptive holographic map*. Forgetting things; pushing thoughts, feelings, or memories down; or over-remembering are all on the continuum of memory.

Examples:
A. Paul pushes back the feeling that his drinking has gotten out of control or that his problem remembering the night's events is not disturbing

to him. He tells everyone that everything is fine and he is doing well, but that is not the truth.

B. Amber and her husband Michael are seeing a marital counselor for conflict in their relationship. Michael cannot seem to remember what happens in their arguments, while Amber remembers everything in painfully vivid details, much to his embarrassment.

Examples from your experience:
(1)

_____

_____

(2)

_____

_____

6. *Negative Hallucinations:*

A negative hallucination is a complex internal *trance* process that edits out one's internal experience of perception. When experiencing a negative hallucination, a person does not see what is seen by others, or hear what is heard by others, or feel what is felt by others, or taste what others taste, or smell what others can smell.

Examples:
A. How many times can you remember looking for your car or house keys, only to discover that they were right in front of you the entire time? Think

of the times you were deeply engrossed in a good book, watching a fantastic movie, or really enjoying a close ball game and suddenly became aware that someone had been calling you for several minutes, and you had not heard the first sound. Objects, sounds, textures, and many other stimuli from every area of the senses are at times out of one's awareness are somehow altered or removed from the sensory mapping.

Examples:
B. Laura talks about the time she was concentrating on her artwork and did not hear her daughter calling her because the soup was boiling over and the dinner was nearly ruined.

C. In the movie "What the Bleep, Do We Know," the Native Americans could not see Columbus's ships because they had no previous frame of reference through which to interpret the new stimuli. (What the Bleep, Do We Know, 2004)

Examples from your experience:
(1)

(2)

7.   *Positive Hallucination:*

A positive hallucination, like its opposite twin, the negative hallucination alters one's perception of the experiential world. With the a positive hallucination, a person can hear, see, feel, smell, or taste what is not there. Positive and negative hallucinations are part of the editing function of the organism as they assist in the adding and the subtracting of the sensory stimuli and perception of those stimuli in the creation and synthesis of the *sensory perceptive holographic mapping.*

Positive hallucinations can be simple or complex and like other *sensory perceptive alteration*s will work in concert with other alterations. These hallucinations are often observed with completion errors where the organism is filling in, subtracting, or distorting sensory perception to keep harmony in the mapping process. The need of the organism to have or create closure may be a driving force behind these alterations. Some types of hallucinations are state or context dependent and only occur when specific emotions or events are present.

> A. When Jennifer ask Monte if he wants to go to lunch, he hears her saying she's interested in a relationship with him.

> B. A child's imaginary friend is a type of positive hallucination, such as John has a friend, "Mr. Elf" whom he plays with for hours when no other playmates are available. This is often context dependent as it goes away when other people arrive. Some types of phenomena are state dependent and occur when specific emotional states are present.

Examples from your experience:

(1)

_____

_____

(2)

_____

_____

8. Confusion:

Confusion is a sensory alteration that can occur when an individual experiences being overwhelmed, threatened by new information or unfamiliar sensory stimuli. This includes role confusion, task confusion or self-generated confusion. The following are examples of each type of confusion.

Examples:
A. Self- generated confusion:
Tyler, usually a quiet and reserved young man, becomes quite agitated, creating much yelling and screaming in the house, when he notices the argument between his parents. His behavior escalates to the point that the parents have to stop what they are doing in order to stop the confusion created by his behavior.

B. Task Confusion:
Susan, an accomplished pianist, turns to her husband Billy and says, "I can't program this VCR. You know I never could do any type of

technical things, and my father always told me to stay away from electronic objects."

C. Role Confusion:
Freud, who coined the "Whore-Madonna Syndrome," identifies confusion as a "syndrome." This case involved an individual who enjoyed having a sexual relationship with a performer whom he perceived as being promiscuous, only to marry her and then find after the marriage, he had transferred all the feelings he had toward his mother to her, and had absolutely no sexual desire for her.

Examples from your experience:
(1)

---

(2)

---

9. *Time Distortion:*

Time distortion is an alteration in the perception and interpretation of time. There are several things to notice about time; the individual creates an experience of time in his body. The individual sustains the experience of time by putting it on automatic and the individual can subjectively alter how he experiences the sense of time he has created. Milton H. Erickson is reported to have said "time" is a construct. Time can be perceived as moving at different rates of speed. Have you ever felt like time just disappears or that it just seems to drag. Individuals describe that they experience themselves as going through time or are in time. Time is treated as if it were an object; however, time is a fluid concept.

Examples:

A.   David's girlfriend insists that they go to a movie he designates as a "chick flick." As David sits there, he munches his popcorn, attempting to make the time go. He continually reminds himself how bad the experience is and how the time just seems to drag. For David, instead of two hours, the movie seems to last ten.

B.   Sally, on her way to work, is involved in an automobile accident. As she is going through the intersection, someone runs the red light. They tap the end of her car, sending it into a spin. Sally feels as though the whole world has gone into slow motion. She experiences, a sense of spinning, a sense of trying to control the steering wheel, and a sense of trying to grapple for control of the brake. She reports after the car finally stops, "It seemed like an eternity before the car would stop."

Examples from your experience:
(1)

(2)

_____

_____

10. *Hypnotic Dreaming:*

Hypnotic dreaming takes the place of healthy action toward realization of a plan or goal. It often takes place automatically without the person's conscious direction.

Example:
A.   Jackie dreams about being a motion picture star. However, Jackie has never been in one play. She has never answered any of the advertisements with a local college to work as an extra in any of their plays. She has refused the offers of friends to be involved as an extra on a film being shot nearby. She spends hours thinking each day in a fantasy world, about the mansion she will live in, the limousine she will ride in, and the rewards she will receive as a star.

Examples from your experience:
(1)

_____

_____

(2)

_____

_____

11. *Sensory Distortion:*

Sensory distortion is an alteration of the sensed stimuli at variance with what the individual may normally experience. There are three types of sensory distortion: These are psycho-physiological sensory distortion in which unwanted sensations are numbed, dulled, or overly intensified; hyper-or hypo- sensory distortion in which environmental stimuli are amplified or obliterated; and pain sensory distortion in which only the afflicted portion of the body is perceived.

Examples:
A: George, while talking with his therapist, begins to notice the ticking of the clock. The noise becomes more and more irritating as he tries to think about what he is discussing with his therapist, to the point he almost feels as if he will scream, the ticking of the clock is so disturbing to him.

B. Jane plans to attend a formal event that is very important to her. The day prior to the event, she notices a slight pimple near her left cheek. As the event approaches, she sees the pimple becoming larger, redder, pulsating more, throbbing more, and becoming monumental in terms of her face. Instead of a slight imperfection, she sees it as almost covering half her face.

C. After Carol, a pain patient, leaves the room, the physician remarks to the nurse "given the injury and procedures she has received, there is just no structural or physiological reason why she is experiencing so much pain in her lumbar region."

Examples from your experience:
(1)

....

....

(2)

....

....

Cluster Trances: (The next two *sensory perceptive alteration* states are what we consider cluster *trances* because they actually utilize and incorporate several different *trance* states to accomplish their effect.)

12. *Gestalt Closure or Completion Trance:*

Gestalt closure or completion *trance*s appear to be part of the hard wiring of the organism in that the nervous system constantly seeks to complete the unknown. A completion *trance* occurs when we expect someone to arrive at a particular time, and the person does not arrive. Anytime there is confusion, insufficient information, or no information, completion *trances* occur. The nervous system will begin to create answers about what has happened disregarding the fact that it has no idea what has occurred. This completion error *trance* is created in relation to past, present or future events, the meaning of other's behavior or the intentions of others. After a completion *trance* occurs, the organism is often amnesic about having created the answers. Thus, it may become part of the mapping system adding to the confabulatory nature of one's beliefs and maps. Think of all the sensory illusions there are. Most people are familiar with optical illusions, one of which is the figure-ground phenomena. In this phenomenon when you focus in one way you see a cup/chalice, and when you shift your focus, you see two people facing each other.

Example:
A. Laine's friend Kinsey has not called her about the upcoming wedding rehearsal. After some time has passed, she begins to tell herself that Kinsey no longer likes her and may have invited another friend.

B. John notices that his friend Richard is unusually quite. He starts telling himself that John must be angry with him for forgetting his birthday yesterday. After some time has passed, John begins to notice that he is feeling angry with Richard.

Examples from your experience:
(1)

_____

_____

(2)

_____

_____

13. *I am or Identity Trance Clusters:*

I am or identity *trance clusters* are at the core of having a particular life, particular time lines, particular expectations, dreams, hopes, or lessons to be learned. Sri Nisargadatta Maharaj once suggested to an enquirer "Wear the uniform; don't become the uniform." He also said, "You can have it as you like. You can distinguish in your life a pattern, or see merely a chain of accidents." The authors see identities as *persistent patterns of trance clusters* brought about by the structure created and imposed over reality by the *sensory perceptive holographic mapping* of the organism's nervous system. Whenever there is an "I," there is an identity, such as the "mommy" identity, the "daddy," the "teacher," the "clown," etc., There are endless examples
.

Examples:
A. Jane believes that in order to be a "good mother" she must do everything perfectly. She uses her grandmother Sarah as the epitome of what a mother should be.

B. George is attempting to follow a particular belief system. He believes that he must dress a certain way, eat certain foods, and only interact with certain people. In addition, he has never met anyone from this faith. He read about it in a book.

Examples from your experience:
(1)

Summary

Sensory perceptive alteration is essential to the creation and maintenance of *homeostasis*. Maintaining balance and congruence in a world of sensory data that is incongruent with the organism's map is an ongoing process. The adding and subtracting of sensory stimuli is critical in the creation of a *sensory perceptive map* that stays harmonious. Therefore, confabulation and closure are two of the primary forces in *homeostasis* that drive the need for *sensory perceptive alteration*.

Basic biological functioning is balanced and congruent until the process of *socialization* whereby the basic functions of eating, breathing, sleeping, safety, and comfort, are altered and affected by it. Stephen Wolinsky, Ph.D., a noted psychologist and author once taught, "The interruption in the outward flow of energy is what creates neurosis." The authors see what Freud termed neuroses as the development of *SPA* states not congruent with the environment and thus a disruption of the energy flow.

Ways to Change Sensory Perceptive Alteration (*SPA*)

1. Becoming aware of "hypnotic" phenomena, as discussed, and labeling it frequently leads to deconstruction of environmentally incongruent

states and reconstruction of environmentally congruent states.

2. Addressing *cognitive programming errors* by utilizing "testing for programming errors" will lead to deconstruction and frequently replacement of an incongruent *SPA* with one that is environmentally congruent.

3. Utilizing diagramming, spoon-feeding, and *neural information centers* updates will change *SPA*.

4. Utilizing communication directly with *neural information centers* may change *SPA*.

5. Practicing "staying" in the present with the use of *present time sensory alignment* will deconstruct and reconstruct *SPA*.

6. Changing body postures and motor movement intertwined with the *SPA* will deconstruct *SPA*.

Explanations are meant to please the mind. They need not be true. Reality is indefinable and indescribable.
Sri Nisargadatta Maharaj

Chapter Nine

Trance De-Confusion

"You will not admit, your conclusions bind nobody but you."
Sri Nisargadatta Maharaj

It's Saturday afternoon. The old black and white movies are rolling. In a castle far removed from the valley below, a very dark and mysterious man is holding a young, pale, and blonde heroine. Amid the surrounding gypsy camps with their infiltrating, mournful music of violins, the dark and mysterious man with his "hypnotic" eyes mesmerizes the beautiful heroine who is held captive by his glance. In a very automaton-like mechanical way, she rises from her chair and with flat affect, fixed gaze, and a mechanical and awkward walk, moves across the room at the bidding of her psychic captor.

Another familiar scene associated in popular lore with *trance* and hypnosis is the following. A friend runs into an old Army buddy at the airport or train station and invites him home. As they begin to enjoy dinner with some of the neighbors who have been invited over, the friend who is hosting asks the old acquaintance, "What are you doing now?" The guest responds that he is a traveling hypnotist. He reports that he helps people stop smoking, learn at a faster rate, or overcome the fear of flying. He adds that frequently to augment his income, he works as a stage performer, assisting people in barking like dogs or flapping their arms like chickens for the amusement of others in the audience. All at the table are intrigued and insist upon a performance by the "hypnotist." They finish their coffee and adjourn to the adjoining room. There the hypnotist begins to select a subject as the others give him their rapt attention. The so-called hypnotist suspends a pendulum pocket watch suspended on a fob, or other such dangling implement, mid-center of the would-be subject's face, and begins to sling the object back and forth. Speaking in very low but authoritative tones, he commands the subject to relax. The subject begins to develop a fixed gaze, and his eyes begin to flutter. Upon the cue of the hypnotist's voice and the command, "Close your eyes," the subject closes his eyes. At this point, the hypnotist begins to suggest that the subject is holding a collection of helium balloons in his right hand, while the hand, itself, is somewhat detached from the body and that as the balloons move higher and higher, the subject's hand will move higher and higher all on its own. The hand levitates, rising higher and higher, and the subject appears to "slump" in posture, indicating that he has gone into a very deep state. The hypnotist then says to the subject, "Now that you are in a deep state of hypnosis, you are subject to my commands. Each time that the phone rings for the next twenty-four hours, you will cackle like a goose, flap your arms like a chicken, or begin to sing "The Star Spangled Banner." Do you understand?"

The subject blankly nods as if an automaton, under the control of some mysterious and dark power. Upon counting up, the subject opens his eyes and says, "Wow, what happened? And when are we going to do the hypnosis?" Everyone in the room laughs and then takes his or her turn in the hypnotic arena. Again, this is the same blank expression, the mechanical-like movement, and the simplistic and much filtered screening of the environment. So as not to agonize further with this travesty, the phone rings, and people begin to cackle like geese, flap their arms like chickens, howl like wolves, become Napoleon, etc.

Movies have had their place in both education and distortion of what *trance* is and what *trance* must be. The box office horror thriller, "The Exorcist," shaped for many what would be considered "hypnotherapy." One scene is almost unforgettable. A very "shrinkly" looking practitioner accompanies the neurologist to the home of the disturbed Reagan. The practitioner, in tones and manner not much removed from that of the entertainer discussed above, initiates a "*trance.*" Arm levitation is evidenced, which has been observed as one of the classical signs of a deepening hypnotic state. As the story unfolds, the hypnotist begins to utter phrases, such as, "Reagan is hypnotized. If you are inside of Reagan, you also are hypnotized. You must speak to me." The scene develops in which there is a roar (somewhat like the roar of the lion, which scared the Tin Man in *The Wizard of Oz*. Reagan, who is not quite under the hypnotist's control, attacks the hypnotist and once again to this collage of the concept of *trance*, another image has been imprinted for millions (The Exorcist, 1973).

Legitimate, documented views of *trance* work that have also shaped how we view these phenomena typically have been associated with inducing profound states of relaxation. *Trance* has also been noted as a "deep, sleep-like state" (The term "hypnosis" itself, as coined by James Braid, is a misnomer, but nonetheless, has shaped the idea that *trance* is somewhat like sleep.) (Kroger, *Clinical and Experimental Hypnosis*, 1963, page 2). *Trance*, as documented for clinical training has frequently demonstrated a very simplified state of behaving, acting, and responding to the world. In and of itself, the portrayal has indicated a very simplified way of being and responding to the greater world. The simple *trance*, evident to the observer, often created the impression, "Yes, indeed, this is different. This is markedly different from the way a person usually is. This is something strange." Known early in the annals of hypnotic literature and work that there was something called "waking state hypnosis." The speculation of the early explorers into this field of hypnotic phenomena, such as Charcot, Bernheim, and Mesmer, all indicated confusion about what *trance* was. Was *trance* something that was brought about by animal magnetism and involved an actor, acting on a subject by his or her mesmeric powers; or was it that suggestions or ideas were given to the subject, who upon picking these up and assimilating them, began to modify and change his or her behavior? In addition, certainly from the camp of hypnosis as suggestion, was the idea of a "waking state hypnosis" with the idea we are encountering suggestions all the time. Some of the ideas or suggestions have a profound effect upon us and lead to different, significant life changes. This is a form of waking state hypnosis. Of course, if the idea of waking state hypnosis exists, the corollary to this is that *trance* must be "a waking state *trance*," and therefore much more complex, on a continuum of human experience, and much less simplistic than is frequently and historically portrayed.

When I (Hellams) was a boy of fifteen, I was able to acquire employment with a local grocery store. The grocery store, albeit it was busy, was located in a very congested area of the downtown city in which I lived. Because of this, frequently the "bag boys" would be required to take groceries, not to a parking lot, but around the corner to someone's apartment or around the block to a distantly parked car, consuming time in the process. It was decided that the most efficient way to achieve this was that one of the baggers would stand at the end of the counter, rapidly bag and box the groceries, load them into a cart, and then hand the cart to another worker for the somewhat lengthy carryout and delivery process. Being an individual who bores very easily (given my ADHD bent), I found the first Saturday almost intolerable. Several times, I considered "packing up my career" in the grocery business and walking out. However, I decided to give it a second chance. The next busy Saturday of this assembly line work, I found a mental phenomenon was occurring. Shortly after entering the store, I would have people tap me on the shoulder and say, "Hey, take a break. It's break time." Time had condensed. Time was distorted. I felt calm, relaxed, at ease, and somewhat as though I had been in a sleep. After the break, I initiated again only to have the same, kind fellow tap me on the shoulder and announce it was time for us to go to lunch. I found my thoughts frequently going to distant places, becoming involved in little adventures, and yet another part of me was doing quite a good job of bagging, listening, moving the major and smaller muscle groups to facilitate the efficient order of bagging. I noticed that when I was given less monotonous duties, such as outside deliveries, that this phenomena did not occur. However, it was very remarkable to me that nobody noticed "my absence." That is, this was a private, internal state without any outward manifestation. Others were totally unaware that there was anything different in my behavior other than I was very focused, very directed, and efficient, although I needed continual reminding of when to go on breaks and when to go to lunch. Years later, I realized that what was going on was something that had been termed as "auto workers' hypnosis" or "assembly line workers hypnosis." However, in this state, I was able to respond. I was able to receive input and obviously give appropriate output in terms of movement, conversation, etc., In doing so, there was no evidence outwardly of the "shift" that had occurred. Later when I was trained in the classical methods of self-hypnosis, I became aware that this same kind of shift, this same kind of experience from the grocery store, was very much akin to the shift I would experience when doing self-hypnosis.

Tobias Schreiber has coined the phrase "*sensory perceptive alteration.*" This is used throughout this work interchangeably with the word "*trance.*" In viewing the spectrum of human behavior, you are viewing a spectrum of *trances/sensory* perceptively altered states that range in complexities from the simplest form of *trance*, which is that classically associated with the hypnotic state. However, as you have found through your readings in this work, (and I feel certain you will discover as you examine your own realities and the realities of life), far from any Svengali associated state, *trance* is a part of our on-going life stream. It is how we interface with our environment, adjust to our environment, and survive the stimulation and at times chaos of the environment. Frequently when we have facilitated talks and workshops, an obstacle has been the word *"trance."* In explaining *sensory perceptive alteration*, there usually is an awakening, an eye opening, a kind of "aha" experience, and we have been asked, "Why do we even introduce the word *trance*?"

"Trance" has become such a part of our on-going culture and has been so integrally tied in with the whole concept of hypnotic phenomena that it is difficult, if not impossible, not to use this word as a bridge into the broader concept of *sensory perceptive alteration*. Just as hypnosis has been acknowledged for well over a century as a misnomer because of its power as a catchword to explain a collection of states, practices, rituals, and techniques, it continues to be used in order to become a bridge in our sharing of ideas. *Trance* is *sensory perceptive alteration*. It is an ongoing natural state of our existence and not the artifact of some ritual.

We are not stating that *trance* or *sensory perceptive alteration* is merely a concept. It is our assertion that it is a direct extension of the biology of a living organism. *Trance*, whether it is a simple "freezing" of the organism in a catatonic like function, or whether it is as complex as the commercial airline pilot's *trance*, it is all one continuing phenomena.

Without this state of *sensory perceptive alteration*, it would be impossible to survive. The organism would overly stimulate, frozen, and unable to adapt to the changing environment to which the complex organism is exposed. Cognitive Behavior Theorists speak of mental filters. It is our observation that there are always mental filters. This is a part of the on-going, *sensory perceptive alteration*. A driver filters out many things in the driver's seat that he does not filter when he is in the passenger's seat. The instructor at the head of the classroom filters out many outside sounds and events as he focuses on the reactions of the students, the material to be presented, the time constraints, and perhaps outside monitorship of his performance that when assuming a different role in the seat of the pupil, he does not, filter.

It is important to understand that when we are speaking of *trance* or *sensory perceptive alteration*, we mean that there is a complex interplay between the neuro-chemical/electrical environment of the brain and the outward environment that we call frequently the world.

A useful metaphor in understanding this is to imagine the following. You are in a simulator. The simulator is based on previous experiences within the world. As you walk through the world, there is a part of you similar to a camera mechanism that electronically tracks, sound, smell, sight, etc., bits of the environment and translates them into electrical code into your simulator. However, at no point in time do you leave the simulator, and at no point in time are any of your internal reactions (moods/physiology) influenced directly by the environment. Your internal state of feeling from which your actions stem is totally reliant upon the simulator's presentation. Contained within the camera system of the simulator is also a certain type of programming of the simulator that there are certain things that you will see and certain things that you will not see reflected from the environment. There are things you will see to some degree or not see, smell or not smell, experience as a tactile sense or not experience as a tactile sense, or some variance on the continuum of awareness. The complex range of your responses is dependent upon this encompassing simulator. The simulator with its selective screening in and screening out function is, of course, in this analogy, the state of *trance*. As mentioned in the overview, we do not readily discern this state unless we define it in a very simplistic and highly circumscribed way. What generally has been held as "*trance*" is the most simplified end of the continuum of this experience.

The reader at this point may be asking, "Are you saying that we never directly deal with reality?" The answer is "yes." We are always dealing through this simulator with its bleed-through, sensing system of what's out there, which is filtered through the programming of the simulator. Reality, as we know it, is more a consensus of what the majority agrees it to be than what actually exists in the world.

Trance phenomena ranges from the most simplistic, which is that which has been classically thought to be true "hypnotic phenomena" to the very complex, highly trained actions of the neurosurgeon.

As an individual standing in the forest is desensitized to any particular tree, unless it is of very striking departure from the corpus of trees around him, the human recognizes only shifts in his trance states if they are very striking shifts.

Since each individual develops from birth *persistent patterns of trance clusters*, those knowing the individual and perceiving the individual only see the illusion of a unified experience, rather than seeing the individual as flowing through individual trance states. This failure to recognize this flowing of trance states and continuum of trance states leads us to label others and ourselves in very solid terms. We speak of ego structure, personality structure, and formations instead of appreciating the fluidity and therefore the great capacity to change that an understanding of trance can present.

Chapter Ten

Chapter Ten

Persistent Patterns of Trance Clusters
The Development of the Personality Illusion

"People have a limited number of physical and psychological postures."
George Gurdjieff, The Gurdjieff Factor

s we begin to explore deeper into the nature of homeostasis and *sensory perceptive holographic mapping*, there is often a question about personality and the core nature of the organism. Personality is an illusion in that we assume because we see some patterns of response that the individual is always that way. Trance clusters are those groupings of responses that manifest as part of the ongoing repetition in the sensory perceptive world and are triggered in stimulus response scenarios. The temporary and transient nature of personality is observed if there is some illness or injury to the organism. People often make statements such as "I'm just not myself today." On the other hand, they make inaccurate statements, like "I always tell the truth," or "I never forget to clean the house." These are all ways that we deny the inconsistencies or variations in the ways we act and attempt to maintain the illusion of sameness, congruence, and *homeostasis*. Some very interesting reading can be found in the works of Antonia Damasio in both "*Descartes' Error*" and in "*Looking for "Spinoza"*. These works explore the neuro-physiological, biochemical underpinnings of mind/body, thought, feeling, and emotion construction from a biological and philosophical view. The illusion of a unified person is part of the biological response to the mind/body's interaction with the living environment of which it is a part. We are now beginning to be able to study and explain the complex interaction of thoughts, feelings and emotions as part of the total organism and its continuum of responses to internal and external stimuli. These interrelated manifestations of biological responses as demonstrated in our patterns of behavior are more readily explained by the on going patterns of neural mapping and networking, than a fixed construct of a personality structure.

Identity Creation

There are an infinite number of identities created, as they spontaneously appear with each experience and disappear when the experience is over. Identities are a construction within the s*ensory perceptive holographic mapping system* as part of the nervous system's effort to organize chaos. The nervous system uses identities to deal with the feeling of being out of control, not knowing, being overwhelmed, or the fear of disappearance (annihilation). As you go through life, you may notice that people, places, things, experiences, thoughts, feelings, and really everything appears and disappears. Some things last longer than others do. Some things appear for millennia, while other things are here for a nanosecond. The mind/body gains skills to meet its needs. It learns these skills from others (parents, siblings, teachers, and others) by observation, instruction, or accident. In taking on the behaviors or mannerisms of others, the person may do this by modeling what is observed or by being instructed. He can fuse with what is observed, or he may resist that behavior or tact and develop what appears to be the opposite. Remember, that in observing others the underlying motives, intentions, or needs are not known, so external behaviors may be duplicated without understanding the internal mechanisms.

The fear of disappearance creates the *need to know* which prompts the mind/body to create the *mapping system* with an illusionary world that is *knowable, predictable, and controllable.* The mind/body has to abstract the sensory information in the environment because of its inability to accurately sense and assimilate all of the stimuli available. There are limitations to the abilities of the sense organs, themselves. Thus, distortions occur due to the inability to accurately detect or sense environmental stimuli. The limited sensory information is then deleted, distorted, generalized, added to, and confabulated in order to make it knowable, predictable, and controllable. Confabulation here is to indicate that sensory information from the environment is mixed with information from within the *mapping system.* The Gestalt closure phenomenon is an example of when the organism answers its own questions in order to fill in a blank area in information. The nervous system decides what to know and what not to know thus editing the sensory information to make it congruent with the *mapping system* already in place. Adding and subtracting the various elements that make up the mosaic of life makes interpretation quite fluid and malleable.

"I" dentities Are:

Identities are biologically encoded response strategies to stimuli encountered in the environment as mediated by the *sensory perceptive holographic mapping system* and shaped by the *socialization* process. Identities are conceptual frameworks that are imposed over the biological core of the organism during the *socialization* process. Prior to the *socialization* experiences, the organism had no conceptual frameworks interfering or altering its experience with the environment. The acquisition of identities occurs during the interactions with mom, dad and others as the developing person seeks to meet biological and interpersonal needs that are required for survival. These identities can be described as roles, positions, points of view, *trances (SPAs)*, strategies, frames of reference, and *persistent patterns of trance clusters*. Each of these descriptions can be further explained as to their functions.

Roles are prescribed patterns of social behavior and interactive rules of behavior, such as son, daughter, mother, father, cousin, husband, wife, businessman, deacon in a church, counselor or, teacher. These roles may be learned in the family, in the community, or prescribed by the society, religious or social group.

Positions refer to a defined point in reference to others. These positions can be points of reference such as young rather than old, happy as opposed to sad, good as juxtaposition to bad, democrat rather than libertarian or republican.

Identities as strategies can be described as the ways we think, feel and behave in order to meet some need or want. Identities always reference the philosophical core (the central belief about life); that is supported by the various belief systems of the individual and carried out in the form of strategies. Needs and wants may include but are not limited to food, shelter, safety, learning, love, sanity, knowing, or being in control. Being the "good son," the "cute daughter," the "faithful servant" are all different types of strategies. Strategies can be learned by interacting and observing others interacting. They can be developed by trying to be like others or by being the opposite of others or even some combination of the behaviors used by others.

Persistent patterns of trance clusters are those identities, roles positions (psychological, physiological, and philosophical) and strategies that are most often demonstrated by the individual, observed, and recognized by others as their persona or personality.

Dr. Stephen Wolinsky an expert in identity and trance states said, "You will suffer to the degree that you believe that you are your identities." He also said, "You don't have problems, your identities do." (Personal telephone conversation, June 2005). If identities are viewed as frames of reference or strategies then they can be seen as flexible and changeable. Identities only become problematic when they become frozen, fixed or when we are fused with them and refuse to or cannot detach from them. Sri Nisargadatta Maharaj said, "Pain is merely a signal that the body is in danger and requires attention. Similarly, suffering warns us that the structure of memories and habits, which we call the person, is threatened by loss or change. Pain is essential for the survival of the body, but none compels you to suffer. Suffering is due entirely to clinging or resisting; it is a sign of our unwillingness to move on, to flow with life" (I Am That, Sri Nisargadatta Maharaj, 1973).

There is a Sanskrit saying that is useful to keep in mind as it relates to the *Identity* and the *sensory perceptive holographic mapping system* or the world of the person. The saying is *Dristi, Shristi, Vada*, "The world is only there as long as there is an "I" there to perceive it." (The Supreme Yoga, Swami Venkatesananda, 1976). As we begin to explore the identities that appear and disappear within the m*apping system* keep in mind that the map is not the territory and the identity is not the person

Posture, Breathing and Eye Movement are Part of the Pattern

The physical postures of the body match or pace with the identity's internal pictures. Pauses and shifts in breathing indicate alterations in emotions, feelings or other internal states. As the Neuro Linguistic programmers learned from Milton Erickson, M.D., eye movements may give a lot of information about internal states. There is at least anecdotal data to indicate that eye movement may give clues to the sense being used to access or create information. The patterns are idiosyncratic but can be useful when there is out of awareness sensory accessing. An example of out of awareness sensory accessing is when an individual may be utilizing visual images or auditory sounds without being consciously aware.

Jennette says that she is remembering how her mother disciplined her because she can see an image of a time that happened. As you notice her eye movement, it appears that she is also responding to some inner dialogue or sounds and when you ask her what she is saying to herself or listening to, she says she can also hear her mother's voice. Additionally, she notices a kinesthetic response of a knot in her stomach.

The eye-accessing chart on the next page comes from a compilation of examples found in the works of. Steve Lankton, MSW. Practical Magic, 1980; Bobby Bodenhammer, The User's Manual For the Brain, 1999; and The Neuro-Linguistic Programming Home Study Guide, developed by David Gordon, Leslie Cameron-Bandler and Michael Lebeau, 1984.

The chart gives some suggestions as to what sensory area or apparatus is being accessed when the eyes move in certain directions or into certain positions. These eye movements give clues and hints to the mapping area that is being used when creating or remembering information

Eye Accessing Cues

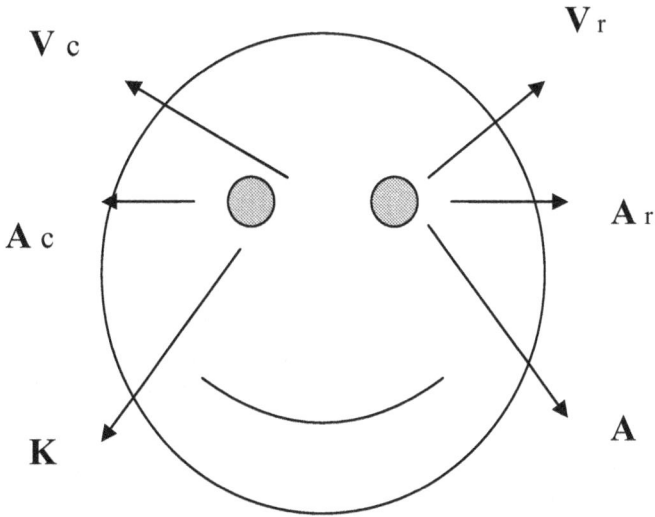

V c = Visual constructed images
V r = (remembered eidetic) image
(Eyes defocused and unmoving also indicates visual accessing.)
A c = Auditory constructed words or sounds
A r = Auditory remembered sounds or words
K = Kinesthetic feelings (also smell and taste)
A= Auditory sounds or words

These are Visual accessing cues for a "normally organized" right-handed person

People will say that they are "visual," "auditory" or "hands on learners" when in fact all senses are being used when experiencing life. Individuals may have modes of perception that they prefer, are most familiar and find it easiest to use when describing their experiences. More information can be found concerning eye movement in the works of Richard Bandler and John Grinder, the founders of Neuro Linguistic Programming.

Intrapersonal Nature of Identity

Identities appear to be interpersonal or interactive but most of what is going on is intrapersonal in nature. Although there appears to be an observer identity, in actuality there is only *observing* taking place. The *observing* creates the *observer* and the *observed*. Below there are several different types of identity labels to explore and experience.

Identities

Hearer	*Hearing*	*Heard*
Seer	*Seeing*	*Seen*
Observer	*Observing*	*Observed*
Feeler	*Feeling*	*Felt*
Thinker	*Thinking*	*Thought*

Identity's Intrapersonal Loop

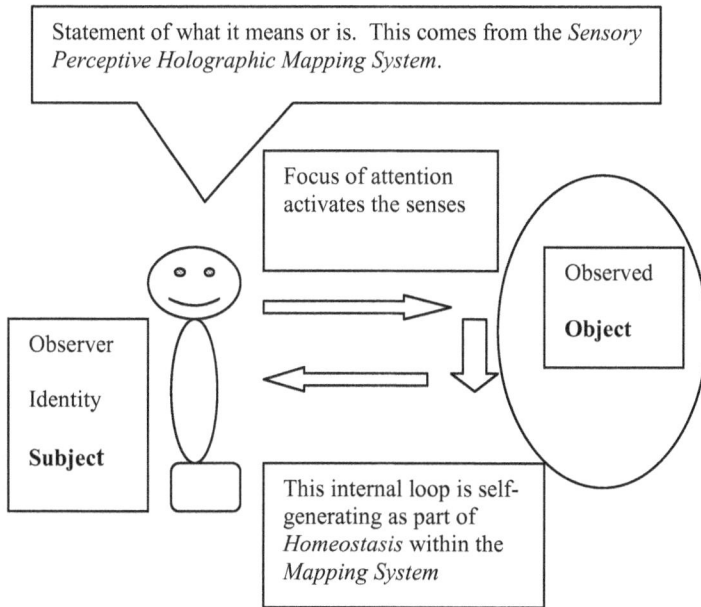

Statement of what it means or is. This comes from the *Sensory Perceptive Holographic Mapping System.*

Focus of attention activates the senses

Observed

Object

Observer

Identity

Subject

This internal loop is self-generating as part of *Homeostasis* within the *Mapping System*

The observer identity appears simultaneously with the object it observes and then goes inside to access the meaning of the object from within the *mapping system.* Therefore, what starts as an interpersonal interaction ends up as an intrapersonal interaction.

Questions for Identities (Trance States)

In each identity or observer identity, you wish to explore or examine, ask the following questions.

What am I paying attention to or what am I focusing on? (Image, thought, feeling, person, place, thing, energy, space, mass or time.)

What am I saying that it is or means?

By saying that it, means (X) that what am I wanting, creating, doing, or expecting. (Also, not doing, not wanting, not creating, not expecting?)

By wanting all of the above, what am I resisting?

Notice shifts or changes in your physiology, primarily breathing.

Watch for energy flow or blocks in the body (muscle tension, numbness etc.)

Let the experience dissolve in whatever way is comfortable for you.

Notice that each "observer identity" is a different window into a universe that has its own unique meaning and experiences.

You are the source of your experiential world.

Identities are a unique response to the stimuli as interpreted in the context of the nervous system's *sensory perceptive holographic mapping system*. The first created association or meaning will be the meaning and association that remains primary and will be accessed when similar stimuli are encountered. Alteration of any aspect of sensory perception will cause shifts in the meaning, association, and what is experienced. This is one reason for the activation of *SPA* states that maintain the appearance of congruence within the mapping world.

Chapter Eleven

Semantic Reversal Mechanism

and

Other Mirroring Phenomena

"The opposite of what we say and hear is often what is true."
Unknown

*P*roblems can occur when there are mixed or confused messages contained in the *neural information centers* that are a part of the *sensory perceptive holographic mapping system*. Mirroring responses are those responses that result when the projections or introjections are confused, and the location of the reference becomes mixed up. An example of this confusion can be when an individual cannot see himself as being successful or competent due to programming errors. *Semantic reversal mechanisms* are a part of the *homeostatic* system that is designed to protect the *sensory perceptive mapping system*. Their function is to neutralize incoming information that threatens *dissonance* to the organism. These mechanisms may involve semantic reversals of the incoming stimuli, such as the addition of "not" and the inclusion of "yes, but" formulations and pseudo-logical argumentations. Further, they can be visual with images that attempt to counter the incoming threatening information.

Mind/Body Inclusion

This discussion emphasizes that the mind/body is one, and as this theoretical model unfolds, it is clear that the entire organism is included. Mind/body integration and inclusion move our thinking and awareness beyond the divisive errors of Descartes' reasoning when he divided the organism into separate parts and created an artificial barrier in the unity of the organism. This arbitrary division of the organism is an illusion created by language, and it further leads to the separation of thoughts, feelings, and emotions. *Neural information centers* contain and may abstract symbolic representations of sensory stimuli, such as color, sound, texture, odor, and smell, as well as the various distinctions within and between these sensory typologies. The words that represent these are visual, auditory, tactile, olfactory and gustatory. The mind/body encodes this data and references and/or associates present stimuli with earlier or variant stimuli as encoded within the experienced neuro-chemical mapping system. Kinesthetics are a subset of proprioception, which is the recognition of organs and body organization, placement, and sensation within the spatial world of the organism. Vestibular orientation places the mind/body in harmony and balance with gravity. Kinesthetics appear to be the internal orientation and recognition response as noted by alterations within the physiology to position the organism as to approach/avoidance or neutrality in relation to the stimulus field. The fight, flight or freeze response is contained within this response set. Curiosity may also be within this orientation approach.

Energy, mass, and space-time are experienced, represented, and created by the flow of "energy" or "sensory data" through the organism. Sensory stimuli as they are experienced, associated, and/or referenced within the sensory perceptive mapping system are rapidly converted to an organic response of energetic orientation that is labeled as a feeling or emotion. This represents the energetic potentiality of the mind/body in relation to its stimulus mapping. Contained within the *mapping system* are references and associations to original, past objects and the emotional connection or response to them. Visual and/or auditory stimuli are rapidly converted to kinesthetic response. The changes in heartbeat, respiration, digestion, hypothalamic changes, muscles tensing and relaxing as well as a myriad of other changes, are all part of a harmonious, concerted effort to maintain *homeostasis* and survival.

Referencing within the organism creates a looping mechanism of orientation to incoming stimuli, as well as its own response to the incoming stimuli. Stimuli are associated and referenced with the *sensory perceptive mapping system* as the pool of *neural information centers* and center programming sensitizes the organism to varying levels of neuro/biochemical change within the organism at different states of energetic potentiality. Gestalt closure is an integral part of this referencing and associating within the *mapping system*. The biological system responds to stimuli by referencing previously experienced "models" and then projecting outcomes, associations, possibilities, and the emotional states aligned with these experiences, both future and past, to notate the present experience. This again indicates the internal looping of the individual's world and world experience.

Chapter Twelve

Chapter Twelve

The Diamond of Awareness

"This is the mystery of imagination that it seems to be so real. You may be celibate or married, a monk or a family man; that is not the point. Are you a slave to your imagination or are you not? Whatever decision you take, whatever work you do will invariably be based on imagination, on assumptions parading as facts."
(*I Am That*, Sri Nisargadatta Maharaj, 1973)

*T*he Diamond of Awareness is the name for a method of p*resent time sensory alignment* that includes considerations of how we describe and experience energy, time, space, and mass. All location is relative to position. From the point of where we are, all distance is measured and perceived. We are the central focal point from which all things are perceived. This way of observing how we experience and label life is a way to create interruptions in the conscious framework and to increase the possibility of our awareness of the ongoing *"trances"* or *"SPAs"* that shape our perceptions and interactions with the self and others. The sense or concept of "I AM" precedes and necessitates all other concepts. It is the seed of the universal experience. This is the source of our world experience. By creating awareness of our abstractions, we can begin the journey back before the creation of the identity through the various concepts, feelings, and sensations to a place that is freer from programming, *cognitive programming errors*, and dysfunctional *trances*.

To begin, we start at the "I" which is our sense of presence, and then *I AM,* which is noticing one's sense of consciousness and the recognition of existence. *I Am Here* references the notation of location being here rather than anywhere else. It is the source position from which to notice other things. To be here, we cannot be there. *I Am Here Now* notates now rather than in the past or future.

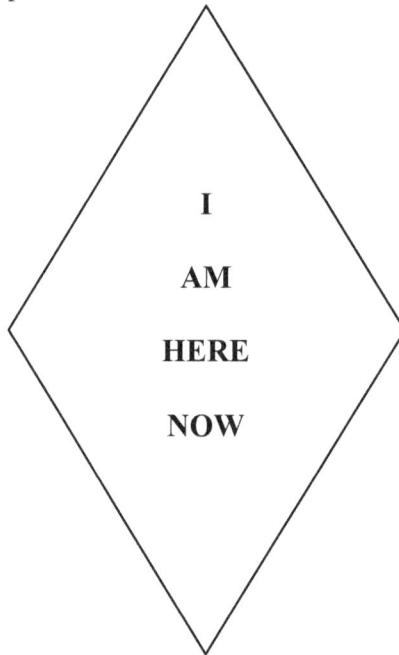

I

AM

HERE

NOW

The diamond is a beautiful stone when cut and polished especially when the debris is cleared away. The diamond is one of the hardest substances known to man and can be used to cut other hard substances. The Diamond of Awareness can be used to clear away all that is not part of the essential self and clear away the illusion created by the nervous system. There are three major sections of this Diamond. They are I *Am*, I Am H*ere,* and I Am *Now.* Coinciding with these are three areas of illusion or trance created by the nervous system's programming and programming errors as influenced by the *socialization* process. These three areas are I Am *this* or *that,* I Am *There,* and I Am *past* or *future.* Sri Nisargadatta Maharaj, a rogue Hindu Saint stated, "Most of what you know about yourself came from outside of you. Discard it." Before deciding which descriptors to discard, it may be useful to first notice what they are and where they came from. Maharaj also instructed, "To find out what you are, you must first find out what you are not." (I Am That, Sri Nisargadatta Maharaj 1973). When we speak of discarding, we are simply referring to examining, exploring, or stepping back from the particular identity structure. As we begin to explore the identities in their various shapes and sizes there are several things to consider as we try different exercises. Not every exercise is for everyone, so try different things, keep whatever is useful at the time, and leave what is not useful behind. If something seems confusing try it again, if it is still confusing, keep going. You can come back to it later if needed.

Confusion means to fuse with some aspect of the experience or belief. The identity (*SPA*), position, or frame of reference you are knowingly or unknowingly in could be fused with and distorting the perception or experience of another area of the territory. It may be necessary to stay with the experience to burn off excess energy or attachments. The willingness to stay with the confusion initially could be beneficial. Trying to get "clear," "enlightened," or to know is also a position and an identity.

As we start to investigate the identities, *trances (SPAs)*, reference points, frames, or lenses, the exercises are not designed to create a better, clearer, more beneficial "I". The exercises may expand awareness or loosen associations, assumptions, and references.

When we talk about frames of reference, positions, associations, assumptions, *trances* and ask that we create a frame, this means to move through and away from the concepts and abstractions about the experience toward the original stimuli. Then step back from the stimuli and observe anew. When we reframe this means to experience the stimuli from a different perspective, filter, position, or angle. To de-frame is to step away from all known frames of reference.

I Am: This or That

The I Am this or that applies to the descriptors of the "I," and along with the description comes the categorization and judgment of the descriptor. To become clearer about the *descriptors,* one must notice if they have *judgment, preference, or significance* attached to them. Notice if any description appears automatically, and if so, where did it come from? Notice who or what authority the descriptor may have come from. Often we describe ourselves on a continuum or in polarities. The list below is just a small sampling of descriptors to start you thinking.

Descriptors

Tall
Short
Thin
Blonde
Red haired
Brunette
Hairy
Bald
Green eyes
Hazel eyes
Strong
Smart
Man
Woman
Child
Adult

These descriptors may be placed in pairs that are seen as polarities. When these polarities are interpreted to be in binaries, they are viewed as one being superior or preferred to the other. At times, they are seen as dichotomous.

Descriptors

Short ---------------------Tall
Fat------------------------Thin
Brunette----------------------Blonde
Weak----------------------Strong
Dumb----------------------Smart
American----------------------Latino
Black------------------------White

As you begin to go through these descriptors, notice which may apply to the way you describe yourself or others. Then ask yourself, or notice if there are judgments, preferences, or significances associated or fused with the descriptors. There are often evaluators paired with descriptors. *Evaluators* give the descriptor a value judgment, which may be in either a positive or a negative direction. Some evaluators are words like.

Evaluators

Good --------------------------Bad
Right -------------------------Wrong
Should------------------------Should not

If you notice that there are judgments, preferences, or significances associated with the descriptors, ask yourself who or what authority told you that. If you notice whom it came from, then notice how you decided that it was true. Ask yourself what you assumed, decided, or believed to get you to create that association.

What does it mean to have judgment, preference, or significance associated with a descriptor? Judgment is indicated by labeling something as good or bad, right or wrong, positive or negative, superior or inferior. When we say that some quality, trait, or description is something that is either an enhancement or a deficit, we are issuing a judgment. *Bill is very strong, but that is not a good quality for an artist.* Preference is noted when one trait, quality, or attribute is seen as superior or inferior to another. Being thin is a desirable trait but to be slender is much preferred. *Susan's musical ability is far more useful than Mary's dancing.* Significance is applied when it is seen as more or less important to have or not have certain identified traits, qualities, or abilities. *Isn't it wonderful that Kristie has such a brilliant sense of design?*

Dr. Stephen Wolinsky, noted identity and *trance* expert, presented the following formulation: That "I" + (word-descriptor) = identity (Personal telephone Conversation, August 2005). One example could be *I am a man*, or *I am happy*. A fusion of meanings can occur when we say "**X**" means "**Y**". We associate meanings and then forget that we associated them, we then believe the associations to be true. An example of this could be, *I am a man, and therefore, I must be strong and confident.* We begin by pretending X, and then pretend that we are not pretending. Therefore, we become that in our *mapping system.* Remember, most of what you know about yourself came from outside of you, therefore discard it. This means that we may want to examine this knowledge or explore its origins and meanings further. Others tell us who we are, should be, or need to be. We are then told how to act, and what our actions or statements mean.

Words as Containers of Experiential and Associational Meaning

As we explore the world of words, we need to keep in mind that words are abstractions. As we move away from the original sensations into images, emotions, feelings, and word descriptions, we are moving further and further from the original stimulus-sensation and therefore the meaning is more abstracted. Words create their own world of meanings and associations. Words are unique to the experiences and connections of the individual and the environment that he has been exposed to. When a young child is told *the stove is hot,* he reaches out to touch the stove because without the experience of what hot is, the word "hot" has no reference, or associational meaning. The next exposure to the word "hot" will bring new adjusted responses. For just a moment, think of all the words that have multiple meanings, depending on the spelling or the context of how they are used. Words like *bear or bare, see or sea, and here or hear.* Words like love, hot, bad, mother, and father (etc.) have varying meanings and associations. Each individual accesses different experiential, associational, and emotional references for any word. That is part of the miracle and complexity of language.

Communication is difficult and errors in interpretation and understanding occur frequently.

Words are part of a complex symbolic representation system that attempts to describe and explain what happens in the individual's *sensory perceptive mapping system.* Some writers such as Wittgenstein and Derrida have described words as, simply referring to other words and as part of a complex game that defers its explanations to other abstract representations and never reaches the concrete level of the territory. (On Certainty, Wittgenstein, 1969).

Remember the representations in your mapping world are symbols and are not the territory. Words can be used as descriptors, they can serve as evaluators, and some words can act as *modifiers* that shift or alter the meaning of the word. Modifiers can be words like *very, extremely, not, barely, and hardly.* Words have different meanings depending on the individual, family, social group, culture, or time. Words are used as if they never vary in meaning, and as if the object or experience the word describes is the same thing as the word and interchangeable with the word. The word and the thing it refers to are not the same thing. For example, the *word "apple" cannot be eaten. You cannot sit in the word "chair." You will not swim in the word "sea," nor can you breathe the word "air."*

Next, we will begin to explore descriptors, evaluators and where they came from within the *sensory perceptive mapping system.*

I Am This or That: Exercise

List your *descriptors*, then list any *evaluators* then list *who or what authority* said them.

Descriptor	Evaluator	Who or What Authority
_____	_____	_____
_____	_____	_____
_____	_____	_____
_____	_____	_____
_____	_____	_____

As you become aware of an identity you assume, then become aware who or what authority made that statement or gave you that example. Become aware that we believed that we knew the meaning, motivation and intent of the person, when in fact we may not have known.

Identity Exercise

Find an identity that you wish to explore. The identity may have a positive or negative association for you. We suggest that you do not pick your most difficult identity or the most traumatic. An example could be I am a mother-identity; I am a counselor-identity; I am happy-identity.

When you select an identity, create the identity. Merge with the identity by stepping into it. Experience it in whatever way you do that. Then detach by stepping out of it.

(This helps us to notice if we are associated or dissociated with the identity) If you cannot step into it then you are experiencing some dissociation.

If you step in but have difficulty stepping out of it, you are experiencing being overly associated. You may need to experience it more to burn off the excess energy of attachment.

Notice who or what authority told you that or modeled that for you.

Listen for the voice and various elements of sound, tone, loudness.

Look for any images, and other visual attributes such as colors, black and white, and distance.

Be aware of any sensations and the various elements of kinesthetic or tactile sense representation intensity and duration. Notice if there is any numbness or lack of sensation.

Where do you experience this identity, notice the location in the physical body, face or head.

Notice any energy. Does the energy seem to have movement or does the energy seem to be frozen. If there is movement, is it fast or slow and in what direction.

Now step into the identity frame, now change the frame.

Now de-frame, and notice what changes.

Enneagram Fixations

The Sufis, who are Middle Eastern wise men, developed an ancient system for identifying nine personality fixations called the Enneagram. These nine fixations are false identifications that result in attempts to compensate for the fixation. Keep in mind that anything you think you are, you are not. False conclusions lead to false solutions. The Enneagram is similar to the Meyers-Briggs Personality Inventory, which looks at personality types, preferences, or styles. This work looks at *persistent patterns of trance clusters* as a way of meeting needs and the structuralization of the energetic space that appears as a personality.

Enneagram Fixations

Perfection
Will
Harmony
Origin
Omniscience
Strength
Truth
Wisdom
Love

Enneagram Fixations and their Compensators

```
Perfect--------------------------------Imperfect
Worthy---------------------------------Worthless
Creative-------------------------------Inability to Do
Adequate-------------------------------Inadequate
Something-----------------------------Nothing
Oneness--------------------------------Being Alone
Wisdom---------------------------------No Wisdom
Truth-----------------------------------No Truth
Love------------------------------------Loveless
```

The area of the Diamond of Awareness that deconstructs the *trances* associated with I am are quite extensive and are only limited by your questions. Being awake helps us to stay aware of whom we are. By balancing the interaction between the territory and the *mapping system*, we are able to be clear about whom we choose to be.

I Am, Here

The next section of The Diamond of Awareness deals with location. You are the location of awareness, and from this position, you locate yourself in space. Distance is measured from this position to all other objects or positions. The body is always here. It is never there. Within the Diamond of Awareness is the *here* and being here is what we can experience. Outside of the Diamond is the *there* and the there is not experienced, it is only imagined. Notice we can imagine being across the room, across the street, across town or the state but imagining is not the same as being there. We may even imagine being in a magical place or nowhere. We spend time making up or trying to figure out what is going on over there. Noticing what is going on with another person or object is projection or pure imagination. How often have you tried to think about what is happening somewhere else or what another individual is thinking feeling or experiencing only to find that you were entirely off in your story. Think about location. Where are you now, what room, what building, what town, what county, what state, what country, what continent, what hemisphere, what galaxy are we in.

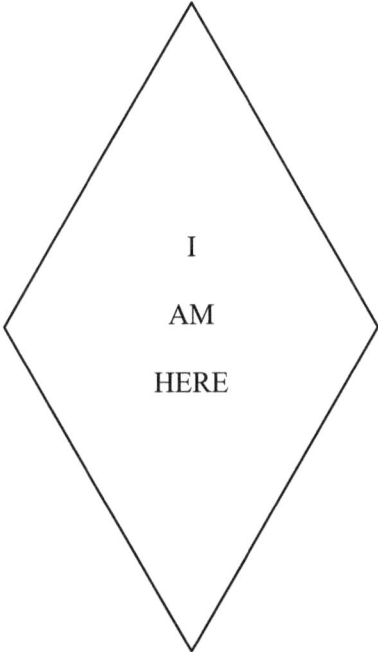

I

AM

HERE

I Am, Now

The next section of the Diamond of Awareness assists in the deconstruction of the *trances* around time. We experience ourselves as being in time or as going through time. Our sense of time is created internally, and then set on automatic so, it appears to function separately from us. The physical body is always present in the now. It is not found in the past or wandering around in the future. Consciousness reconstructs the past or projects the future over the present experience...

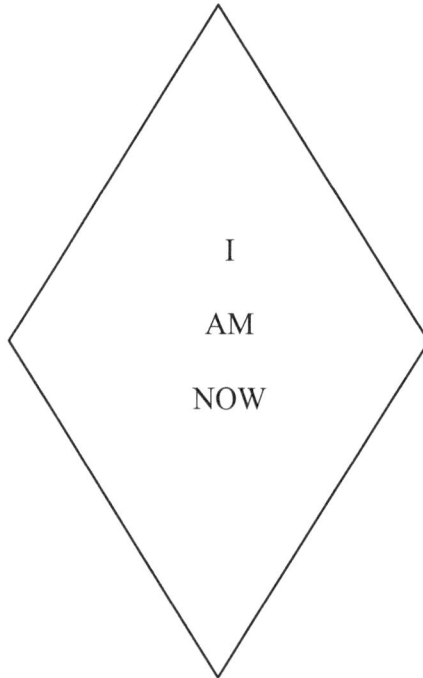

I

AM

NOW

Time Lines

Being In Time

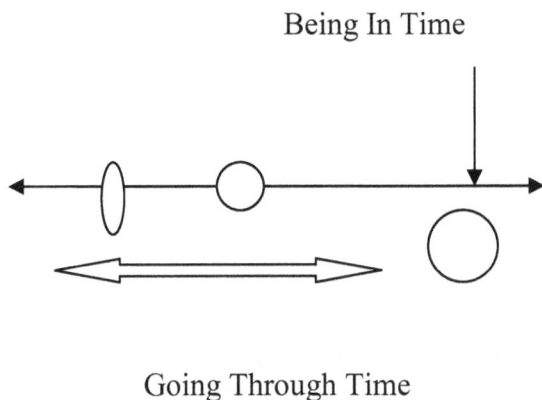

Going Through Time

People are aware of being present, fully being where they are, and enjoying the event they are engaged in as if time were fluid and flowing. People may experience themselves moving from event to event as if time was solid, fixed or frozen and they are moving through it.

Become aware of how you experience time. Does time seem to move slowly or does it move quickly depending on whether you are enjoying the experience or not? Experiences, identities, emotional states all have a beginning, a middle and end. Here are some questions to get you thinking about time.

Time Exercise

*In relation to (*love, loss, person, place, or experience*)*
X what was?

*In relation to (*love, loss, person, place, or experience*)*
X what is?

*In relation to (*love, loss, person, place, or experience*)*
X what will be?

Also, ask
*In relation to (*love, loss, person, place, or experience*)*
X what was not?

*In relation to (*love, loss, person, place, or experience*)*
X what is not?

*In relation to (*love, loss, person, place, or experience*)*
X what will not be?

Another type of questioning regarding time, deals with the things that you assume, decide, or believe about objects, people, places, or things. Whenever a decision, assumption, belief, or philosophy comes up trace it to its origin or earliest remembrance.

Assume, Decide or Believe Exercise

Notice something that you assumed, decided, or believed and ask the following:

I know that when you were X years old, etc. - you assumed, decided or believed that then. Are you still assuming, deciding or believing that now, and if you can, notice who or what authority told you that?

Is there any associated judgment, preference or significance affecting the assumption, decision or belief and is there any interaction of the judgment, preference or significance?

162

An example of this would be as follows: *When Susan was 8 years old, she believed that her mother knew everything and could read her thoughts. Now that she is an adult of 25, she sometimes feels that she cannot hide things from her mother because of this old belief.* If she says that it is *good* that she tells her mother everything about her life, it is an effect of a judgment. Beliefs that we create in the past if not examined now in the light of present information, automatically popup and affect how we perceive things. Once a belief is formed, the original belief is the strongest and if it is followed by positive results, it will become part of the *mapping system*. If this interaction is repeated, its functioning may become automatic. A point of interest may be that energy is said to be neither created nor destroyed, it just changes form or is transmuted. Within the *neural information centers* are contained all references to known objects and within those centers and their interconnectedness are the rules for how they are associated or referenced. This is based on the idea that contained within the *sensory perceptive holographic mapping system* is not only the original object construct (representation) but also all references and history of varying associational linkages and their rules of acknowledgement, use and nonuse of the object. We consider that our personal or idiosyncratic interpretation of stimuli is dictated by the original representational object as modified by the association with all representational objects within that class or category. This would bring up some references to category and scope. Category is a designation of a certain set of similar objects, stimuli or experiences while the range, limit, and rules for inclusion or exclusion and there defined functions would be the indicators of scope. Category can also be used to indicate distinctions of classes that objects can be divided into.

Recognition of Present Time Stimulus, Objects, and Experiences

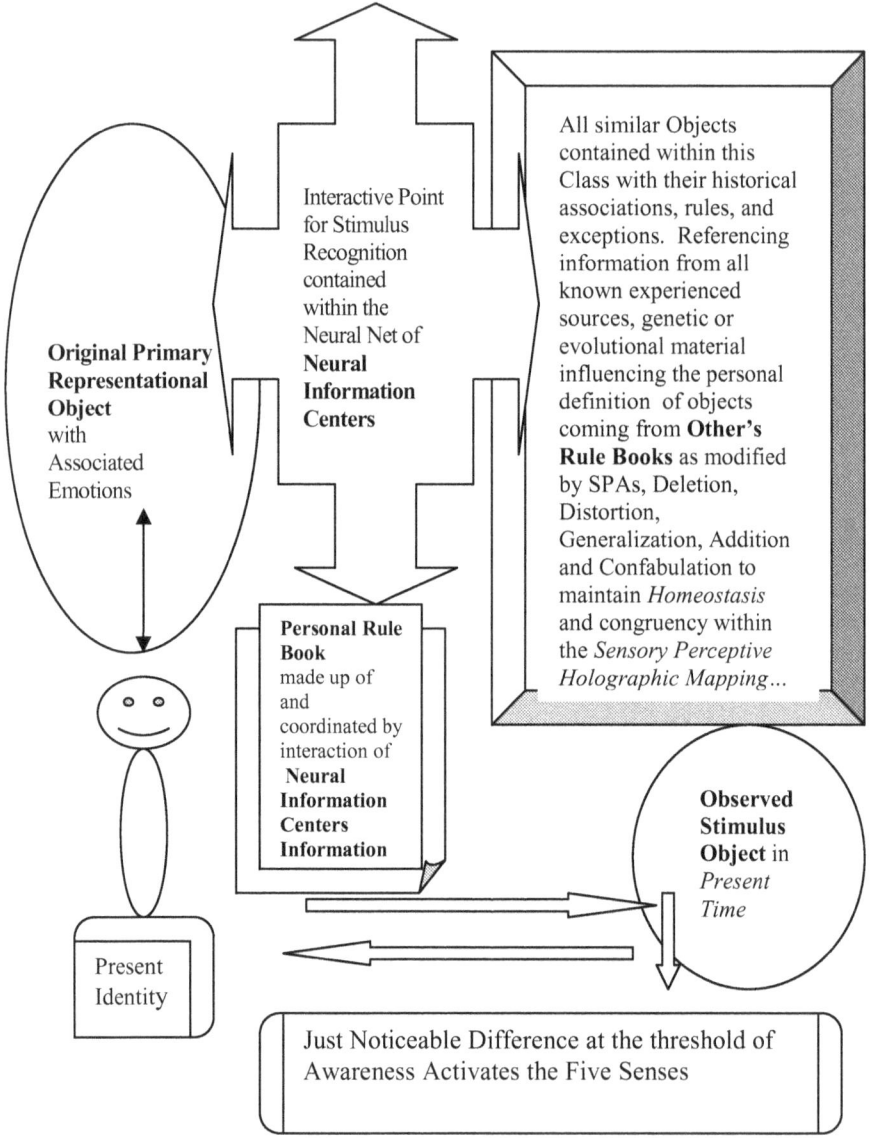

Original Primary Representational Object with Associated Emotions

Interactive Point for Stimulus Recognition contained within the Neural Net of **Neural Information Centers**

All similar Objects contained within this Class with their historical associations, rules, and exceptions. Referencing information from all known experienced sources, genetic or evolutional material influencing the personal definition of objects coming from **Other's Rule Books** as modified by SPAs, Deletion, Distortion, Generalization, Addition and Confabulation to maintain *Homeostasis* and congruency within the *Sensory Perceptive Holographic Mapping...*

Personal Rule Book made up of and coordinated by interaction of **Neural Information Centers Information**

Observed Stimulus Object in *Present Time*

Present Identity

Just Noticeable Difference at the threshold of Awareness Activates the Five Senses

The genetic/evolutional need and survival indicators dictate or guide the original biological response to stimuli. Biological needs are safety, water, nutrition, comfort, attachment (merging), learning and information completion, which are all geared to the nervous system's primary focus of survival. The natural essential interaction with the environment and the energetic flow is interrupted and mediated by the *socialization* process of interaction with others. The rules and injunctions from others' interpretation (*others' rulebook*) of the world begin to be the foundation of our *personal rulebook* and the giving of judgments, preferences and significances in relation to need acquisition and behavior. The impact of others is a natural part of development, but it begins to compartmentalize the thinking, feeling, and responding of the organism into an unnatural responding to the environment self and others. An internal considering of internalized rules of interpretation and their judgments, preferences, significances and their interaction, interrupts the natural flow of response by the organism. So within the neural net is contained the original stimulus, all the biological indicators, the interpreted rules of others, and the organism's created rules of response. The conceptual world and the constructed rules overlays the natural biological interaction with the environment. Within the *mapping system*, the construct of the personal identity is created as an interface of interaction with the world. The survival mechanisms of the nervous system do not or cannot differentiate between the biological and the imagined, so any perceived threat to an identity is seen as a threat to the biology. Then we begin living in a world constructed by metaphors and interpretations of what the environment means or should be according to the mythological constructs of our family, group, culture and our biological progenitors. Within the messages of judgments, preferences and significances are the stories or rules (beliefs and philosophies) of how to survive better. The message is we need to learn these rules and apply them to living and that we need to or should know them. There are instances when a child makes errors and is told, *you do not know what you are doing, what were you thinking, you should know what to do, haven't we taught you anything.* The biological being is separated from the environment and looses its harmony with its essential self. Remember, *the spirit is willing, but the flesh is weak* is a message about the subjugation of the flesh and a judgment of its inherent weakness and badness. Within this rule is also the preference for the higher functioning spirit as opposed to the body thus separating the organism from itself. Since, we are told that we should know things (the rules) to survive; we have developed a biological learning response and a biological completing response (Gestalt closure). Therefore we should, *know, predict and control* in order to survive better. The organism's natural responses to danger are a search and scan mechanism along with the flight, fight, or freeze response. Since the nervous system can only respond to things it recognizes and knows, the things it is looking for have already happened and are in the past. Therefore, the nervous system is constantly projecting an overlay of the past over the present so it can survive in the future from events it has already survived. *Present time sensory awareness* creates a null set, or reset point to momentarily disrupt this mapping overlay of the present with the past. Therefore, enlightenment is a return to the natural connection of the environment (territory) and the biological self (self in territory). The biological being and the environment are one and are congruent when they interact and are not mediated by a conceptual, mythological world.

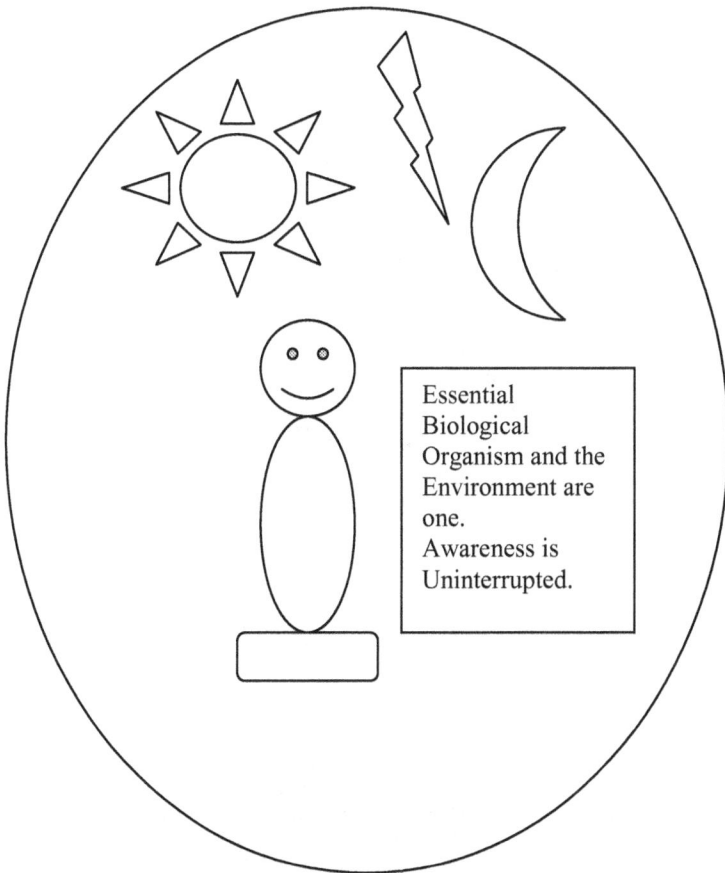

Essential Biological Organism and the Environment are one.
Awareness is Uninterrupted.

The Person and Environment as One

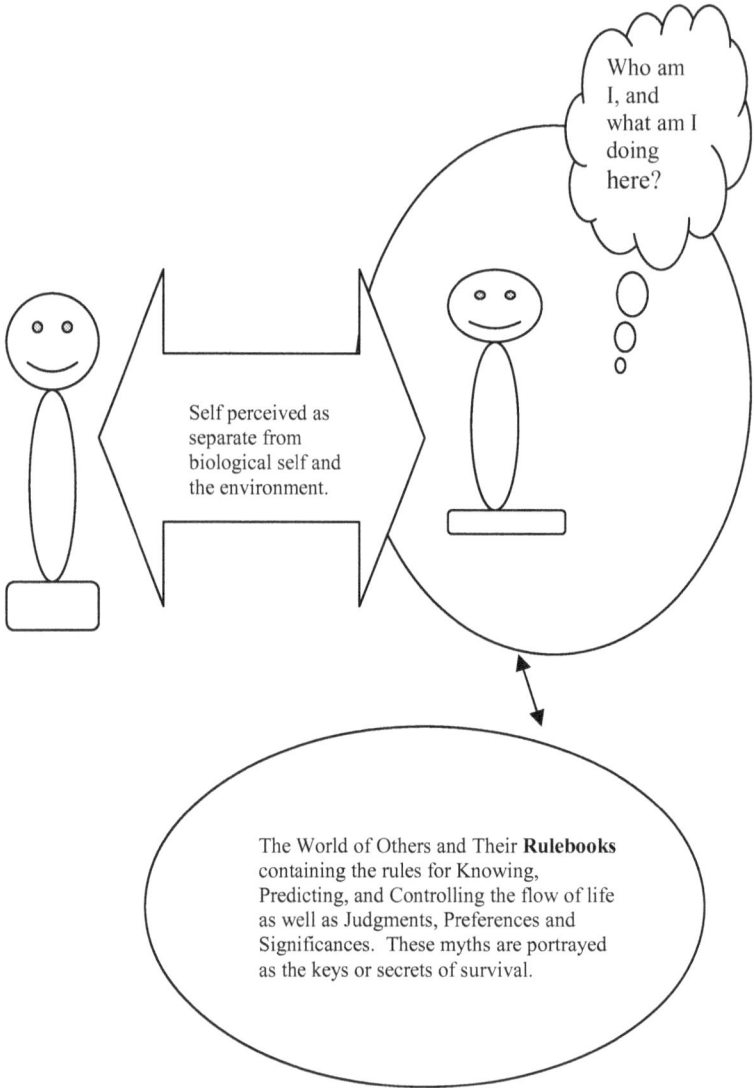

**Socialization and the Conceptual
World That Compartmentalizes and Separates**

Rulebook Metaphor

The rulebook is a metaphor for the *neural information centers* and their ability to acquire, categorize, respond to, and utilize stimuli (information). The Sensory Rulebooks may be similar to books in that they contain information but they are additionally multi sensory. They use all available senses to construct the sensory representations, their associated emotional states, and any accompanying editorial explanations. The representations can be various visual images, auditory sounds, dialogues, tactile sensations, smells, tastes; and they may contain access to a singular stimulus or a complex interconnection and interaction of sensory stimuli that construct a multi-sensory, multi-dimensional experience or memory. Within the *sensory mapping system* is a massive library complex that maintains a referencing system of all experiences and a history of experiences and their explanations from all known sources. The library complex is a way of describing the categorizing sensory information into the various classifications and subjects. The books separate sensory material into their designated areas and scope of reference. Although, not fixed there are rules of connection and categorization and usage that are both universal and idiosyncratic and made up by the nervous system.

Inherent Sensory Perceptive Mapping Errors

The Diamond of Awareness assists the user in remembering *to be aware* of the *Here* and *Now*. This is useful because the *mapping system* is always referencing the past. The nature of the biological system is to reference incoming sensory data to past objects, experiences and the associated emotional, energetic orientation toward that object. Thus, the images, sounds, and emotional orientation are experienced as if they are occurring now, but in fact, they are referencing objects, experiences, and emotions in the past. The *mapping system* is an abstracted representation of the territory as constructed within the nervous system. Survival and navigation through the territory are the goals of this representational hologram. Remind yourself that what is being experienced is always being filtered and altered by the *mapping system*. This is a continuous challenge. Remind yourself to be aware that the linking of present stimuli with past-created representations of similar stimuli creates a representational blend within the sensory *mapping system* and is not accurate. Distortions, deletions, generalizations additions, and confabulations (blending of stimuli, past, present, created, with their associated meanings, and emotional states) are the tools used by the nervous system to keep the *mapping system* congruent and maintain *homeostasis*. This is where s*ensory perceptive alteration* assists with the maintenance of internal and external stimuli referencing by altering sensory data and its integration into the ongoing storyline created by the nervous system through the lens of an identity.

The Diamond of
Awareness

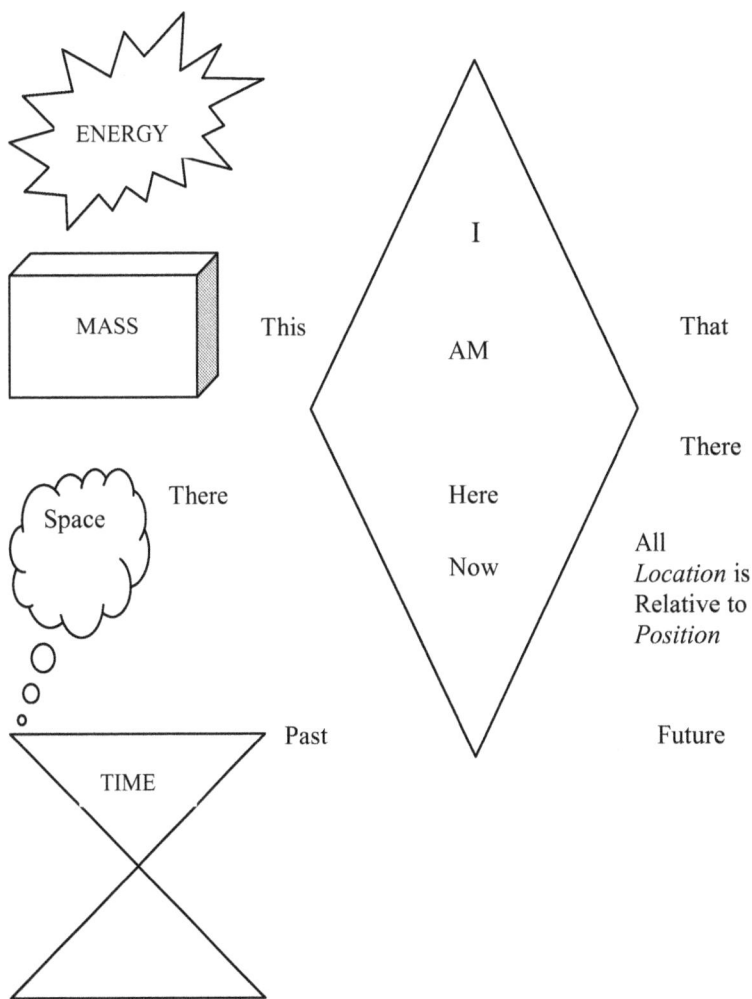

Figure 4

The Diamond of Awareness is a method of increasing awareness of *present time sensory alignment* and disruption or interruptions of s*ensory perceptive alteration*s or *cognitive programming errors*. This particular way of working with the organism, was developed during studies with Dr. Stephen Wolinsky, the founder of the Quantum Psychology Institute. It is simply a method for increasing awareness of the focus of attention and the various underlying stories, beliefs, lies, and imaginings we call reality and life. The Diamond of Awareness can be used as a tool to be used for *enquiry*, that is to question and confront the concepts that are created. The Diamond can be used to assist with trance Deconstruction or interruption and the Diamond can be used in a similar way to the meditations dealing with the space between two (2) breaths to dissolve the experience.

Exercise

Sit comfortably and notice as a thought comes up or materializes. Ask yourself where does that thought come from. Then if you notice another thought, ask where does that thought come from. Do this with several thoughts. Pause

As the thought goes away, ask yourself where does that thought go. Do this with several thoughts.

Now notice that these thoughts come from the space and return to the space. This is a dissolving exercise; it helps you to notice the space.

The Diamond of Awareness will also bring you back to the space.

Each section of the Diamond is used to cut away the layers of illusion, programming errors, and *sensory perceptive alterations* that distort or prevent the organism from more clearly experiencing reality. The center of the Diamond contains what "I" consider experience-able. The individual is encouraged to notice the "I am" without additions or subtractions from the *sensory mapping*. The "I" represents the conscious sense of presence. The "I am" is what is known. The "I am" *this* or *that* is what is created and generally comes from outside the experiencer's internal world. The "I am" a man, a woman, an American or any other descriptor such as likeable, ugly, stupid, smart etc. is what is created. It is also the foundation of identities or *SPA* states. Remember that "I" + anything (Statement) = an identity. When you begin to notice the body or physical organism, where do you experience or sense its location? It is usually experienced as *here*. The time you notice the physical form is always *now*. The experiencing of the physical body is always *here* and *now*, however the experience of the "mind" or conceptual person can be *here* or *there* and can be in the *past* or *future*. The mind has no location in time or space or so it imagines, so it can tell itself things about what may be occurring in other parts of a room, a city, a country or in distant galaxies. It "the mind" can make decisions about what other people feel, think or intend without bothering to question or confirm its accuracy. The mind can respond to things that are occurring in the present as if they are events that happened in the past. The mind predicts and anticipates the future as if it knows what will occur. As you, explore the world inside the diamond of awareness (I Am Here Now) notice that the area on the outside of the diamond is filled with things that are imagined. These things are interpreted to have meaning but those meanings are derived from associative and assumptive meanings. When the mind or "consciousness" asks a question and there is no answer, "consciousness" will answer itself. This is what we have called the completion or Gestalt closure error. In the absence of information, the mind will create its own and conveniently forget that it is the source. This is one of the reasons that our *sensory perceptive mapping* world is confabulatory and filled with distortions and misinformation. The use of the Diamond of Awareness simply increases awareness and frees consciousness to be present.

The Diamond of Awareness is to assist you in becoming more aware of the creations of the mind/body. It is like an iceberg that you have brought into the sun exposing more and more of what was below the surface to your awareness. Whatever you are doing unknowingly, unconsciously and unintentionally begin doing knowingly, consciously and intentionally. Most of us imagine that there is only one identity or observer but in fact, there are identities for each experience. There is an observer for each observation. Become aware that identities come and go. In fact, they appear and disappear. The nervous system resists the void, space or emptiness and the chaos of not knowing by creating. The mapping is an attempt to know, predict and control the flow of energy and the outcome.

Mapping construction, deconstruction, and reconstruction is a natural ongoing process of the nervous system. *Neural information centers* are the neuro-chemical imprinting or copying of the stimuli within the five senses. The associative, assumptive, and referential meanings are a neuro-chemical response to the stimuli as they are referenced within the *mapping system*. Meanings are created through interactive perceptions. The *mapping system* engages in a process through biology, *socialization* integration, and emotion that engages the multi sensorial and multi associational *mapping system* and it is balanced by *homeostasis*. When we observe and do not know, we create knowing through the Gestalt closure process. We select the meaning from what is already available in the *mapping system*. The *mapping system* assimilates and accommodates new experiences and attempts synthesis. The memory of pain creates fear and the memory of pleasure creates desire. The mapping system of the organism is continually learning. It merges and then detaches from various experiences and stimuli. There are times when this process is fused in the experience. Either fusion creates an agreement with what is experienced or there is a resistance. Confusion may occur during this experience. This confusion is the *fusion confusion illusion* where the identity we have taken on is believed to be who we are. This may happen when a child tries to help depressed parents by trying to take on the depression. The child then forgets taking it on and begins to think and feel it is their depression. We often take on the injunctions or descriptors given to us by parents, siblings, friends or teachers, forgetting that it is not who we are. We observe or interact with others such as (parents, siblings, friends, teachers, and authorities) and hear, see, feel the interactions and this is how we learn to get our needs met. We have biological needs such as those listed in Maslow's Hierarchy including food, shelter, safety, love, belonging and self-actualization. The areas that the nervous system through identities is engaged in are as follows:

Developmental Areas of Focus

Safety
Needs
Boundaries
Esteem
Will (freedom)
Love/Sex/Competition
Sexual/Asexual

Dichotomy

Presence--- ---------Absence
Needs-----------Other's needs
Autonomy ----------Enmeshment
Grandiose----------Worthless
Control---------------Controlled
Sexual-----------------Asexual

In an attempt to find ourselves, we look outside of ourselves for the answer and get lost. The primary loss is the betrayal and loss of self to get something. In an attempt to find ourselves we create an image and pretend it is who we are, there is effort to maintain the identity but then we become fearful thinking it may be false and we create a new identity? Identities appear spontaneously in response to stimuli. By focusing inside, we loose contact with the external territory, by focusing externally we loose perception of our internal state. A balancing between the external territory and our internal map is necessary for accurate perception. Awareness of these factors is useful in creating a bridge between the two.

Energy, Space, Mass and Time

All things in the known universe have the qualities of energy, space, mass and time. Energy is noticed in the strength, intensity, or movement of things whether they are thoughts, emotions, elements, or objects.

Space is all around and it is measured in distances close or far. All things require space to occupy.

Mass can be heaviness, lightness, ethereal or dense. Mass can occupy great areas of space or be very dense and take up very little area.

Time moves quickly or slowly and measures all things.

Notice how things have movement, or are they frozen? Is the movement fast, or slow? What about the intensity. Where do things appear, and what is their location? What is the duration of the object or experience? Who decides what it means?

Location Exercise

Notice how you locate yourself. (Name, family, or city)

Who are you? (Name, sex, race, religion, or role)

Where are you? (Location)

When are you? (Past, present, or future)

Create an identity, feeling or experience.

Step into the experience, now step out of the experience.

Step back in the experience. Pretend that it is you.

Pretend that you are, not pretending. Now let the experience dissolve.

What observer observes that?

What experiencer experiences that?

What decider decides that?

What believer believes that?

Now, turn your attention around and notice what if anything did all of that?

The organism develops a survival response, which is called the fight, flight freeze response, with it there is a scanning and search response that assist with the survival response. Subcategories of the survival response include a learning response and a completion response. We resist not knowing and being out of control by developing the knowing, predicting and controlling response. There are infinite positions or frames through which to experience life. The Diamond of Awareness assists you in loosening associations and frames so you can expand awareness, increase experience, and offer choice.

"I"dentity Exercise

When you step into an identity, ask yourself the following questions.

What are you doing?

Who or what are you being?

What are you, having?

What are you creating?

What are you expecting?

Who or what are you resisting? In addition, consider,

Who or what are you not doing, not being, not having, not creating, not expecting, and not resisting?

You need to be aware of the combinations, permutations, transmutations, and conditioning of identities.

There are *mapping errors* where there is misinformation within the *mapping system* itself. There are *mapping misapplications*, which is when a map is used in an incorrect situation or in a time or location where it does not apply. Then there are m*apping transpositions*, which is when one map is placed over another map as if it was not there or did not matter.

Chapter Thirteen

Chapter Thirteen

Life on Life's Terms or Things Are as They Are The Dream is a Dream

"No matter what happens, keep your feet moving."
Bill O'Hanolin, (Training Seminar 1983)

"If what you're doing isn't working, do something else."
R. Reid Wilson, Ph.D., (One-Year Training Program in Strategic
Psychotherapy and Clinical Hypnosis 1986)

*P*eople often become confused between life and their stories about life. All of us would certainly like to have things our way all the time, but we learn through the years of experience that we do not always get what we want. However, as Mick Jagger sings, "If you try sometime, you just might find, you get what you need..." Moreover, even that may not be true. Life is not like the advertisement at Burger King, "Have It Your Way." Life is lived on life's terms, and things unfold the way they do. If you have many expectations, then you may experience disappointments and resentments. You may find yourself spending time trying to beg, negotiate, or force the territory to conform to your "map," "story," or "picture" of the world. This struggle is futile and is what we call incongruence. If you can function in the present and become aware of more accurate, sensory information, you may find yourself coming to *acceptance* of things as they are. This does not mean that you like or agree with things as they are. It simply means you are aware of things, as they are, not filtered through some illusion or story of how things *should* be. Those are the things we term myths, stories, and lies, based on programming, programming errors and *sensory perceptive alterations* within the *sensory perceptive holographic mapping system*. Acceptance leads to greater congruence with the territory, and therefore may lead to decisions that are based on the territory, not on a story or fabrication.

There may or may not be structure to reality, however, the nervous system through the s*ensory perceptive holographic mapping system* imposes a structure, so it can know, predict and control the outcome and survive better, or so it believes. We live in a conceptual world created by the nervous system through its symbols of words, images, sounds, and sensations.

"You have invented words like effort, inner, outer, self, etc. and seek to impose them on reality. Things happen to be as they are, but we want to build them into a pattern laid down by the structure of our language. So strong is this habit, that we tend to deny reality to what cannot be verbalized. We just refuse to see that words are mere symbols, related by convention and habit to repeated experiences." (*I Am That*, 1973, Sri Nisargadatta Maharaj).

Sensory Flow and the Nature of Chaos
Or
"Life on Life's Terms"
Events or occurrences in life

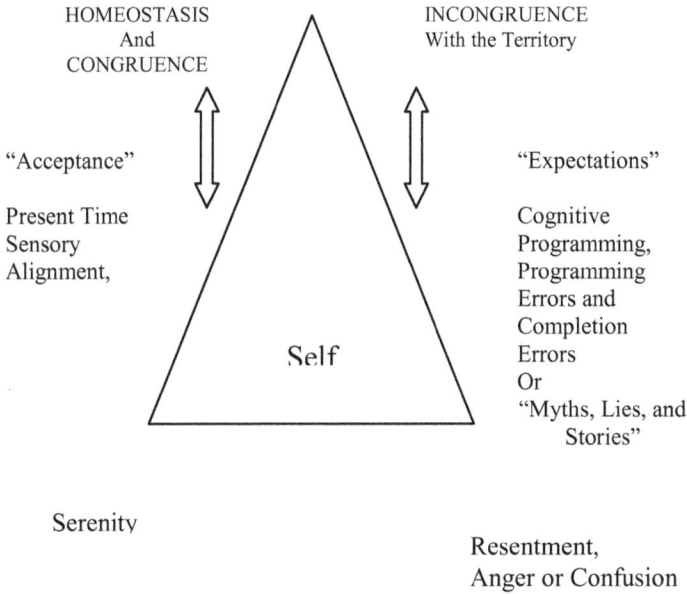

HOMEOSTASIS
And
CONGRUENCE

INCONGRUENCE
With the Territory

"Acceptance"

Present Time
Sensory
Alignment,

Self

"Expectations"

Cognitive
Programming,
Programming
Errors and
Completion
Errors
Or
"Myths, Lies, and
Stories"

Serenity

Resentment,
Anger or Confusion

Figure 5: This illustration is an outlined approach for dealing with the energy or events of life on life's terms. Acceptance does not mean that we must like or agree with what is occurring. It means that we comes into alignment with sensory information without extra distortions.

Resentment, anger, and confusion are the fruits from the seeds of "expectations" or *cognitive programming errors*, which we impose over the world.

Leads to
Congruence

Leads to
Incongruence

Sensory
Perceptive
Mapping in
Alignment
With the
Territory or
Sensory-
Based World
through an
interactive,
Co-operative
Relationship

Attempts to
force the
Territory to
conform to the
Map or the
Personal
Dream; made
up of
Programming
Errors, Myths,
Lies & Stories.
This is a
False
Relationship
based primarily
on
Manipulation
and Coercion.

Self

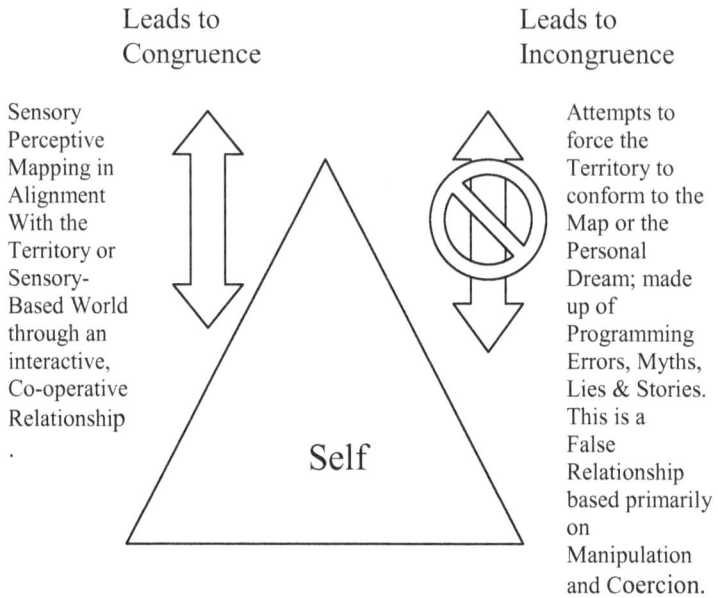

Figure 6: This illustration represents errors which move awareness away from sensory-based reality and toward the internally generated error laden *mapping*. *Errors* within the *mapping system* indicate that the representation of stimuli is influenced and altered by pre-existing programming, *cognitive programming errors* or *sensory perceptive alteration*s rather than *present time sensory alignment.*

Chapter Fourteen

Chapter Fourteen

Trauma, Homeostasis and the Sensory Perceptive World

"Trauma comes in chains of similar events."
Sigmund Freud

"There are no similar events, just a Sensory Perceptive Mapping System that appears to create similar events."
Tobias S. Schreiber & Wilton Hellams

"Living well, is the best revenge, but then you forget revenge and just live well."
Yvonne Dolan, M.A.

rauma, as we are defining it for this theoretical model, is any perceived threat to the organism, its sensory map, or any perceived necessity in its created world. As the trauma is perceived, whether it be the loss of a loved one, a physical threat to the organism such as an assault, deprivation, a molestation or some environmental danger such as a hurricane, tsunami, or some threat to the constructed images and/or meanings of the *sensory mapping world*, the organism will

185

organize itself in some manner to know, predict, and control the effects of the perceived threat. With the flow of sensory data, such as auditories, (sounds), visuals (images), tactiles (touch, sensation, variations in pressure or texture), olfactory (smells), and/or gustatory (tastes), there may be some shifts in the kinesthetic experience (the internal muscle tonus and chemical state) which are labeled as "feelings." When these feelings reach the energy level of outward movement, they are labeled "emotions" which may prepare the organism to respond to the changes in the perceived external and internal world. Interioceptive and exterioceptive changes occur as the organism constructs a *sensory perceptive holographic map* to navigate the altering terrain and adjust its energetic state to approach, avoid, or freeze in response to the sensory flow. Along with the changes in the neuro-chemical state, there will be shifts in the associated metaphors and meanings as a referential search takes place. Depending on the perceived degree and primacy of threat, the organism may organize and respond from the various organism structures such as the amygdale area or the hippocampus region. The triggering of response and orientation will activate previously created *cognitive programming errors* or engage the *"Gestalting"* or *completing mechanism* which contributes *confabulatory* material to the *sensory mapping system* which is influenced and boundaried by the *homeostatic system*. *Sensory alterations* will occur as the referential and associational search ensues, and the organism edits the incoming sensory flow to maintain congruence with the previously created *mapping system*. The activation of adding to, deleting from, generalizing, and/or distorting sensory stimuli or meaning as the organism seeks to maintain *homeostasis* and *congruence* in its mapping and response set. The collapsing of the "ongoing conscious set" or common everyday *trances* now creates major upheavals and shifts in the organism's created life experience and deconstructs the sensory state, resulting in fluctuations in *sensory mapping* and the previously constructed meanings associated with this s*ensory perceptive map*. As the organism works to re-establish *homeostasis,* it seeks to stabilize, neutralize, and harmonize divergent energies and sensory stimuli and to re-create its *sensory perceptive map* of the universe. Things, people, places, and their associated meanings appear and disappear, as they transform and transmute. Thus challenging the organism to locate itself in energy, space, mass, and time along with the "functional fiction" it calls its particular life. We all share a consensual confabulatory experience we call life, and although the internal *mapping system* is quite "idiosyncratic" in nature, we speak of it as if we are all having the same experiences and the same sensory representations.

This theory explores the importance of *trance* as an extension of *cognitive programming* distortions (thought errors) as the source of pathology. It further introduces the concept of h*omeostasis* and s*ensory perceptive alteration* as the underlying mechanisms for the generation of what is commonly termed "*trance.*" The presentation further explores the continuum that exists between healthy *trance* states and those that are currently not serviceable to the organism. The writers suggest that the concepts of h*omeostasis* and *sensory perceptive alteration* are biologically based mechanisms whose function is to prevent change and disequilibrium. The writers further see this model as congruent with the views of an ego, superego, and id or other ego states, seeing intrapsychic conflict occurring out of discordant informational centers held within the *homeostatic* field.

Techniques are suggested for disrupting these *trance* states (states of sensory perception), which are produced and held in check by the *homeostatic mechanism*. These techniques are seen as the on-going extension of commonly used Cognitive Behavioral Therapy techniques to disrupt the sensory perceptive altered states of pathology.

Chapter Fifteen

Chapter Fifteen

Cognitive Behavior Therapy as Trance Deconstruction

"Let's do it once more, and this time with feelings!"
Unknown

It is the 25th wedding anniversary of Frank and Sarah. Sarah has prepared a dining experience for them, reconstructing the first meal that she prepared for Frank. She has gone to great length to provide the same elegant setting, soft candlelight, incense, and background music of their "favorite song." Frank has brought to the event the same type and year of wine they had at their first meal together. Sarah has painstakingly collected photos of memorable events they have shared together, framed them, and strategically placed them around the room in order to create the ambience for this romantic occasion. As Sarah and Frank begin to share the meal, they start reminding each other of the first meal they shared together. as well as other pleasant dating experiences.

The world becomes just theirs. Everything else seems to be screened out as they drift into this wonderful, romantic state, focused on each other, regressing back in time as if this were their first date. The years fade away. They see each other no longer as business partners, conjoint homeowners, parents, but as two lovers who have found something very special. As Frank leans forward to gently kiss Sarah, the doorbell rings, followed by knocking. Then Larry, their rather boisterous neighbor of ten years, throws open the front door and asks, "Why are your lights out, and why are you using candles? We have electricity at my house."

Despite the protests of Frank and Sarah, Larry moves further into the room, flicking on electric lights. He joins them at the table, and immediately with his questions, starts to orient them back to present time. He questions them about who will be driving the next day in the car pool. He further asks if they have heard about a series of vandalisms in the neighborhood, and informs Sarah that his wife and her friend Irene will be back Tuesday just in time for their regular community league softball game. Further, Larry begins to comment on the dinner as he helps himself to the meal, reminding them of the times the "four of us" have had barbecues in the backyard. Larry then comments that the wine Frank purchased is actually inordinately expensive, and a comparable wine and year could be purchased at a local discount beverage store from a regional vineyard. Upon Larry being informed that this is their wedding anniversary, he makes very lame apologies and begins to comment on how rare it is for people's marriages to actually hold together. He begins to introduce conflicts he has witnessed couples have in the past and reflects, "I guess it's lucky you made it this far." Larry apologized again for his intrusion, and then he leaves and goes home.

Frank and Sarah find themselves once again alone. Sarah is now very angry. She begins to vent to Frank, "This is just like in the past, those times which Larry mentioned when you were a 'wimp' and didn't assert yourself, just as you didn't with Larry this evening,"

Frank counters, "You always judge me. You never give me a chance. How did I know what you wanted me to say or do with Larry? Why didn't you say something?"

Sarah's body posture becomes very tense. She then begins to reflect on the multiple failings she has witnessed of Frank in the past.

Frank reveals to Sarah that he is beginning to feel again like a small boy facing his tyrant of a father, and he has no intention of "putting up with this abuse anymore."

Sarah thinks but does not voice, "This is just the way my father used to disregard and take my mother for granted, and here we go again. Frank is doing the same thing to me."

Frank regains his composure and suggests, "Let's try to get back to where we were before that idiot Larry came in."

Sarah retorts, "The evening is ruined. The mood is destroyed. I don't want to even be in the room with you or have you touch me." After saying this, Sarah begins to reflect on images of the past of how her mother would sob when she was berated by her father.

Sarah, feeling very tense and threatened, and retreats to another room, slamming the door and locking it.

At this point, Frank begins to react to all the stimuli, telling himself, "This is just like with my father. You could never please him. No matter what you did, you were always on the short end of the stick. All people want is what they can get out of you, and they don't care about your feelings. This is just like when I was a child. Try and try and try to be accepted, but no matter what you do, you will never have it." Frank then starts to feel very angry, himself, and yells, "I don't deserve this. I want to be listened to. You should listen to me." As Frank's shouting continues, he sees further images of himself being berating by his father. As his feelings of anger grow, he begins to smash furniture, throw chairs, scream, and yell until the police arrive.

Following their encounter with the police, Frank and Sarah decide that they need help and assistance. Given this, they contact a local therapist. As they are seen individually, each begins to recount his or her version of the evening. They find themselves rising and falling through different feeling states. As Frank initially describes the setting of the meal, the table, and the aromas, his feelings soften, and he begins to have very warm and romantic feelings toward Sarah. As he recounts to the therapist the entrance of Larry, he once again feels anger and irritation with Larry, and also notices feelings of being helpless, as though someone is taking over his life, just like when he was a child, and had no control over it.

When Sarah is seen individually by the therapist, Sarah begins to recount how beautifully she had prepared the room. She describes how she even framed and displayed old photos that had been taken of their first dinner together. As she talks, the therapist notes her body posture relaxing. Her facial features become relaxed. Her eyes moisten. There is a slight uplifting of her cheeks as if to smile, and her voice markedly softens. She begins to talk about many of the beautiful moments that she and Frank have had in the past. She reflects on times when they wrote notes to each other, and then laughs, clapping her hands together at one "silly note you wouldn't understand." The therapist observes a marked overall transformation from the woman who initially entered his office. However, she then mentions the name "Larry," at which this point she begins to tense, reporting to the therapist how she feels victimized by Larry. She explains, "I'm still angry with Frank. He is just like the people in the past that would not protect me." As she is saying this, Sarah becomes aware of images of old school episodes, an incident in which she felt she had been physically violated by an older cousin, and other images as she continues to run an on-going movie with associated dialogue of being verbally, physically, and psychologically abused. The therapist notices that Sarah behaves "as though she is not there." Her eye movements suggest she is scanning something, but when the therapist calls her name, she is unresponsive until her name is called with an increase in tone and volume. She is then somewhat startled, shakes herself, and says to the therapist, "I'm sorry, but I didn't hear all of what you said to me."

Between therapy sessions, the therapist, who has a lengthy history in classical hypnosis, reflects on how this couple when seen individually began to respond just as a hypnotic subject responds when a post hypnotic cue is given. He had witnessed the same apparent *sensory perceptive alteration* in the couple who, when cued by certain words and questions, retreated back to earlier times. In the case of Sarah, her retreat was so profound that she was removed from the room and the surroundings, oblivious and amnesiac to the therapist's interactions.

At the next session, Frank and Sarah were seen together. The therapist strategically used the key words he had used in the individual therapy sessions. He noticed these cue words triggered different changes the in couple's body postures, vocal responses, attention to each other, and in general, attention to their surroundings. In other words, he noticed that one cue word would generate different *"trance"* (*sensory perceptive alteration*) states in the two people before him. Being the astute therapist and realizing the danger of compartmentalizing his experience (i.e. seeing himself only as a Cognitive Behavior Therapist as opposed to a hypnotherapist or practitioner of NLP), he began to describe the observations he had made and to suggest an experiment. He suggested that as he mentioned certain cue words (stimulus words), he wanted Frank and Sarah to report what they were feeling, and then what they are telling themselves or showing themselves. As an aid to this process, he asked each to write down in abbreviated form and in personal coding his or her experience, to avoid confusion. At the end of the experiment, the couple was surprised to find they had experienced markedly different feelings, as well as pictures and sound bytes in their heads. They were also amazed at how much of this feeling had been from the past as opposed to feelings related to on-going events. Frank reported that at times he actually had felt cold, like "in the old house with my father." Sarah indicates, "There were times when you had to call me back. I felt scared. That is silly. I was here in this room, but when I thought of those times back there, somehow I was no longer in this room."

The therapist began to explain to Frank and Sarah that external cues in the environment can trigger internal states and certainly feelings that do not appear relevant to the surroundings. The therapist suggested another experiment in which he asked Frank to notice Sarah, and he asked Sarah to notice Frank. Then with his assistance, they began to feed each other the audio recordings that were made of them during the session. Further, each revealed that he or she had seen these expressions and gestures before. Each indicated they had placed very different interpretations upon what they had witnessed, rather than framing this as a response to a cue as though it was a "post hypnotic suggestion firing in response to a signal."

Given the "education," the couple was instructed any time there was a change in mood or feeling, to immediately go inside and give himself/herself permission to guess, "What am I telling myself? What am I showing myself?" As weeks went by with the therapist, they reported the *sensory perceptual alterations* began to diminish. They also revealed that they were increasingly present in the circumstances in which they found themselves. They reported that the feelings previously noted, such as victimization, helplessness, anger, being small, and even temperature changes no longer occurred. Rather, they now automatically would begin to think about "What would I like to tell myself? What is more accurate in the present circumstance?" Building on this, the therapist suggested that they quite frequently engage in a dialogue about the now, such as, "I am standing in the room. I am looking at Sarah. Sarah is looking back at me. Sarah is stating her displeasure with me. I am responding to my ideas about her statement." After working with this concept of staying in the now, essentially keeping mind and body together, the couple noticed they experienced less of these "*trance*-like" states (s*ensory perceptive alteration*s). In general, the couple felt more grounded as that they were dealing with here and now issues.

Frank was given the assignment of engaging in future projection at those times which previously he most likely would have engaged in regressive thought. In other words, when Sarah raised her voice, this would become his cue to think about the following constructed episode: Sarah will say something to me. I will reflect to her what I heard her say. I will then add what I have to say. She will then give me her opinion. This will go on. At the end, we will arrive at some successful conclusion. I can see her kissing me, and us hugging. I can see us having a happy day tomorrow.

Sarah is given like programming in that after she performs her deconstructions of the former states by asking herself, "What am I telling myself? What am I showing myself?" and breaking up the cluster of images statements that have led to *sensory perceptual alteration* in a chaining of cognition and behavior, she is instructed to engage in future projection. When Frank raises his voice, she is to see herself standing tall, stating her desire for him to lower his voice, and then seeing him complying with her request in a respectful way, sitting down with her, eye to eye, while actually discussing and moving toward problem solving. She creates a positive outcome in that they arrive at a conclusion, and her "movie" ends with them touching, hugging and kissing.

They both remark at how the "spell" has been broken. The strange phenomena of feeling, perceptual changes, and intense mood, which they felt, were visited upon them as though by some mysterious or external force, is now understood to be nothing more than the generation of their internal complex of auditory and visual cognitions creating *sensory perceptual alterations* or "*trances.*"

However, both Frank and Sarah frequently comment to the therapist that this new state and these new cognitions do not seem "comfortable." The therapist explains *dissonance* as a long-standing concept held among his colleagues of therapists known as Cognitive Behavior Therapists. He describes dissonance as the grinding, uncomfortable, and uneasy feeling that occurs when you interject new thought.

Sarah and Frank report that in addition to the uneasiness, at the time it is difficult for them to remember the techniques of deconstruction they have been taught. They further indicate, as they record their thoughts experiencing them as though coming from some internal force messages, such as, "This isn't going to work; this takes too long; this is just a bunch of garbage." They are presented with images of seeing themselves failing at this task. They see themselves back where they were in the past. They see themselves as being embarrassed that they have attempted to change something that messages inside them say, "this is just the way we are." The therapist explains this is nothing more than *homeostasis*, the same *homeostasis* that gears the body's metabolism up if the weather becomes colder in an attempt to maintain internal body temperature. *Homeostasis* also occurs when we drink too many fluids, and the body seeks to maintain a certain level of body fluids and thereby increases urination and elimination. *Homeostasis* occurs if a virus enters the system, disturbing the balance of the tissue that is accepted as "supposed to be there" as opposed to "not supposed to be there," triggering the muscles to begin to shiver as a way to increase heat to extinguish the virus. This same "gearing," "eliminating" and "shivering" also occur in Frank and Sarah's relationship. The therapist goes on to elaborate that the goal of the *homeostatic* system in the biological realm is to maintain the system as it is. The logical extension of this in the psychic realm is to maintain the thought life, the collection of what we tell and show ourselves, creating no changes or ripples. Maintaining sameness equals no disturbance on the surface of the "mental pond." The therapist assures them if they continue to engage in replacing messages following deconstruction of old messages, in time, the *homeostatic* system will accept the bombardment as part of its own and thus begin a reworking of the programming system. He likens this to reworking the programming of a computer. As the programming becomes more weighted in terms of the new functional input as opposed to the old, dysfunctional input, the material will become accepted, and there will be a feeling of comfort and of it being "natural."

As Frank and Sarah learn to deconstruct their sensory perceptive altered states (*trance*) by asking themselves, "What am I telling myself, what am I showing myself?" and further deconstruct the *trances* by incorporating the on-going dialogue of reminding themselves to be in the now, and what it is like to be in the now, as they neutralize the regression of *trance* to the past by utilizing future progression, they find that increasingly they deal with each other as they are rather than merely the holographic projections of programming errors that were once held within the *homeostatic* system. Frank sees Sarah more for Sarah. Sarah sees Frank more for Frank, rather than each other's voices and movements becoming cues or post hypnotic signals for an internal processing that they previously responded to.

As the therapy progresses and they engage in deconstruction by identifying what they are telling and showing themselves, they find that increasingly they have a feeling of being empowered as they tell themselves, "I can choose not only what I want to tell or show myself in order to create a mood, but I can tell or show myself things in order to create the *trance* state (sensory altered state) I would like to be in."

The therapist, along with Frank and Sarah, comes to an increasing understanding that, indeed the idea of the non-*trance* state for a human being does not exist. There are those states that simply are more reflective of the external reality than other states. There are those states in which there is a broader range of recognition of the stimuli in the environment versus a narrow range. There are *trance* states, such as future-oriented *trance* states, which predict positive outcomes and provide motivations when needed. The therapist, along with Frank and Sarah, comes to realize that the programming within the mind is like a map, but as the philosopher, Korzybski, reminds us, "The map is not the territory." The closer the map is to what is actually occurring around the individual, the more functional the individual will be and the more realistic the individual's adaptation to the demands of the environment. The therapist who previously saw himself as either a hypnotist or a Cognitive Behavior Therapist now has a greater understanding. He realizes the work of therapy, all therapy, is a matter of changing *trance*. Another definition of *trance* is a *sensory perceptive alteration*. This can be an alteration that is beneficial or an alteration that is harmful to the organism. This can be a sensory alteration that can be on the scale of a conversion reaction creating blindness, or can be a heightened sense of the environment so the individual is alert to any possible dangers that might be occurring. Pathology then becomes defined as the wrong *trance* or sensory perceptive altered state for the wrong circumstance. It is perfectly appropriate for a soldier in a war zone to exercise a hyper-vigilant *trance* in response to a sound like a gun being fired. However, five years later for that same individual working as a sales representative, it is not adaptive for that individual to operate in that hyper-vigilant *trance* in response to a car backfiring in the middle of a major American city.

As the work with Frank and Sarah continues with the therapist, it becomes increasingly obvious that at no time in the life of a living human being is there not some type of *sensory perceptive alteration* going on, and therefore, there is no time in which *trances* are not employed by the h*omeostatic* system of the organism.

As the work draws to an end, Frank and Sarah realize their one time villainous neighbor, Larry, was actually nothing more than a catalyst for *trance* change. When they believed the emotions and experiences they were having were due to an external source, they felt at the mercy of the surrounding events. However, when they engaged in Cognitive Behavior Therapy as a means for deconstructing these sensory perceptive altered states, they began to realize the great power they had. They also realized the importance deconstructing dysfunctional, habituated *trance* states and replacing them with functional *trance* states based on maps within the *homeostatic* system that were closely congruent with the external environment, the territory.

As we continue our journey into the world of *sensory perceptive alterations* and the *homeostatic system*, it is important to understand that this is occurring for everyone at every moment. What we refer to as s*ensory perceptive holographic mapping* is the mechanism whereby the mind/body digest, represent and interact with the world. *Sensory perceptive holographic mapping* is a multi-dimensional, multi-sensory, multi-associational system that describes how the mind/body sees, hears, feels, and interprets the experiences and processes of living. This brings up a point made by Korzybski who said, "The only usefulness of a map or language depends on the similarity of structure between the empirical world and the map-language" (Korzybski, Science and Sanity, 1973).

A person by the name of Lyn W. came to an interesting discovery during the process of therapy. This discovery was that the map of the world his mother described contained an item called "mother's rule book." This book, as he described it, contained many wise sayings his mother would share on various occasions if she deemed it necessary. Quotes such as, "you can never make up for lost sleep" and other sayings, left him puzzled over their meaning and relevance in his life. In questioning this *sensory perceptive holographic map*, he discovered his own rulebook, which contained his story of being a "good boy" and the rules, and expected outcomes that went into his particular map. By asking questions and making enquiry into the nature of the map, he experienced a shifting into present-time, sensory experience. When in the "good boy" *trance* or sensory perceptive altered state he felt younger, less powerful, and confused about why things did not work as expected. He began to ask himself, "Where does this rule come from? How did I decide it was true, and what does this belief have to do with what is going on right now?" By questioning the *cognitive programming errors* or cognitive distortions, he experienced a deconstruction of the s*ensory perceptive alteration* state that had previously kept him stuck.

It appears that the *homeostatic* nature of the mind/body creates *sensory perceptive holographic maps* in order to navigate and balance the experiential world. When incongruent features are encountered, the system has the ability to accommodate the variance or create a *sensory perceptive alteration* in the data or its meaning to the system. In this way, the balance is maintained. Particularly during times of trauma, confusion, or when the system is overwhelmed, then problems occur in the ability of the mind/body to maintain its h*omeostatic* equilibrium.

One interesting feature of *homeostasis* is that it is an attempt to maintain balance but it is not related to truth or reality. Therefore, the sensory stimuli in the individual's environment and whatever is focused on by the sensory perceptive system are what affect the contents of the person's *sensory perceptive holographic map*. This map contains *cognitive programming errors* that are congruent with the holographic map, thus maintaining *homeostasis*. The cognitive distortions or programming errors are part of the *sensory perceptive holographic mapping system,* which may be harmonious with *homeostasis.*

Another example of how the *homeostatic system* and *sensory perceptive holographic mapping* creates and maintains cognitive distortions or *cognitive programming errors* is when therapists apply their various theoretical positions to individuals in therapy. The following account illustrates such a problem.

Greg W., a licensed professional counselor intern, made a discovery that there were several *cognitive programming errors* or cognitive distortions in his *sensory perceptive holographic mapping* of how to assess individuals, deal with their problems, and offer solutions. One error in the map was related to the word "mother." The word was symbolic and created a powerful, referential, assumptive, or associational search to find meanings, thus resulting in confusing the person with his theory about the person.

Milton Erickson, the master psychiatrist and hypnotherapist, is said to have exhorted Earnest Rossi, Ph.D. to "Pay attention to the clients, Earnest. They're over here, and they have more answers and are more interesting than your theories." (Hypnosis Training Seminar, North Carolina Society of Clinical Hypnosis, Earnest Rossi, Ph.D., 1989).

Another programming distortion is assuming that we all operate in the same world. The therapists may offer a solution based on his *sensory perceptive holographic map* without considering that the individual may have a completely different map. Therefore, the solutions offered may be incongruent and may cause the *homeostatic* system to defend itself. Simply to remind oneself that the map we are using to navigate the world is not the map someone else is using and addressing this cognitive differential, may serve to improve congruence and to enhance communication.

When attempting to reach a goal, we need to adjust our *sensory perceptive maps* to accommodate the present territory or just like the smart bombs with errors in their programming; we will find ourselves in unexpected and sometimes hostile territory with innocent victims. As Alfred Korzybski reminds us, "If the map shows a different structure from the territory represented (for instance, shows the cities in the wrong order), then the map is worse than useless, as it misinforms and leads astray." As this illustration demonstrates, the effects of *sensory perceptive alteration* when used by the *homeostatic mechanism* of the mind/body to maintain its state of equilibrium and congruence, there are significant *cognitive programming errors*, which disrupt the present functioning of the individual. The dilemma arises in that the s*ensory perceptive mapping* is created in the past and at times has difficulty updating itself; therefore, a state of incongruence may exist when an individual uses outdated maps, which do not accurately represent the territory one is navigating. Most of us share a consensual, confabulatory reality where, although not exact, there is an agreement to appear to think congruently. Each individual has his or her own unique, *sensory perceptive holographic map*. Moreover, there are different maps for different experiences. Each moment, each experience has its own perceptual map. Maps are idiosyncratic in nature.

For quite some time we have been dividing the person into at least two parts, the mind and the body, and this has been especially emphasized since the time of

Descartes. A harmonious existence of the mind/body can be increased by realizing the body is always here and now functioning in the biological world, while the mind is constantly in the conceptual world which has not time or location. In addition, the mind is at times showing the body (itself) images from the past, the future, or some other locality that the body responds to. Since it cannot respond in any other time than now that is what it does. The body produces energy and it utilizes it. Psychobiological *homeostasis*, balance, congruence, or equilibrium is brought about by unity and integration of the whole. So whatever your role, it will be based upon a *sensory perceptive holographic map* and it may contain *cognitive programming errors* or cognitive distortions created and maintained by *sensory perceptive alteration*s in attempting to maintain *homeostasis*. Enquiring into the errors is necessary by asking questions, such as, "What am I telling myself? What images am I showing myself? Who or what told me that is true? Is this occurring in the present time?" By deconstructing the supporting, *cognitive programming errors*, present-time sensory functioning can reoccur, and the person can choose which state to be in. The map is not the territory. However, the map does not need to misrepresent, distort, delete, misinform or mislead its user. With attention to awareness, we can maintain congruence and *present time sensory perceptive mapping*.

David is a tall, sandy-haired, young man who had been through a series of foster home placements until he entered residential placement with a local agency. He was attempting sheltered employment when we first consulted with him. The referral issue was extreme and prolonged episodes of rage. The client has a diagnosis of Aspergers that was confirmed by three independent sources connected to separate hospitalizations in different in-patient settings during his childhood and adolescence.

The rage episodes were quite severe. They would initiate with an almost growling verbalization of being mistreated by others. Reflections on obviously past events (back in school) and present time events would be incorporated in this growling verbalization of current reporting and past memories. Despite the efforts of those in his surroundings to redirect him and intervene, the episode would build to a point of the individual becoming physically aggressive, *hurling chairs, lashing out at people, and concomitantly voicing the desire to harm others along with rather bizarre homicidal ideation (skinning people like a rabbit, cutting their heads off, and disemboweling them). Rather standard paradigms of Behavioral Therapy had previously been attempted in which the client could earn tokens for cooperating with redirection. Various applications of this framework demonstrated little or no efficacy in interrupting the extremely disruptive behavior. The undesired behavior had occurred over a five-year period. It was noted with almost each passing month, that the verbalizations and physical aggression increased in both frequency and intensity. It was noteworthy to the author that those in attendance would frequently describe the individual as "having a spell," "looking like he was in a trance," and even one individual remarked, "He looks like one of those people who has been hypnotized on a stage show."*

The therapy for the individual involved *trance* deconstruction. The individual was able to clearly recount a video-like pattern of thought which would initiate when he saw others laughing in the environment, particularly young, white females. In working with the individual, it was possible to map the sequence of the "video," and it was noted it had a very predictable sequence and flowing scenario.

The client was a "Three Stooges" fan and had quite a collection of "Three Stooges" videos. We suggested the individual pick his favorite video, watch it and then practice replaying the video in his head. This required much assistance by the staff and the author for compliance. The next step in deconstruction of the *trance* involved learning and applying a mantra, "Change the video and change your life." Role-plays were practiced with the individual in which young, white females would laugh. The client would signal the running of the old video, which involved past, taunting episodes back in school. The client would then be signaled verbally to "change your video." He would then be verbally coached in "playing in my head" excerpts of the "Three Stooges" video he had selected. He was led in this process until the previous scenario of taunting was disrupted. This coaching process occurred for a period of approximately nine weeks, at which time the individual began to initiate the disruption on his own with only minor assistance from staff. There was first a reduction in the length of the disruptive episodes from an hour down to several minutes. The behavior then changed to rarely having homicidal ideation voiced at all, with no physical aggression. In a nine-month follow up period, the client reported being very invested and even enjoying replacing his video. The staff reported no incidents of disruptive behavior or voicing of homicidal ideation.

Chapter Sixteen

Relationships and Other Myths

"When you discover the truth, there will be few takers, for the world is only interested in activities and modifications, fragments of the truth."
Sri Nisargadatta Maharaj

Relationships are based on several things. Who we think we are, or who we think we are supposed to be, and whom we think others should be. We call these assumptions identities. Identities can be complimentary, antagonistic, reciprocal, or even polarized. One complaint often heard in therapy is how people have changed. Some examples frequently verbalized are "Well, you are not the person you were when we first met." "Boy, things changed when we were engaged," "You are not the person I married;" or "I have never seen that side of you." This is because we assume, decide, or believe we have one identity, therefore, we assume, decide, or believe that others have one identity also. There is a dating identity, an engaged identity, and a married identity. In fact, there is a new identity for every new occasion. Just like an actor or actress performing in a play, we go to our dressing rooms and select the appropriate costumes and makeup (identities) for our particular scripts (our personal drama roles). This involves imagining and creating the dress up and role creations for all the others in the play. Not known to us, every other individual in the drama is going through a similar yet different process. Each individual is living in the same physical universe, yet experiencing a different internally represented universe of thoughts, feelings, images, sounds and sensations. Whatever I am doing is about me and whatever you are doing is about you, even though we each imagine that our world is inclusive of others. I am the only person in my world; others just seem to appear there. Meaning that I have some self-generated interpretation of others but it is not them and the same is true for your universe.

Chapter Seventeen

Chapter Seventeen

Don't Stay Stuck
Be Free

"Freedom is just another word for nothing left to lose." Me and
Bobby McGee
Kris Kristofferson

This work emerged from our day-to-day practice with families and individuals (both adult and children) over the past thirty years.

When we have been asked to define what it is that we do in our brand of therapy; we have at times labeled ourselves as *"eclectic,* hypnotic, or Cognitive Behavioral Therapists." Simply put, this means that as therapists, we believe that a cycle exists, which is the basis of all appropriate and inappropriate or aberrant behavior. The cycle profoundly affects the way that a person sees, feels, acts, and engages in his or her world. This cycle has profound impact upon the neurotransmitters, which are the basic chemical elements, which the organism uses to communicate throughout the nervous system. It is through these intricacies that a person's thoughts or programming affects such elements as the Endocrine System, and thus the Immune system. It is in these intricacies that we find factors that trigger a rise and fall in blood pressure, as well as the circulation of blood and re-routing of circulation to different parts of the body.

In short, this most fundamental relationship, what we think creates mood, and in turn creates behavior, is the key to stress versus relaxation, happiness versus unhappiness, and in many cases disease versus health. Few physicians would doubt the impact of a patient's attitude as a major contributing factor to healing, recovery, and longevity.

As *Eclectic* Therapists, we are interested in working with clients at the most fundamental part of the programming, mood, and behavior cycle. This, of course, is in reference to thought. Thought is of two basic modes: those things that we tell ourselves (self-talk) and those things which we show ourselves (visualization). Thought sometimes is an auditory tape. At other times, it is a still photo. Yet at other times, it is a running video of self-talk, pictures, and a chaining of these two elements. For purposes of simplification, we will refer to both types of thought as *cognitive programming*.

The most illusive element of the thought/mood/behavior cycle to apprehend, address, manipulate, or change, is the most readily apparent part in our everyday lives. This is mood or feeling. Frequently, we operate out of feeling without ever looking at the basis of the feeling and thought. For example, we feel anxious and upset about small groups, so we avoid them. We feel good about a person for some reason; therefore, we pursue a relationship with that person versus someone else that we do did not have these feelings about. We feel ourselves to be failures; therefore, we hesitate to venture out, expect failure, and therefore produce failure. However, to begin to move through feeling and to give oneself permission to guess, "What am I telling myself? What am I showing myself?" is to begin to make a dramatic move toward changing this cycle by changing the mood, that is predicated on this programming.

After years of working with clients and attempting to utilize techniques that would best assist them in freeing themselves from being "stuck" in unsuccessful paradigms for approaching life, it becomes apparent that all effective efforts are based upon deconstruction of territorially, incongruent, sensory states and replacement with more beneficial sensory states or *SPA* through reprogramming with tools that are more accepted by the client's *homeostatic* system. The form of therapy we have developed is what we refer to as "*eclectic* therapy."

Chapter Eighteen

Chapter Eighteen

The Why is Always the What

"Go back the way you came."
Ramana Maharshi

*G*iven the paradigm previously explored, it would be appropriate to engage in a consideration of where *cognitive programming* comes from. Broadly, speaking, *cognitive programming* is derived from four major sources:

(1) Programming that is directly taught,

(2) Modeling,

(3) Interpretations of new experiences based on previous programming, and

(4)   Synthesis   is   the   evolvement   of   new
       programming as a logical derivation of old
       programming.

Individuals, frequently come into the practice with the
mission of discovering "Why am I this way?" "Why do
I feel this way?" or "Why do I act this way?" "Why,"
with its attachment to its psychoanalytical legacy,
frequently sets the questioner up for a review and
intense search of his history for some pivotal event that
set his mood and undesired behaviors into motion. It is
much more efficient and productive to ask "What?"
rather than "Why?"   "What is my *cognitive
programming*?"   In other words, "What am I telling
and/or showing myself that is creating these mood
states and ultimately these behavioral patterns?"   The
programming, itself, has its origins in a number of
different sources.   None of these sources are very
important in freeing the person from being stuck or
frozen in mood or self-defeating behaviors.   However,
very   broadly   speaking,   sources   of   *cognitive
programming* may be viewed as the following:

(1)   Instructed Messages

Instructed messages are sometimes directly spoken to
the individual.   These would include labels or phrases
that describe the individual's behavior.   This category
also includes descriptions of the individual by others
that the individual is aware of.   An example of this can
be seen with Jack.   Jack's father, known as verbally
abusive to the family, frequently looks for what is
wrong with Jack's accomplishments with schoolwork,
duties around the farm, and performance on the athletic
field.   He openly applies such labels as "awkward,"

"inept," "fat" and "stupid" to his son. Further, when Jack rebuts this, citing positive comments and praises he has received from teachers, coaches, and others, the father frequently responds with the comment, "Remember, you can't believe that. They are just being nice."

(2) Modeling

An example of modeling can be seen with Roy. Roy had a very strong bond with his father with whom he worked within the family store. Roy heard his father frequently make such statements as, "There's no way for us to get ahead. Some people are just meant to be prosperous, and some people are just meant to get by. The harder I try, the more I lose. I just can't win." These thoughts, repeatedly voiced by Roy's father, were assimilated into Roy's *cognitive programming* where they were frequently played, especially when Roy contemplated new ventures or taking any kind of calculated risk, thereby, serving to limit Roy from achieving growth personally, emotionally, and financially. This was the course of Frank's life until he later learned *cognitive programming* identification and replacement techniques.

(3 & 4) Interpretation of a New Experience with Synthesis

Following the unexpected death of his nine-year-old brother, Joe's mother became very restrictive of Joe's activities, forbidding him to play in his tree house, forbidding him to cross even quiet neighborhood streets without her help, and daily insisting that he ingest a regimen of vitamins and herbal formulations. Although his mother withdrew to her own cocoon of grief and said very little about the brother's death, Joe interpreted and formulated new *cognitive programming* that "daily life" is a perilous place to be; individuals must constantly be watchful of not only dangers in the environment, but also disease; and it takes much effort and medication just to survive." This programming grew and connected with other messages, and by the time that Joe was in twenties, he was afraid to move out of his front door without extraordinary precautions and safeguards.

Chapter Nineteen

Chapter Nineteen

Multiple Personality Disorder (MPD)
Dissociative Identity Disorder (DID)

"Personality is a case of mistaken identity"
Sri Nisargadatta Maharaj

(The following is an excerpt from a training session on *trance* phenomena.)

Doug, I appreciate your questions this afternoon regarding how we see dissociative phenomena fitting into our overall schema, and in particular, the phenomena of Dissociative Identity Disorder (DID) as it is now known, and also the associations of role plays.

To begin this discussion and to address your question, I think we need to first state that in our schema, it is not necessary for us to assume either side of the argument that has developed, whether indeed DID or MPD is iatrogenic or naturally occurring phenomenon when certain humans are subjected to trauma. In our model, this really does not matter. I would like to share with you, as I begin this discussion, some work that I did a number of years ago. This was with a young lady in her late twenties who came to me as a referral through a family doctor/internal medicine specialist because of an on-going series of complaints of G-I problems and headaches. The young woman, by profession, was an exotic dancer, and as our initial interview began to develop, she revealed that there were blocks of time that she had literally no memory. She reported that quite frequently, habitually, and regularly she, in the course of her performance, would have no idea of significant portions of what had transpired. She indicated, however, that she had never had any lapses of time or any difficulty retrieving memory of events until she was "trained" to do this by other more established dancers. She indicated that her first several nights on the job were very difficult and very stressful for her. However, she began to assume the role of her stage name and to adopt this persona, with the encouragement of others. It became a matter simply of her walking through the side door of the establishment, being called by her stage name, and then for hours, performing her duties with a great deal of variability and flexibility. From performing, to carrying on conversations with customers, to having conversations with other dancers, to negotiating shifts, she carried out her job responsibilities only to have no memory of the events until walking back in the doors at a later time and being called by her stage name again. When we began to work hypnotically, this individual indicated that there was a great deal of abuse going on. Further, she indicated there were certainly parts of her that felt disrespected by others, and also she felt a sense of letting herself down by performing. However, this was shielded away from other parts of her except through the expression of headaches and G-I complaints. Not to belabor this point, but it is interesting that without any kind of formalized post-hypnotic suggestion, this person had developed the construct of a persona that worked quite well for her. It was accompanied with amnesia for a certain circumscribed event. It was triggered by a predictable set of stimuli in the environment (side door and then being called by the stage name), and thus mimicked very well the type of set up that would be used in formalized hypnosis if one wanted to develop a persona based on post-hypnotic suggestion and cueing. It also reflects very well the phenomena that are frequently seen, as is reported in the annals of MPD and DID, where an alter performs some function while others are amnesic to the event.

Going back to our original schema as presented, it is our belief that *cognitive programming*, working through the *neural information centers*, is ultimately responsible for developing certain *trances*, dysfunctional or functional. The *trance* in and of itself rules in and out certain perceptions of the environment which are congruent with the segment of the person's overall map as dictated by these programming errors, suggestions, or cognitive instructions. As we have offered earlier, each of us is in a process of unfolding *trances*, and that we develop a persistent pattern of *trances* known as *persistent patterns of trance clusters* that we come to know an individual by. However, MPD and DID are extreme forms of role-playing. What we are actually seeing is a rather exquisite example of *neural information centers* in their vast array of functions becoming highly compartmentalized. We are seeing in the development of the disorder greater compartmentalization or merger of *neural information centers*, given the demands of the environment or the suggestions of those important to the person in the environment. Of course, by suggestion here, we certainly mean this in the same way that we would a direct or indirect hypnotic suggestion. In this case, it was indirectly suggested to our dancer that she had a different identity. If she maintained the identity, it would work for her. In fact, it did work well for her in many ways. It allowed the young lady to reconcile the abuse on one hand with the desire to make considerably above what she could earn from a minimum wage job. At the same time, it preserved a sense of dignity by walling off a set of centers that knew and actually performed in an environment where other centers saw her as being degraded and abused.

Historically, this sort of development of the different centers is amplified very well in the work of Morton Prince, M.D... Probably the best-known case of his work was with Marie Beauchamp. However, Dr. Prince, as cited in *Psychological Concepts and Dissociative Disorders*, worked with another female patient who was seen to be a Multiple Personality, and this patient actively engaged in the process, leaving a legacy of her own journaling and written insights into her states and disorder. The following is cited in the above-named work. It is from a letter dated August 4, by the patient, herself, a Miss Bean, and it was written circa 1907-1913: *"Then after Mr. Bean's death, B-, the original B, you know, sank completely out of sight, and she was all A—not this A, but the original A. I am afraid I do not make this very clear. This old A was different from A now, for though she was sad, worn, and ill, she still had plenty of courage. She did not want to die. She expected to live on in the just the same way, and she worked herself nearly to death over business affairs and got so ill she was sent away to the sanatorium. Then after a little, she began to get better, and she became something I will call C-, not your C. I do not know anything about her—but sort of a combination of the A and B I am talking about. I think she was natural enough at that time, only shaken from the long, nervous strain, the self-reproach, the grief, etc., but there came a time when something happened to her (the kiss and its consequences)--you know, and she did change completely, and you can never get old, original B, for she does not exist. I came, but I am not exactly like the old B. I have lost something, and this A is not like the old A. We are both quite different, though we represent the same elements. Besides all this, there is a new element, which is, I think, a part of the real personality. These new elements do not mix with either of us—I do not know what it is, and A cannot bear it. It changes her to me. We are all shaken apart like the pieces of glass in a kaleidoscope. Can you ever get the pieces back in the original pattern? You see, I know all that A thinks, but I do not feel her emotions." (Morton Prince, M.D. in Psychological Concepts and Dissociative Disorders, Duane, Kleine, and Erlbaum, 1994)*

In our metaphor, we have established that there are *neural information centers*, that these *neural information centers* have housed within them different bits of pieces of information, and that these bits and pieces of information can be separate from other *neural information centers* or shared with them. In the center work where we have deliberately merged certain information, feelings, etc. from one center with another, we have actually engaged in stripping down walls for a

223

permanent merger of *neural information centers* to become new *neural information centers* that are a combination yet different from the original centers. We have worked with the centers in developing dialogue between the centers that could range from being temporary to approaching that of being a permanent arrangement. We have worked with executive centers in looking at new ways in which centers might express themselves or their actions in different ways by utilizing executive centers to mobilize other centers to be involved in a decision making process and in a coalescence to derive new alternative behaviors.

We have used executive centers to work and mobilize other centers in forming a hologram of certain *trance* and sensory perceptive altered state so that when certain key stimuli or triggers were given, the state would be replayed like replaying a holographic production. Of course, you will recognize that this is accomplishing exactly what is done in a more ritualized, more classical hypnotic induction and establishment of post-hypnotic suggestion to facilitate self-hypnosis and future *trance* work by using certain cue elements.

To more directly address your question about how we would model the development of DID within our system, we would see it as nothing more than a highly compartmentalized set of *neural information centers* under the direction of executive centers, with these executive centers in and of themselves developing a certain hierarchy. This is seen rather exquisitely in the schemata that have been drawn by patients diagnosed with MPD and DID disorders and the accounts of clinicians who have observed and engaged in dialogue with different "personalities" who seem to be more dominant and less dominant, more knowledgeable and less knowledgeable, more in control and those which felt relatively helpless.

It is also interesting to note that historically these individuals who have been classed as MPD have been remarked to be "hypnotizable" or rather to be hypnotic virtuosos (James P. Bloch, _Assessment and Treatment of Multiple Personality and Dissociative Disorders_ 1991, page 36).

As we work with our model, it is well within the scope of possibility, if desired, for any individual without a rigid, _persistent pattern of trance clusters_ by the direct work with centers to develop with programming/suggestion (either direct or indirect) a hierarchy of centers. To accomplish such a hierarchy requires manipulating various sensory perceptive altered states/_trances_, which would be markedly different from each other but have unified elements of being controlled by executive centers.

To clarify, this is actually seen in an on-going way within everyday life. There are functions of centers that actually click in the business-person _trance_. The centers then coordinate with other centers in clicking in the father-at-home _trance_, or the lodge brother _trance_, or it is the time to be funny versus serious _trance_, etc. MPD disorders simply are on the end of this continuum and are evidence of highly compartmentalized centers. Yet these centers can be merged or integrated.

Our work would suggest that the very nature of referring to centers as "personality" or even "sub-personalities" could, in fact, suggest the need for further compartmentalization, and therefore this programming could produce the "splitting" that has been cited in the literature around individuals with DID and MPD.

Our model, in looking at centers and realizing the centers' reactivity to the underlying *cognitive programming* which can be directly or indirectly installed, also further seems to offer some very good rationale of why MPD has moved from being classed as a relatively rare disorder to a less than rare disorder with an increasing number of "personalities" being cited over the years.

Rather than viewing this in a "Wilburnian sense" of fragmentation (Doane, Kline and Erlbaum, *Psychological Concepts and Dissociative Disorders*, 1994, pages 11-14), we are simply seeing naturally occurring elements that are very pliable, and plastic being mobilized by suggestion or programming to become what they are suggested to be. In short, an individual who for whatever reason lacks a set of *persistent patterns of trance clusters* can be made aware that there is a phenomenon of Multiple Personality Disorder, and that others have had increasing numbers of "personalities." This is well within the scope, from what we have seen, of centers to utilize the information to compartmentalize (rather than fragment) and develop suggested personalities from these centers, just as our dancer had developed her own extended role play that functioned well for her.

Further, centers on their own in response to the environment have the capacity to compartmentalize based on trauma whether sexual, social, or physical. Given the programming, an individual might learn that there are certain circumstances in which being disclosing is read by certain predatory others as being vulnerable. Centers may well then compartmentalize this *trance* of being disclosing and open to certain circumscribed circumstances or acceptable environmental triggers. Given such *cognitive programming errors* as polarized thinking, this can lead to very dysfunctional *trances* in which this vulnerable state is only seen in very rare and infrequent circumstances, leaving the person with a very impoverished social life.

The all-or-none thinking that is frequently cited by Cognitive Behavior Therapists and in our view, polarized thinking, certainly leads to commands, suggestions, which would direct executive centers and clusters of *neural information centers* to provide very sharp, distinct contrast, and thus associated sharp and distinct *trance* states to the outside world.

Without the high level of compartmentalization or polarized programming, people are more likely to present a more gradual continuum of *trance* states rather than marked, sudden, and dramatic presentations of *trance* states, which might be viewed as another personality.

Further, the notations in the literature of individuals exhibiting animal-like qualities, animal sounds, and actions that are not consistent with a human quality are far more consistent with the activity of *neural information centers* and the knowledge that they have housed within them than any notion of a sub-personality or a fragmented personality. In other words, each of us has within us recordings of what certain animals, sounds of animals, and behaviors of animals are like. This can be replayed such as when we read a book, and it mentions a dog, we see a dog, hear a dog, and see the emotions of a dog, horse, etc. The bread and butter of hypnotists who have utilized the work of these centers without realizing it for years has been to entertain audiences by having the person at the sound of the bell or the click of the fingers, cluck like a chicken, graze like a sheep, or bark like a dog. Certainly, in such a performance by stage hypnotists, there was no supposed altering of a personality, but it was simply seen as a function of some mysterious hypnotic phenomena. Of course, by now, you will recognize that this is simply the shifting into and tapping into different centers with the merger of these centers under the direction of executive centers in order to produce the performance.

In short, we see the phenomena of MPD/DID and the development of roles being exactly the same process. We see that this is a matter of working with, compartmentalizing, merging, and triggering *neural information centers*. Executive *neural information centers* will martial centers to produce certain sensory perceptive altered states. All aspects of MPD can and have been produced for years under conditions of classical inductions of hypnosis. Further, we can see the work of centers in such disorders as somnambuliform states, whether in somnambuliform possession as seen in primitive tribes, or somnambulism in which the "sleep walker" carries out complex duties, conversations, etc. triggered either by cues (stressors) in the environment or internal electrical disturbances.

Finally, as we leave this discussion, I would emphasize the following. To change the *cognitive programming* by means and/or of instruction/suggestion means to change *neural information center* functions and their relationships with other *neural information centers*, thus bringing about changes in *trance* states. When we change the components of the map, we begin to change the way that the person interacts with his or her world for we all are interacting within our own maps, and not the actual territory. This provides a very good working model for the phenomena of MPD or DID.

Chapter Twenty

Chapter Twenty

Two Phases of Intervention

"Zen mind is beginner's mind. In the mind of the beginner, there are many possibilities. In the mind of the expert there are few."
Ken Suzuki

G oing back to our fortified city/state metaphor, there are two stages of intervention. One is somehow gaining access through the wall. The other is affecting change after you are on the inner side of the wall. It is our premise that all effective therapists, no matter what their theoretical orientation, have learned to deal effectively with both these phases of intervention. If not, they have not become effective therapists.

In the literature, resistance is noted, dissonance is noted, and transference is noted. All of these are the outer wall phenomena. These are extensions of the *homeostatic* system, protecting and guarding the map, guarding changes to the integrity of the map as a Gestalt, as well as changes within its sub-units and basic bytes of programming. Ultimately, of course, since this is a biological process, there will be changes in the electro-chemical, neuro-chemical, physiological pattern. In their review of the work of master hypnotherapist, Milton Erickson, M.D., the NLP gurus Bandler and Grinder, utilized the term "pacing" (Bandler and Grinder, 1975). Pacing is a matching in some respect to the system so that the system at large accepts rather than rejects the outside or in-putting source, and thereby makes the therapeutic process more rapid, effective, or in many cases, even possible. Basic to the work of hypnotherapy and hypnotism as an art has been the very concept of pacing. In its simplest form, this is been a verbal narrative of what is currently on going with the organism. For example, the subject/client is seated in the chair. The operator/hypnotist/therapist says to the subject, "You are seated in the chair. You can hear many different sounds around you. You are looking at an object. You can feel changes occurring in your hands and your feet. You can feel sources of tension and relaxation in your body. You can feel your breathing. You can feel the motion of your chest moving in and out. If you listen and are very attuned to it, you can feel the beating and pulsing of your heart."

The next step is to lead the system. This simply involves statements such as, "you are relaxing in the chair; you notice one of your hand is becoming warmer than the other. You notice that those muscle groups are becoming more relaxed than other muscle groups. You are noticing, as you relax in the chair, that you are becoming much more relaxed now than you were a moment before, and how much more relaxed will you be in a moment from now than you are right now? What other changes are beginning to occur that you are noticing now, that you did not notice that may not exist a moment from now? As you breathe in deeper and slower, slower and deeper, as the good, rich oxygen moves through your system, you find yourself being relaxed, more and more relaxed, and you allow these words just to move through your mind and be translated into your body, "Relax and be calm." This basic formulation, in one way or another, has been the mainstay for all hypnotic rituals.

Bandler and Grinder further illuminate Erickson's use of matching, which is a form of nonverbal pacing. In matching, the hypnotist might match strides with the subject as he walks, or he might cross match, such as matching the way in which he moves a pencil back and forth with the rocking movement of the subject's chair (*Patterns of the Hypnotic Techniques of Milton H Erickson, M.D., Volume I and II, 1996*).

Another form of pacing utilized as part of the tool chest of master hypnotherapists has been the use of the metaphor in story form (*Therapeutic Metaphors, 1978, David Gordon*). Ostensibly, the story was about something the system was interested in. It could be a daily part of the system's routine, or met a congruency with what it understood its reality to be. However, after the story had begun, there would be interwoven within it messages or programming, implications that would lead to system changes. In other words, the metaphor became the Trojan horse. The horse was welcomed into the city; yet after the horse was allowed to come into the city, the virus inside the horse would begin to move in, work, change, and redistribute the programming and *neural information center* connections.

Another technique of hypnotherapy is the use of the interspersal technique. This is no more adroitly used than in the work of Erickson. Erickson would imbed a command or suggestion, or as we would term it, *"cognitive programming,"* by appropriate pauses and breathing patterns. This underscored a change in the way that the presentation or the command was presented against the context of the rest of the delivery. Rises and falls in pitch and other speech markers would make pertinent *neural information centers* aware of programming while not raising the defenses of the *homeostatic* system (Bandler and Grinder, *Patterns of the Hypnotic Techniques of Milton H. Erickson, M. D.*, Volume I, 1996).

Following and frequently utilized concurrently with the former two methods, again no more skillfully than in the work of the master, Milton Erickson, is the use of the interrupter technique. This means simply to deliver a suggestion or *cognitive programming* byte to the system and then immediately follow it with an interruption of the *homeostatic* system. In other words, the *cognitive programming* byte would send the *homeostatic* system to "chase a red herring", and therefore, end its manipulation or neutralization of the programming that was being inserted as an attempt to alter the h*omeostatic* system. An example of such a mechanism would be the following: "Wendy, you must know now by the evidence that you have accumulated that men find you to be a very pleasant and attractive woman. Why is it so cold in here? Do you feel cold? I tend to be a bit cold natured, sometimes hot natured, but mainly cold natured. Are you cold? Do we need to adjust the heat? What's happened?"

Although the above example comes from the annals and lore of classical and Ericksonian hypnosis, the field of psychotherapy repeatedly offers examples where the "master psychotherapists" utilize and address the *homeostatic* system in order to be effective. A prime example of this is Carl Rogers' therapy in which there is reflection and paraphrase of the client's own wording, forming an outside loop that folds back into the programming system of the individual. Although non-directive in its presentation, the elements of suggestion are always there (Carl Rogers, <u>*Client Centered Therapy*</u>, 1951). Any time any two individuals are together and ideas are shared, the non-verbals, changes in breathing patterns, experience of being a human being, and reacting as human being do, to information that is input into its system, these activities form an on-going holographic type of programming back into this loop. It is also important to note that many times in looking across hypnotic therapies or non-directive therapies, they simply come into an agreement with the *homeostatic* system, itself, allowing that system to move to present time congruence, bringing about a re-shifting and a recalibration of the individual's response to the world.

Frequently shared vignettes of individuals who trained with Erickson was to meet him and several hours later find themselves waking up from a "*trance*," feeling they had learned nothing, yet later finding they had learned "oh so much." The highly non-directive manner of classical psychoanalysis with its sparingly but poignantly made interpretations is yet another example of the *homeostatic* system being allowed to play its agenda, unwind its programming, set its own stage, and in a supportive fashion, move itself toward a more internal balance that is congruent with the existing "now."

Eye Movement Desensitization and Reprocessing (EMDR) is a system, which almost totally paces with the *homeostatic* system. With the exception of an initial statement of negative cognition about the traumatic event followed by a positive statement of the individual's placement within the event, there is very little suggestion/programming/input. The therapist largely functions as an encourager and provider of moving visual stimulation, bi-lateral tactile stimulation, and alternating bi-lateral auditory stimulation in order to "free" the person from trauma.

The question has been raised in training seminars, "What about the Gestalt masters?" Addressing the *homeostatic* system as viewed in the Gestalt work of the modern founder, Fritz Perls, it is not that the Gestalt master is pacing with others, but produces an environment in a very authoritarian posture. This is a system in which individuals will elect to play the game or not play the game by pacing to the demands and the persona of the Gestaltists. In other words, a phrase, such as "being on the hot seat," connotes a system in which the client's *homeostatic* system has already elected to be there, to be present, and to be "obedient" to the dictates, demands, and nuances or suggestion from the Gestalt Therapist, or has elected to avoid and refuse participation. There is a very famous incident cited involving the founder of modern Gestalt Therapy, Fritz Perls, in which a young woman, very much taken not only with the techniques, but also persona of Gestalt Therapy as projected by Fritz Perls, began to attempt a conversation with the master. She attempted to express flattery. She attempted to express appreciation to the

Gestalt Therapist. Perls, as the anecdote relates, stood motionless, totally ignoring the individual as though she was not there. At some point, out of frustration, she began to insult Perls and denounce him for being cruel and indifferent and at this point Perls turned, looked, and said, "Now we can be real." The accuracy of this recorded moment is not as important as the embodiment of this moment suggesting the overall philosophy of Gestalt Therapy as projected by Perls (Gestalt Training Seminar, 1978). In its own way, it is the Gestaltists suggesting, "If you want healing, relief, or correction, then pace with me."

Paradoxical therapy, in its essence is built around the *homeostatic* framework. Rather than oppose the framework, the paradoxical therapy seeks to actually pace and extend the elements of the framework and the underlying map. For example, if you are afraid that you might expel gas, then I would suggest you indulge in eating these beans and learn to modulate your flatulence as to produce a discernible tune (*My Voice Will Go With You: The Teaching Tales of Milton Erickson*. Milton Erickson and Sidney Rosen, April 1982).

If you fear that you are going to faint and feel a compelling sense that you are going to faint, then seek to bring this fainting about to the best of your ability, a form of symptom prescription as seen in Frankl's Logo Therapy (Man's Search for Meaning: An Introduction to Logotherapy, Frankl, 1992).

The following represents an extension of this respect for the *homeostatic* system in a therapeutic encounter engaged in by one of the authors. A young man having a lengthy history of violence presented with his family. There had been multiple fighting incidents in school before the individual had been removed to a series of camps. Ultimately, after several combative episodes there, his family removed him, against the advice of the camp director. The youth now at home was virtually holding the family "hostage" (as they saw it) by his acts of property destruction, explosive episodes over which he claimed to have little or no control, and at times, the menacing of younger siblings and others with such things as kitchen knives and slats or such weapons. The family, feeling immobile to address the situation and frequently expressing compliance to keep peace with this individual at any cost, presented and saw themselves in their maps of the world as his victims. The youth, too, saw himself as a victim to some force beyond himself. Yet, by the same token, it was indeed part of his map that he was tough, a fighter, played by different rules, and was somewhat of a warrior breed as expressed through his admiration of professional wrestlers he watched on television.

In pacing with his *homeostatic* system, (which obviously by now is understood to be protective of his underlying map through which he navigates the world), the therapist began to simply repeat the various actions that the youth had engaged in. The youth was noted to smile, nod, acknowledge, and frequently make comments, such as, "I would do it again. Nobody pushes me around. I can take care of myself." Then he would look at his parents who had adopted a posture of almost cowering. It was suggested by the therapist in pacing with the *homeostatic* system in congruency with his map that, indeed, it sounded like the young client was a very tough guy. This young man was a guy who was constantly wanting action, a guy who was afraid of little and sought to prove it and someone who felt himself almost invincible in the face of other males. He was someone who felt himself unchallenged, unrivaled and almost invincible in the face of other males. As these statements were made, there were a number of non-verbals, such as the client frequently moving forward, nodding his head, smiling, and orienting his head by tilting one ear more in the direction of the therapist. The therapist then concluded after these accolades that since he was such a violent individual he was; probably a "natural-born killer" whose instincts, talents, and abilities were being largely wasted; and given his abilities, his warrior-like talents, and his age, he was fast approaching the time when he could join the Marines.

At this point in the session, the non-verbals of the individual (which it should be remembered are guided by the *homeostatic* system and map) were noted to first be a smile, a sudden halt, followed by an obvious stance of being taken aback as his head recoiled, and his jaw dropped. It was explained that the Marines have a proud tradition of training men to become the most dangerous fighters in the world, and since their very inception, Marines have been trained to live and die by a code of warrior combat. It was noted that obviously, if he continued in society with this expression of talent in the civilian sector, he was headed for prison or jail. However, in the Marines, he could engage fully with other warriors who wished to harm and kill him as much as he wished to harm and kill them, and thus all would be fair in the art of war. It was pointed out that this would be a win/win situation. He could rise to a point of high honor and be decorated, even if it cost him his life. It was then suggested that very little time should be wasted. Given his approaching age, it was recommended that he contact the local Marine recruiter and additionally enroll in some rapid courses of martial arts that would make him more desirable to the Marines.

The young man then uttered, "There's a war going on right now."

The therapist responded, "Yes, and that's something we can't always count on, so the sooner you get into this, the sooner you may have an opportunity to explore the full range of your killer abilities."

The young client then began to shift position, stating, "Well, I didn't really ever want to hurt anybody." The therapist remarked, "Don't be so modest. You have spent almost an hour telling us about your great exploits, your fearless encounters with others and, your desire to be head of a gang, etc. Given the history that you have voiced, yourself, you certainly seem the caliber of man the Marines would want, perhaps going on suicide missions and other almost deadly assignments, assignments that would assure you of having the opportunity to give your life or take life. However, that's all in the day's game for a man that has a "natural-born killer/warrior instinct." The youth then stated that he felt he needed more experience in school.

The therapist, again pacing with the original mapping that was presented, explained he probably needed no more school than he had right now to buy his ticket into the Marines. There the marines could finish perfecting, training, and instilling in him the desire to complete the mission, whether he came back or not, stating to him, "You know, to learn to do it, dead or alive."

The parents, sensing the change in the overall rhythm, began to voice that there was actually somewhat of a family tradition in that one of his grandfathers had served proudly in the Marines and had been wounded in a charge, one of his finest hours, as he would report years later. It was then suggested that perhaps these genetics were being passed down through the generations, and this "warrior instinct", this savagery, was presenting itself in the flesh of their young son who could carry on the tradition.

On a one-week follow-up period, the family reported absolutely no violence. There had been no use of weapons. The father and mother stated that they had attempted to follow up the suggestion by taking the young man to the Marine Corp recruiter, but the young man had stated that he did not think he was ready for such action. On a two-month follow-up, violence had markedly decreased as measured by a reduction in threats to others, property destruction, and zero fights with peers. At four months, it was noted the individual was giving no regaling of his history of wishing to be in any sort of combat with anyone. At every turn, the therapist and the parents insisted that he seriously consider either joining the Marines, the Army, or become a member of something like the Special Forces, Rangers, or even a Navy SEAL suggested it.

This example of therapy is obviously one of a paradoxical nature. However, it was effective in that instead of challenging the map that the individual held of himself and his world and thus challenging the *homeostatic* system, it rather agreed with it. It not only agreed with it, but it assisted the map in going where it had yet to go. At that point, in time, the map began to review itself through its *neural information centers*, arriving at a new level of congruency, which was more realistic to the on-going environment. With this review, there was a behavioral change.

The examples given in the afore-mentioned pages are not meant to be exhaustive. They only serve as a limited sampling of the much larger set of therapeutic interventions.

What happens after we have been invited inside the wall into the city? What happens after we have breached the wall and are inside the domain? In the metaphor of our model, we work with the *neural information centers* directly. We do this by the following means:

(1) Addressing underlying *cognitive programming errors*, directly or indirectly. These filter through the *neural information centers* and *neural information center communities* and thus produce distortions within the map and dysfunctional *trance* or *sensory perceptively altered states*.

(2) Directly or indirectly updating and giving information to *neural information centers* that are attempting to perform a function without sufficient information.

(3) The therapist can directly or indirectly promote harmony or unity within the system by promoting communication between *neural information centers* that are at odds and in conflicting function.

(4) Directly or indirectly assisting the organism in developing new *neural information centers* associated with new skill development and expression, and new administrative, executive, and organizing functions.

This classification of interventions is merely for a sense of convenience and communication. It is most helpful to understand that it is quite artificial in nature and that the boundaries between the interventions frequently are very blurred.

The idea that there are groupings or forces behind the wall to which these afore mentioned interventions are addressed can be readily seen in the monumental works of Eugene Gendlin, Bandler and Grinder's NLP parts work, and Milton Erickson's appeal to the subconscious and his "confusion" technique of functions within the subconscious. There is very lengthy history dating back to the ancients of classical hypnosis making appeals to the various parts of the sub-conscious to receive information, change behavior, and understand the "underlying meaning" of the overtly manifested behavior. All these therapeutic approaches indicate that unless something is connected internally within the organism, change does not happen. Unless there is a "felt sense" of connecting with some inner part, the patterns of behavior and perceptions continue unabated.

All of the different types of therapeutic interventions that are not part of the pacing and "wall breaching" of the *homeostatic* barrier fall into the category of *trance* deconstruction and reconstruction by various forms of communication with n*eural information centers*. In fact, once *trance* deconstruction has begun, the n*eural information centers* very often begin *trance* reconstruction spontaneously.

All techniques, from classical hypnotic suggestion, cognitive restructuring, scripting, Gestalt work, EMDR, TIR, and any other effective modality of therapy, bring about changes by the interaction with n*eural* *information centers.* In other words, effective therapies could be viewed as working towards an en*trance* into the centers and reworking the underlying programming connections and intracommunication between the centers. Therefore, the hypnoanalysts, Cognitive Behavior Therapist, Gestaltists and all other effective therapists and therapeutic modalities have as their ultimate goal the individual's freedom from incongruent or inaccurate programming while allowing for congruent realignment with the sensory-based world of the organism.

Chapter Twenty One

Workshop Excerpts

What About EMDR?
(Excerpted from Workshop, Spring of 2005)

"EMDR is one way of approaching and conceptualizing solutions TIR is another."
Hellams and Schreiber

*A*n excellent question is about how EMDR fits in the schema of what I have laid out so far today. We have talked about dissonance as a biological mechanism. We have further discussed the nature of *homeostasis*, maintaining things as a status quo, defending the organism against change. We have discussed *neural information centers*, how they comprise individual programming, and how this individual programming is connectively linked to form the map of the organism. We have further looked at how *trance* states or *sensory perceptive alteration* is an extension of the programming within the *neural information center*s and thus the map. It has also been presented that any effective therapy can be broken down into two major components: (1) Addressing and working with *homeostasis,* and (2) after accomplishing the acceptance by or entrance through the h*omeostatic mechanism*, addressing reprogramming within the n*eural information centers* and therefore changing the map and the associated sensory perceptive altered states.

Given these assumptions and building blocks, our study and practice of EMDR is found to be totally congruent with our model. In many ways, it is even more congruent with our model than with other therapeutic schools we have explored.

EMDR is a highly effective tool. I would recommend training in EMDR to any therapist. EMDR was certainly one of the schools we looked at extensively as we were developing our metaphor.

Please note that in EMDR, it is almost a total matching with the organism's *homeostatic* system.

You question the client to make sure he is in a comfortable seating arrangement and that he is comfortable with the place in which he is working. You test out and offer several methods of stimulation from bilateral auditory to eye movement to bilateral tactile stimulation. In this process, you are sensitive to the responses given by the client as to which vehicle is comfortable for him. For instance, if the initial mechanism chosen was to use eye movement and the pace or distancing of the hand of the therapist is uncomfortable, then this is adjusted. If the use of a light bar or hand waving in front of the client's face is too distracting, then you may well shift to tactile or bilateral auditory. Further, in respecting *homeostasis* and not inviting *homeostasis* out to fight, you are suggesting nothing to the client in the way of new information. You elicit from the client what he is telling himself about a traumatic event from the past. You further solicit from the client's system what he would like to tell himself about the past. The client's own reworking of the experience is internal, or if you will, "behind the walled city," as in our metaphor. Any responses given by the client are accepted and not challenged. The entire process to include the SUDS ratings that are an integral part of EMDR are totally based on reports, which are unchallenged from the client.

There is an obvious reworking of the programming within the n*eural information centers* as gauged by reports of the client of his or her internal experience of seeing past events from new angles, new lights, and with new interpretations.

The abreactions that are witnessed and reported obviously contain a physiologically-based element, as frequently has been witnessed in regression work in classical hypnosis, which, of course, by now in this workshop, you would have understood to be a sign that n*eural information centers* are certainly involved in some type of processing.

Frequently, clients experiencing EMDR therapy state that something has "changed" or "shifted." Upon exploration, EMDR clients often talk about feeling that something has physically shifted or moved in a definite sense of a physical change. I would ask at this point, "Does this seem to mirror what we have cited as that sense of inner change noted in Eugene Gendlin's focus therapy?" We see all of these latter experiences and transformations being highly congruent with reprogramming within n*eural information centers.* Further, we see this also as indicative of *neural information centers* changing their relationship to each other inside the map.

Frequently in utilizing EMDR, we have encountered individuals for which their experience does not seem to "move." We have developed a technique in working through centers in order to open the gateway and pathway to help the EMDR be more effective. However, this is beyond the scope of this particular workshop and would need to be addressed with individuals who have previously been trained in EMDR from an EMDR-certified center.

Good question, short answer. EMDR, in all respects, is highly congruent with our metaphor.

Quantum Psychology/Quantum Mechanics

"There is no Quantum Universe, just a Quantum description."
<u>**Quantum Psychology**</u>
Stephen Wolinsky

(Excerpt from workshop in summer of 2006)

e have not engaged this topic in our presentation because of the sheer, very broad scope of quantum mechanics and quantum psychology. The presentation today, as well as our upcoming book, is largely based within the macro world of Newtonian physics. However, you can see in our book, MAPPING, that we have included references from the movie, "What the Bleep?"

It is necessary to have a grounding in understanding how we are using "*trance*" and "*trance* states" and how this has been transformed in viewing these as states of *sensory perceptive alteration* that are an integral part of *homeostasis* and *mapping*.

Let's look at it this way. One of our basic premises is that appropriate programming, which is programming that is congruent with the outside environment, yields appropriate or functional *trances* or states of *sensory perceptive alteration*. Dysfunctional programming within n*eural information centers* yields dysfunctional states of *sensory perceptive alteration* or *SPA*. In this way, we are largely addressing the world within a macro, more Newtonian concept. In other words, visualize if you will, a Venn diagram with the larger circle being all possible known experiences at any given time, and a smaller circle, which would represent the *SPA* and the *SPA*'s experience of that subset that it allows to filter through to the organism. Of course, the view is that the larger circle of possible experiences does not radically change, but that the smaller circle of the *SPA* is an on-going flow and transformation of changes of what is seen, what is experienced, what is distorted, what is filtered in, and what is filtered out.

Now to take this a step further, we must visualize three circles. One circle, the larger, is the set of all possibilities, and therefore is a rather infinite set. The next inner circle is a circle of the created reality between that larger set of infinite possibilities and the observer out in the universe creating this reality by observation. Within this circle, there is yet another circle of *Spa*. Now picturing this diagram the way that our system would extrapolate into the quantum world would be the following. As our n*eural information centers* dictate certain states of *SPA*, at the same time there are certain levels of expectancy. So that as the levels of expectancy change, the impact upon the reality, itself, changes so that not only is *SPA* filtering in/filtering out, distorting information consistent with the process, but is actually functioning as a co-creator with the universe as to what is happening within the environment.

Now, like most things in our world for pragmatic sake, it is easier to view most of our work, especially at the very beginning of being introduced to these concepts, within that larger block of a fixed physical Newtonian world. However, as you can see by the latter Venn diagram that we have described here, this metaphor is very consistent and can be quite workable, even when looking at the quantum universe.

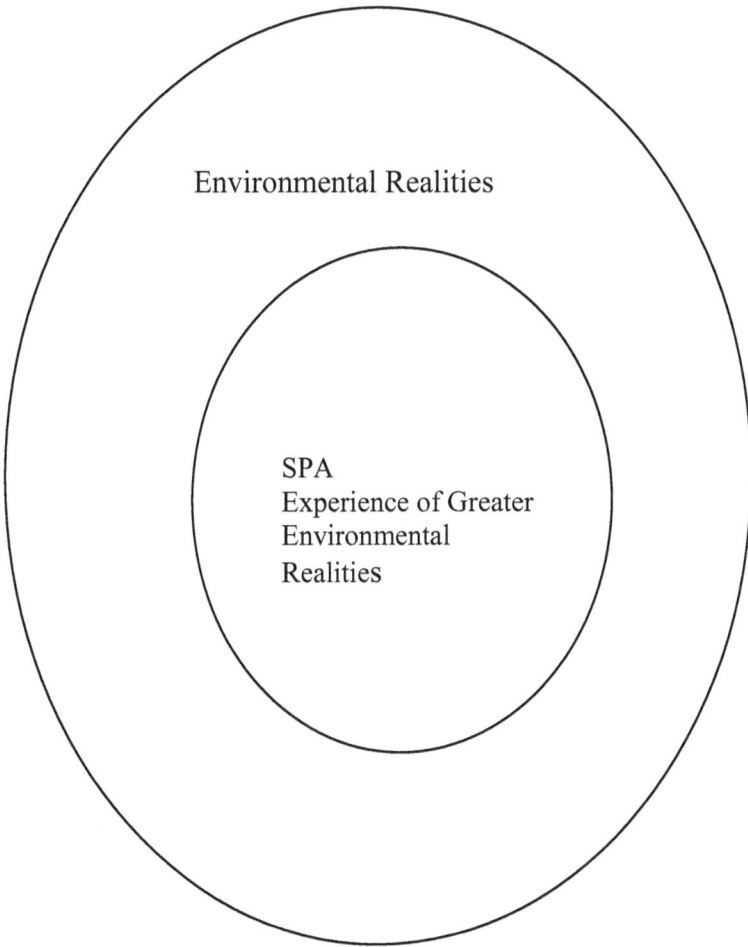

Environmental Realities

SPA
Experience of Greater
Environmental
Realities

SPA Model in the Newtonian World

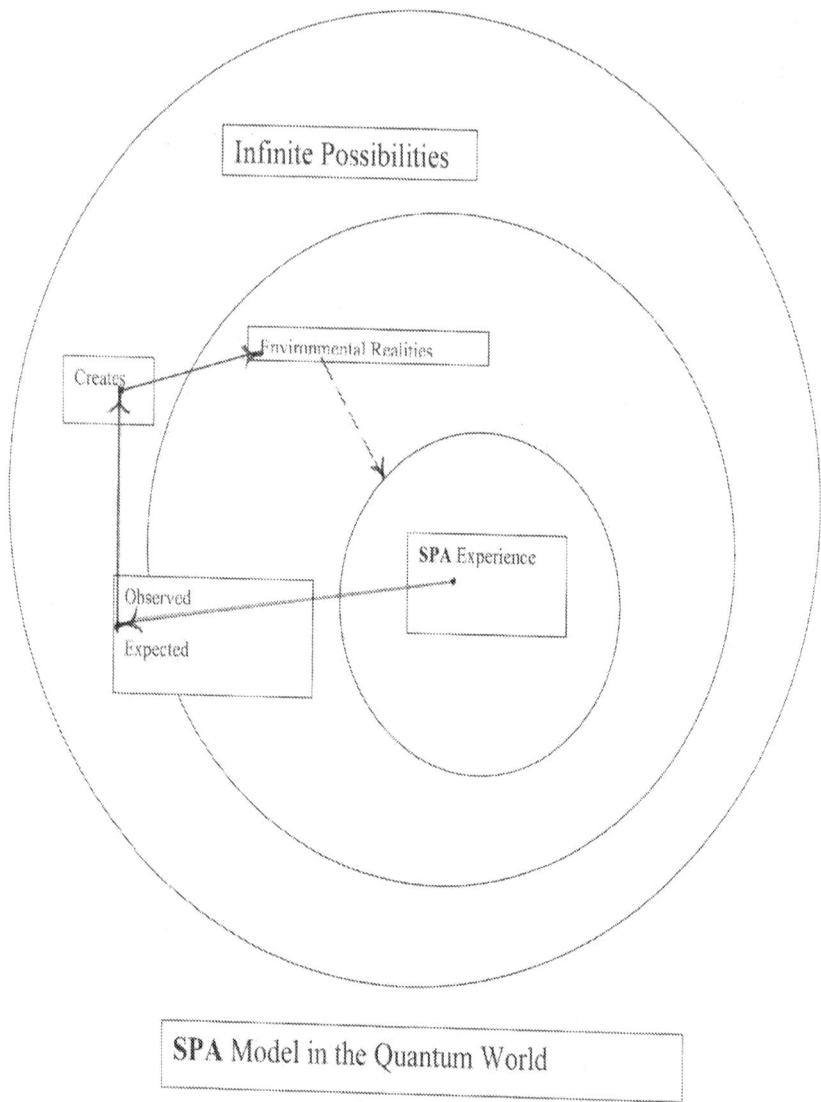

Infinite Possibilities

Environmental Realities

Creates

SPA Experience

Observed
Expected

SPA Model in the Quantum World

Chapter Twenty Two

Chapter Twenty Two

Trance Deconstruction and Pattern Interruption

"There is no fundamental reality."
Buddha

"It is all a play of perceptions and concepts."
Stephen Wolinsky

The use of interruption techniques can change the types of stimulus patterns within the *sensory perceptive mapping system*. Sometimes associations inhibit the ability to learn and to expand your awareness. Here are some methods for loosening association at those times when you might choose to loosen them. As you become aware of your *sensory perceptive holographic mapping system*, you can become more familiar with its editing functions and abilities. Within the *mapping system*, there are many areas that you can observe and adjust. In the sensory arena, there are visual, auditory, tactile, gustatory, and olfactory dimensions. Some descriptors that apply to each of these sensory areas are as follows: visual, [*color/black and white, brightness, contrast, focus, texture, detail, size, distance, shape, border, location, movement within the image, of the image, orientation, associated/dissociated, perspective, proportion, dimension, singular/plural],* auditory [*location, pitch, tonality, melody, inflection, volume, tempo, rhythm, duration, mono/stereo*], and kinesthetic [*quality, intensity, location, movement, direction, speed, duration*]. You can adjust the kinesthetic responses and the associated and referential meanings. In each of these dimensions, these descriptors can be edited, and the effects observed. The *sensory mapping system* can be treated as an object, and it and its contents can be observed. In the old school, this would be called "observing ego." Sensory data, energy, mass, and space-time can be observed, and their functions and effects can be altered. Using the pattern, interruption "map" it is suggested that you can vary the following elements:

1.   *Change the frequency/rate of the pattern.*

2.   *Change the intensity of the pattern.*

3.   *Change the duration of the pattern.*

4.   *Change the time (hour, day, week, and month) of the pattern.*

5.   *Change the location (in the body and in the world) of the pattern.*

6.   *Change some quality of the pattern.*

7.   *Perform the symptom without the pattern.*

8.   *Perform the pattern without the symptom.*

9.   *Change the sequence of the elements of the pattern.*

10. *Interrupt or otherwise prevent the patterns from occurring.*

11. *Add (at least) one or subtract (at least) one new element to the pattern.*

12. *Break up any previously whole element into smaller elements.*

13. *Link the symptom/pattern to another symptom/pattern.*

14. *Reverse the pattern (O'Hanlon, William H. 1987. Taproots, Bruner/Mazel, New York).*

In energy, mass and space-time, there are qualities that can be observed. Energy can be observed as strong, weak, fast, slow, intense, or mild. Mass can be observed as weight, density, size, and shape. Space can be observed as distance, location, position, empty, full, infinite, figure, or ground. Time can be defined as movement, speed, duration, or direction. All of these elements of the *sensory mapping system* can be observed, experienced, and altered, and the effects noticed. The movement of the eyes can be one method to assist in loosening associations. Think of a word, image, or sensation that has a positive association for you. Notice the location of the feelings. Now as you listen to the words visualize the image or feel the sensation. Follow these arrows with your eyes. This can also be used with uncomfortable or negative associations or simply associations you wish to loosen.

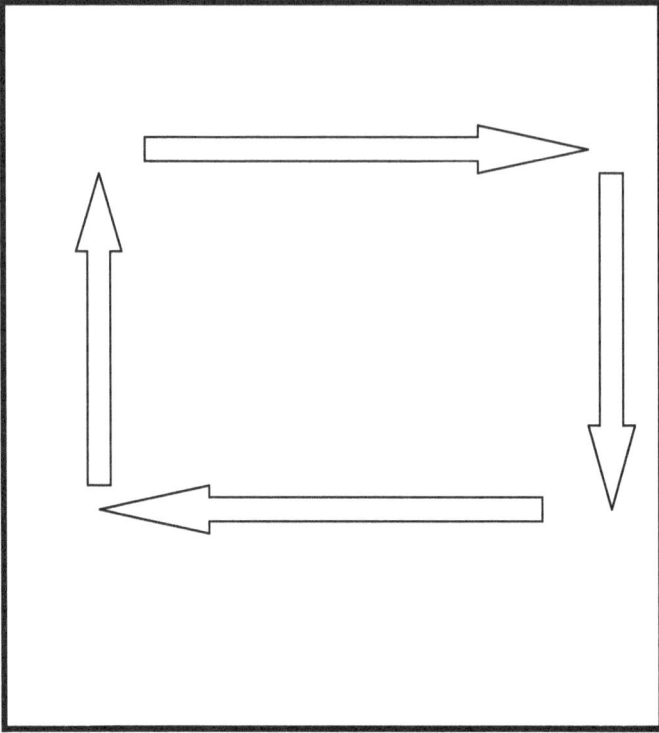
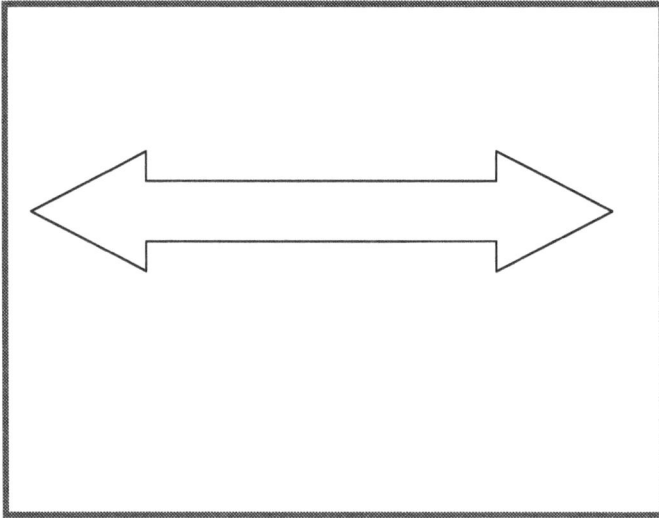

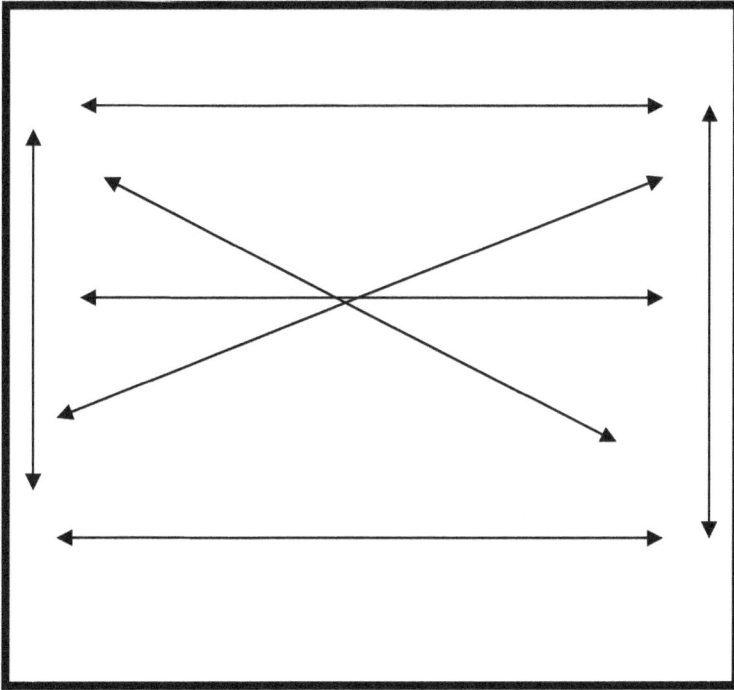

As you gaze at the arrows and allow your eyes to follow the direction, you can do so in straight lines or angles, or you can go in figure 8's or in other combinations of directions. The movement does not have to be rapid or at an uncomfortable pace. Notice any change or variation in the associations. This is only one way among many ways of altering or editing the associations, references, meanings, or sensory data configured within the sensory perceptive holographic mapping system.

Chapter Twenty Three

Learning Models and Teachers

"The inner teacher is you" (I Am That, 1979)
Sri Nisargadatta Maharaj)

As you look at different models and theories for counseling, become aware of your inner consciousness. The clear consciousness within is the teacher, the questioner, and the observer. As you absorb a teaching or theory, digest it, and discard things that are not useful to you. Keep things that are useful to you. If you can, become aware, then, go beyond the concepts, ideas, or beliefs that you have or will be indoctrinated into. Remember, you cannot get outside of a paradigm, belief system, or identity from within that system. All systems of understanding are vehicles to be utilized and discarded. In order to be free it is essential that you remain unattached to ideas, beliefs, systems, and creations within the domain of consciousness. Become aware of any underlying errors and move beyond them. Teachers, trainers, and experts demanding that you must follow their particular dogma or rituals have their own agenda. Be cautious when becoming involved

259

with them. Any map that claims to be "the one" is not. Move on. Be aware of the traps of infantile grandiosity and magical thinking.

"All paths lead to unreality. Paths are creations within the scope of knowledge. Therefore, paths and movements cannot transport you into Reality, because their function is to enmesh you within the dimension of knowledge, while Reality prevails prior to it." (The Ultimate Medicine, Sri Nisargadatta Maharaj)

Chapter Twenty Four

Chapter Twenty Four

All Maps are Maps and Are Not the Territory

"We say that everything is an abstraction, an abstraction is a metaphor, a metaphor is a map, a map is a representation and that's the best we can do. We operate with sensory perceptive mapping. Homeostasis is the gyroscope."
Hellams & Schreiber 2006

Maps can be useful, or maps can lead us down a path away from our goals. As Alfred Korzybski has said, "The map is not the territory" and "a map that misplaces the cities or the directions of the streets is worse than useless as it misleads and misinforms." (*Science and Sanity*, Alfred Korzybski 1993). The difficulty with *cognitive programming errors*, assumptive errors, associative errors, and/or completion errors is that they place within the *sensory perceptive holographic map* cues, references, and directions that misguide the organism, generating responses that not only mislead, but that also could endanger the organism. One reason that we choose to reference

261

sensory perceptive holographic mapping rather than simply refer to a map is that mapping is an ongoing process of sensing energy flowing through the organism and being synthesized as the organism locates itself in energy, mass, space and time as opposed to   a frozen mapping phenomenon.

The freezing of stimuli within the framework of the past and projected into some imagined future or created present is part of the confabulatory nature of referencing, associative, completion, and/or assumptive errors as the organism seeks to maintain bio *homeostasis*. On one occasion while studying with Dr. Stephen Wolinsky, a well-known author and therapist in the area of *trance* phenomena, he stated to the group that one challenge that we face is to tolerate the flow of energy through the form or organism. As energy bombards the organism via a sense apparatus such as (the skin, eyes, ears, nose, and/or mouth), it gets transmuted into thoughts, sensations, images, sounds, tastes, smells, emotions, feelings, reactions, and actions as the organism channels the energy in ways that interpret and respond to the energy. We also utilize the energy in the form of oxygen, sunlight, fluid, plants, animals, and other chemicals that are converted by the organism into itself. Thoughts are also converted into the organism. In all respects, the organism and the environment are the same and never separated.

"As a man thinketh in his heart, so is he." (Proverbs 23:7). The metaphor becomes the reality. The dream and the dreamer are synonymous. In the end as the dream merges with the silence, the dream, the dreamer, and the silence disappear, reappear, and disappear, for they are not. This particular way of working with people is not just a technique, but it is a way of thinking, observing, and questioning. It incorporates into itself all other useful and effective schools of thought, philosophies, and therapies as being various windows of interpretation to be used to interrupt the present sensory perceptive altered states allowing for a reconfiguration of the *mapping system*. This is an ongoing, developing and changing process.

Don't be concerned if you do not "get it" at first glance. Stephen Wolinsky once shared a story about himself as a young developing therapist, attending training and hungry for knowledge. He was studying bodywork with a trainer who had twenty plus years of experience. During a break as Stephen was asking the trainer questions about the technique, the trainer responded with the question, "You want it all right now, don't you?"

Wolinsky responded, with an emphatic *"yes"*.

The trainer said, "That's bullshit! You can't have it all, you can only have the piece you can digest and absorb, and then you may get more." (Training Seminar on The Enneagram in Seattle, Washington 1993 with Stephen Wolinsky).

There is a story that Herbert Lustig, M.D. had been studying with Milton Erickson for a period of years when he asked Erickson, since several of Erickson's students were calling themselves Ericksonians, what he should do. Erickson responded, "I believe it's a little late to change your name."

Bill O'Hanlon, an Ericksonian and solution focused therapist states in the foreword of his book <u>Taproots</u> that Erickson said, "Develop your own technique. Do not try to use somebody else's technique... Don't try to imitate my voice, or my cadence. Just discover your own. Be your own natural self. It's the individual responding to the individual... I've experimented with trying to do something the way somebody else would do it. It's a mess!"(Taproots, 1987, O'Hanlon).

One time Dr. Wolinsky shared that he was with Sri Nisargadatta Maharaj and asked him the question, "Sometimes I think the thought , 'I like myself,' and I go with it ...and then some time later the thought appears, 'I, don't like myself,' and then I go with that thought. Why, does that happen?"

Maharaj responded, "You have been here long enough, you should know this. There is no birth. There is no death. There is no person. It is all a concept. It is all an illusion, and now you know the nothing and you can leave." Wolinsky says it took him somewhere in the neighborhood of ten to twelve years to get that (Personal Conversation with Stephen Wolinsky, 1993).

I am not sure that any of us "get it". We probably get some abstracted version of what we imagine something means within our self-constructed universe. As the teacher Sri Nisargadatta Maharaj has suggested, "You imagine that you are a person; therefore, you imagine that others are people, or gods, or beings, but I am universal consciousness." Further, he said to a student "It is all a dream" and the student said, "So, if I go with it's all a dream, where will that take me."

He responded, "Well, it will take you nowhere, for it is still a dream. It is not that it is all a dream that causes the problem. It is that you like one part of the dream and dislike the other." (I Am That, 1973, Sri Nisargadatta Maharaj).

The sayings of a wise man and the babbling of an infant are equally valid. It is all in the interpretation. Therefore, this is a gift, a way of discovering your own, natural self and by discovering yourself; you may assist others in their attempts to discover themselves, or at least a way of being congruent within themselves, in spite of whom others tell them to be. When you discover yourself, where is the need to ask others if it is correct or ask them to confirm your right to be you? I have discovered that I must spend a great deal of time with myself and if I have to spend that much time with someone perhaps I should like them and make it a pleasant place to be. Maharaj was once asked by a student "Don't I deserve peace?" He responded, "Those who deserve peace do not disturb it." (Sri Nisargadatta Maharaj, I Am That, 1973). Therefore, do not disturb the peace, if you discover it.

We often tell therapy interns do not confuse your theories, concepts and ideas about the person with the person. Your solutions may be effective in your version of the world but may have very little if anything to do with the client's 'world'. (Hellams & Schreiber, 2006)

Bill O'Hanlan tells the story of what psychology has taught us. He says that psychology has shown us that rats can be taught to run mazes, and people love stories so much that at times they will hang on to their myths and stories even when confronted with the reality. Such is found in the story of the Supreme Yoga where the teacher, Vasishtha is instructing Ram in the ways of Kundalini energy and its awakening, piercing the chakras, purifying the 72,000 Nadis, etc.   Ram says, "Now I understand."

Vasishtha asks, "What do you understand?"

Ram repeats everything Vasishtha has told him.

Vasishtha says, "No, none of that is true."

"Then why did you tell me those stories?" Ram asks.

"It's for the unenlightened, to give them a story to talk about," Vasishtha continues.   "None of that exists. Everything is consciousness, nothing exists outside of consciousness." (The Supreme Yoga, Venkatesananda, Swami, 1976)

Remember consciousness creates questions and then answers them so it can pretend that there is an orderly world that is knowable, predictable, and controllable. Therefore, the story begins. Have fun.

Your friends on this journey,

Wilton and Tobias

The End/Beginning

"Knowledge is bondage"

Vedas

Appendix:

Techniques for Working with Neural Information Centers and The Homeostatic System

The following techniques are not to be used as a "how to" or as a "cookbook.". Work within the limits of your training, education and expertise. Best practice principles need to be applied.

Technique No.1
Present Time Sensory Perceptive Alignment:

Step 1.   Ask the client to gaze at some object, which has neutral association for him or her.

Step 2.   Sit or lie comfortably.

Step 3.   Describe to yourself what it feels likes to position yourself in the seat, chair, or bed.   For example, I can feel my entire body sinking into the fabric of the chair. I can feel my left foot (sensing) it feels heavier than my right foot.   My muscles are beginning to feel limp. My breathing is beginning to slow and is now deeper in my chest.

Step 4.   Take three deeper than normal breaths –
slow, deep breaths, and upon each breath think to
yourself R-E-L-A-X, allowing the air to slowly, leak
out with each exhalation.

Step 5.   You can allow your eyes to close. However;
you can be in a deep comfortable state with your eyes
open or closed.

Self-Pacing

Step 6.   Try to hear and become aware of as many
elements (sounds) in the environment as possible.

Step 7.   Allow the sounds to be linked by the centers
with images. Allow any images to be linked with the
sounds. Allow any thoughts of the past or the future to
be redirected back to the present streaming of thoughts.

Step 8.   Now allow your thoughts to be projected
onto a screen that you visualize out in front of you,
about ten feet away and slightly above eye level. The
screen becomes the channel through which and by
which thoughts are conducted.   Sound thoughts are
even heard as running through the screen display.

Step 9.   Now give your n*eural information centers*
permission to operate independently performing the
following:

    (a)   Redirect all thought to the present time
        (no past or… future thoughts).

    (I)   Start one center counting down from
    1000 to 0 by 1's.

(II)   Start another center counting from one to 1000.

(III) Have another center send commands to the body to "be calm – relax."

(IV) Have yet another center narrate and create healthy body state.

Step 10.   Remind yourself if you start feeling overwhelmed to let go and allow the centers to do their work. A center can check in from time to time on it's status, but let them do their work. Trust the centers.

Step 11.   Continue to allow the centers to develop their autonomy.

Step 12.   Recognize any source of tension in the body and request that the center in charge provide "release and relaxation."

Step 13.   Allow the steps above to become a more fluid and flexible schema under the direction of the *homeostatic* system, rather than a rigid schema. Remember the *homeostatic* system is seeking balance and congruency.

Step 14.   Count from one to five when signaled by a *neural information center* to do so. Allow your eyes to open, and be fully alert and present.

Technique No. 2
Dislocation Trance:

Step 1.   Begin by shaking off any tension in your arms, legs, neck, or shoulders, and be here with me now.

Step 2   Generate the *present time sensory alignment* state from the previous exercise (Steps 1 through 12). When you are fully relaxed, ask a center to give you a special place or a series of places that you can go.

Step 3.   When you have an image of a place, move into the image. Look to your right, look to your left, and now in an internal way describe to yourself what you see. Allow yourself to see, hear, and feel the textures. Notice the contrast of dark and light and any other variations in the scene. Feel your movement and rhythm as you move through the scene, and allow yourself to notice or become aware of any scents or smells.

Step 4.   Expect the experience to unfold through the associated links of the *neural information centers*.

Step 5.   Allow the outside world to fade as you experience this new state of awareness or *trance*. (*sensory perceptive alteration* state*)*

Step 6.   If you drift away from your pleasant scene, allow the *neural information centers* in charge to redirect you back into the description and experience of the scene.

Step 7.   Count from one to 10 and experience the present time sensory state with eyes open. Describe the surroundings to yourself and re-ground. For example, "I am sitting in the chair and I can feel the fabric of the chair. I can see a desk, bookshelf, and a window. I hear the heating/air conditioning system operating."

Technique No. 3:
Connecting With Your Centers

Introducing yourself to neural information center work.

Step 1.   Close your eyes and pace with yourself, (I am sitting in the chair, I am taking relaxing breaths. I can feel a tingling in my right foot. My left foot feels heavier than my right or vice versa. I can feel my back sinking into the chair.)

Step 2.   Allow a center to direct you to your right or left hand by initiating a question "which hand?" and then accepting a signal. The signal can be any type of sensation.

Step 3.   Thank the center for the communication.

Step 4.   Ask the right (or left) hand center to communicate with you and give you a signal that it will work with you by signaling through one of your fingers (ideomotor). Creating a small level of movement in one of your fingers is requested. This signaling consists of one (1) movement for "yes" and two (2) movements for "no."

Step 5.   If a "yes" signal is given, ask the hand center to connect with any other centers necessary to change the sensation in the selected hand. Ask the center. "If you are willing or ready to change the sensation in the right (or left) hand, let me know by giving me a signal. One X for "yes" or two Xs for "no."

Step 6.   If "yes" signal is given, ask the center to start at the tips of the fingers and very gradually moving back, make the hand more like a cloud hand (light, fluffy, floating), a shell of a mannequin hand, or more not there than there. Ask the center to connect with any other centers or resources that it may need to create the change.

Step 7.   If the answer is "no," move to the next paradigm (*Homeostatic System Check*).   The no indicates that some other centers need to be consulted, or resources are not present within the system to establish the request.

Technique No. 4:
Homeostatic System Check: (HSC)

Step 1.   Access a *neural information center* simply by making the request "I would like to be in communication with the center in control, responsible for, or having the information regarding (subject of inquiry)." (This could be right hand, left hand, or a sensation such as butterflies in the stomach, etc.).

Step 2:   Ask, would you be willing to give me some information about the change to be made or history of the problem? Give a signal, one movement for 'yes' and two movements for 'no' (Most frequently, especially when requested, this will be an ideomotor signal. However, we respect the idiosyncratic nature of the system and will accept any signal.)

Step 3.   If the answer is "yes" (usual occurrence), proceed to step 4-5. If the answer is "no," then ask the center to give more information about "What would be necessary to have such information?"

Step 4.   Ask the center to search the system and recruit any centers for necessary information and resources addressing the desired change or problem.

Step: 5.   Ask the center to give you a definite signal when the task is completed.

Step 6.   Ask the center to arrange the following:

(a)   To give information about the problem or change requested (Be prepared to accept visual or auditory messages.)

(b)   Ask if the change or the problem can be safely addressed, "yes" or "no" answer (Wait for signal.)

(c)   If the answer is "yes," then ask the center to go inside and connect with all centers necessary to make this shift.

(d)   Ask the center when this connection has been made.

(e)   When signaled, ask the center to show or tell you the option(s) you have available.

(f)   If option(s) is (are) clear, thank the centers for their work. Then instruct the centers to reconnect to make the change happen.

(g)   If the answer is "no" in step (b), then ask the center to signal "yes" or "no" (1X or 2X respectively) to the following queries:

        (I)   Can this change be made safely?

        (II)   Do I have all of the resources available to me to   make the change?

        (III)   Is the time right to bring about this change?

        (IV)   Is some part of the system in opposition?

(h)   If the answer to I – IV is "no," then ask the center to go inside and connect with any and all centers to access more information to illuminate what elements are necessary to bring about this change. Ask the center to signal when you have information.

(i)   When signaled, thank the centers for their cooperation.   Then ask them to show or tell you what elements are necessary to lay a foundation for future change or resolution.

(j)   If the answer to IV was "yes," then proceed with the following:

        (I)   Ask the center if it will contact the opposing center (one signal for "yes" and two signals for "no").

(II)   If "yes," thank the center and ask it to connect with the opposing center.

(II)   Ask the opposing center if it will speak with you (one signal "yes" and two signals "no").

(IV)   If the answer is "yes," thank the center and explain that you understand that it is trying to assist the system by doing its part. Begin queries of "yes" or "no" of variety based on signal system. Ask the opposing center to work with the other centers to show you its point of view.

(V)   Use the information from above for resource building and acquisition of information to be used in an information update technique.

Technique No. 5
Neural Information Center Updates:

After conducting a *Homeostatic System Check*, an opposing center may be discovered whose opposition may be based on outdated information. This is a common occurrence for Cognitive Behavioral Therapy as illustrated by the following:

A young lady persisted in experiencing mild headaches and nausea, growing to near panic, on her morning drive to the office. This was despite the radical, positive change in her work environment. When challenged to log or record what she was telling herself, she revealed the following statements: "Here I go again... another bad day at the office. I hate the way I must live. Life sucks." Upon discussion of the reality of the changes, she agreed that the statements were not valid. Accurate statement replacements were made, such as, "That's the way things use to be, but not now. I now like my boss. I can easily get my work done and it is helpful to others."

The previous represents a more classic, Cognitive Behavioral Therapy process of thought replacement and cognitive restructuring, utilizing the neural information concept for cognitive restructuring, *trance* deconstruction and replacement. The model for the same issue would be as follows:

Step 1: Access the *neural information center* associated with the symptom or issue (Frequently this will be the opposing part discovered through the *Homeostatic System Check.)*

Step 2: Thank the *neural information centers* for its communication with you.

Step 3: Move from "yes" or "no" signaling to the thoughts of a talking picture nature.

Step 4: Ask the center to convert pictures to thought of a word nature. (i.e. You see yourself in a bubble. What might you be telling yourself in that bubble? What word thoughts would replace the pictures?) What might other centers be saying about this picture? Pursue active dialogue with you and the centers. Put each word thought to the following test:

      a.   Is this thought accurate with current or present time?
      b.   Is this thought helping?
      c.   Would I teach this to a child?
      d.   Could I defend this thought based on facts?

Step 5: Replace word thought that not does meet the test.

Step 6: Ask the center to signal acceptance (yes or no) of thought.

Step 7: Ask the center to check throughout the system for acceptance or resistance to the new thought and signal "yes" or "no."

Step 8: If the center signals "no acceptance," then ask the center to give the reasons. Continue with updates based on new information, if necessary. Check again, and if the center stills signals "no," perform the *Homeostatic System Check*.

Step 9:   If there are other centers resistant to the new thought, then (as above) request dialogue and begin any update necessary.

Technique No. 6:
Promoting Dialogue between Polarized Centers:.

Polarized centers are those *neural information centers* of which one is usually highly organized but seemingly encapsulated.   These are revealed in the client's dialogue regarding his or her life with others.   The following example illustrates this.   Jane reports that prior to her first child, she frequently enjoyed sex with her husband, noting, "I would dress in my naughty lingerie and fantasize that I was a high paid call girl, but after I became a Mom and all, it just did not feel right. I would have sex with my husband to satisfy him and wait for it to be over.   I don't know what happened."

Step 1.   Establish two chairs or locations.   (More may be used, if necessary.)   Have available one tape recorder if desired.

Step 2.   Place yourself in one position, and while sitting, "go inside and get in touch with one of the polarized centers" (in the previously proposed case the "Mom" center).   Ask the center to begin to share with you information, memories, (visual and auditory, etc.) associated with the center.   Allow this to continue until you "feel" emotional and/or physical changes.

Step 3.   Experiment with pictures/thoughts/talk thoughts, bringing up colors, contrast, textures, pitches, volume. etc. that allow the center to disclose this position.

Step 4.   When the feeling of this experience is "strong," count to 15 and rise from that position.

Step 5.   Stand, engage in several deep breaths, and facilitate *present time sensory alignment*.

Step 6.   When you are fully in present time and (only then) step into the opposing position.

Step 7.   Repeat steps 2 through 4 again, this time working with this polarized *neural information center*.

Step 8.   Stand.   Again, reestablish *present time sensory alignment*.

Step 9.   Still standing go inside and ask, "Which one" were you preferring to change Allow an exchange from the *neural information center* to guide you.

Step 10.   Start the tape. Allow the *neural information center* to speak to its polarized counterpart.   Give yourself time and permission to allow the *neural information center* to ask questions, chastise, communicate, discuss, etc. to the empty chair, which is the projection of its counterpart. When signaled by the appropriate *neural information center* to change chairs or positions–do so. When reseated, allow that *neural information center* to respond, argue, vent, and communicate with its projected counterpart. Continue this interchange of positions and voicing or dialogue between counterparts until signaled by an executive *neural information center* which indicates, "It is time to stop." Please note that the *neural information center* executive may signal throughout this venture in a fashion very similar to what has been described as a "felt sense" (Gendlin).

Step 11.   After the interchange has stopped, it will mean that the centers have become much more aligned and have begun to merge.   To complete this merger, listen again to the tape, writing down indications of distortions held by each part.   As the newly merged *neural information center* is operating, go inside and ask the merged center to work with other centers to give accurate updates or cognitions for each distortions or programming error noted on the tape.

Step 12.   One by one, ask the merged centers, "Can you accept the new cognitions?" (Signal 1X for "yes" and 2X for "no.")

Step 13:   Subject any "no's" to the *Homeostatic System Check*.   Then again, ask the center if it can accept the cognition.   At this point, the answer will frequently be "yes."   If the answer is "no," query for any opposing center.   Ask the center for its cooperation.   (Signal 1X for "yes" & 2X for "no.")   If "yes." begin dialogue with the center to update for change.

Technique No. 7:
Installation of New Auditory or Visual Messages:

Step 1.   When installing an updated visual or auditory replacement message present the message, with these three tests."

    (a) Would you teach it to a child?

(b) Would you advise your best friend to use it?

(c) Would you be willing to defend it in court as fact?

If the message passes these three tests, then you can begin this installation.

Step 2.   Have the *neural information center* in charge of visual messages begin with a dim, distant, colorless picture that incrementally increases in color, closeness, and intensity until it is a complete picture.

Step 3.   If this is an auditory message, have the center in charge of the message begin with a soft message that increases with volume and intensity until it is a strong message.

Step 4:   Once the message is at full intensity, check for any opposing centers.

Techniques to Stimulate Thinking Methodologies for Interrupting Pathology of the Conscious Set

1.   Trance Labeling

This type of technique gives us an opportunity to describe and interrupt the *trance* that takes us out of the here and now and distorts the experience by creating a confabulatory experience.

Throughout the day, we are engaged in any number of roles and/or activities, each of which can be labeled as a *trance* or altered state. When Susan is with her child Gregory, she can be in the "mommy" or "teacher" or "playmate" *trance*. When she is painting watercolors, she finds herself in the "artist" *trance* and when she is with her husband, she may be in the "partner," "friend," or "lover" *trance*. Some of the *trances* are specific and are reinforced by others and their expectations or the interactions we have with them, while some states of alteration have locations, times, duration, functions, and social meanings. Some of the alterations we experience are multifaceted and multilayered with other states of alteration. In other words, they may be state or context dependent or independent. Some alterations happen so frequently and may seem so natural that we barely notice them, if at all. While other alterations seem strange and awkward, there are altered states that we purposely create, such as meditation or acting in a play.

2. Video Camera

This particular intervention allows the individual to gain perspective by asking him or her to approach the scene, memory, experience as if viewing it through a video camera with the ability to change the view or the sound narration. When using this technique, ask the individual to notice anything that a mechanical recording device would not pick up and record.

This technique is an extension of a standard technique in the practice of Cognitive Therapy. The camera technique, in particular, is associated with Albert Ellis. However, extending this to the video camera, we are using it as a *trance* deconstruction mechanism. It is suggested to the client that in entering a situation in which he feels upset or inadequate, that the next time he begins to move into such an identified situation, to become a video camera. The video camera is to become one that is highly sophisticated. It sees nuances of shades or colors, can detect chemical compositions and report them as smell, and records a wide range of audio events. However, what it cannot record are emotions and descriptors of emotions. In essence, the video camera is a reductionistic mechanism that strips the client's interpretation of the event and reduces it to bare facts. This reduces the elements that are feeding into the dysfunctional *trance* and provides a means for *trance* shifting. The following is an example.

"John, I know that each time you go into your boss's office to ask for a raise, you start feeling like a small child, and you report feeling a great deal of discomfort in the pit of your stomach. You have reported to me that at the time you entered the boss's office, you began to make statements to yourself, such as, 'This is like it was back in the principal's office.' This is just like when I had to face my dad with a bad report card,' etc. You then have reported to me that your boss had an angry look on his face. You reported you saw the boss as growing larger, and you growing smaller. You reported that the room seemed very large, and you felt at a distance from it. For your homework, I want you to engage going into the boss's office. As you go into the boss's office, I want you to be the video camera. The video camera will see the doorframes, see the chairs, record colors, record shades within the room, and record high and low pitched voices. Being a sophisticated camera, it also will notice those chemical elements and identify smells. However, the camera will obviously not record anything that cannot be directly seen, heard, or sensed as a chemical element in the environment (such as taste or smell). Thus, the camera will not be recording such things that are non-existent to it, such as an angry posture of the boss, an angry look on the boss's face, scowling, a non-approving look, a large, threatening desk, etc."

"Now what I would like for you to do is to practice this technique in the park or at home. I would like you to feel free to have some fun with it. Become this video camera that is running reels, recording motions, recording action, but is not recording descriptors of any emotions nor making any guesses as to what any of the compilations of colors, movements, or gestures might mean."

3.   Present Time Sensory Trance Alignment *(Reference to page 267)*

Present time sensory alignment is an intervention, which is described in detail on page 267.

4.   Dislocation Trance/Noticing it as a Perpetuation of Trauma

Safe place teaching at will to create the changes. Notice when it is happening and give it a name. *(Reference to page 270)*

5.   Diagramming the Trauma to include Sensory Representations

Diagramming the Trauma will also include associative meanings, referential and associational searches and the associated kinesthetics.

We can read a beautiful poem and experience sadness, anxiety, love, or hate because the power of the words with their associations on the paper begin to stir and connect with the associations within us and fire a complex chemical interaction of associations and firings which lead to emotions. However, if we take the same poem and we diagram it, we break it down to nouns, verbs, or gerunds, and we critically examine it for comma splices, run-on sentences, paragraph construction, etc., we begin to disrupt and destroy the meaning of the poem in terms of its *trance* effect or otherwise *sensory perceptive alteration* of it that has brought about these feelings. In other words, we destroy the art by disrupting the *trance* associated with the art in the same way as has been highlighted by workers in visualization, transformational grammar, and neuro-linguistic programming. It is possible to perform the same type of deconstruction technique with the *cognitive programming* that is running a trauma *trance*. The essence of this is that we actually ask the client to go inside and get in touch with the thought, to identify thought in the form of pictures, thought in the form of auditory experiences, and identify any associated physiological reactions in the body (nausea, tight muscles, headaches, flushing around the ears, etc.). We then painstakingly go back and have the client bring the trauma programming up. Systematically, we begin to analyze if there is a picture, then a sound, or if there is a sound and then a picture, and if the sequence initiates with a sound and then a physiological response followed by a visual response followed by a sound and a physiological response. In other words, we begin to make a recording of the chaining of thought, noting where in this chain a physiological response occurs. We graph this. We then have the individual go back and reconstruct the trauma based on the diagram, checking to see if we are getting the same physiological responses. Failing the same physiological responses, we then adjust our chain of events until we produce them (Caution: Sometimes, what happens is a deconstruction begins to occur when an individual becomes aware that his thought has such a chaining relationship and that this chaining relationship has a relationship to physiological responses). The individual is then instructed to draw a different diagram of the trauma experience using the diagrammatic elements previously recorded so that this time the sound might occur and then the picture, as opposed to the established, on-going sequence of the trauma chain, with the visual and then the sound. After a new sequencing is developed, the client is asked to follow the diagram and begin to run this newly constructed, programmatic chain in place of the old one. This is done three times. The client is then asked to produce further combinations of change within the programming chain, and this, too, is run three times. To address the physiological responses in the trauma chain, if an individual reports having a very tight chest, at the point in the diagram where this is indicated as a physiological response, the client is encouraged to take a very low, deep breath, hold it, and then gradually let this breath seep out. Another way of altering the physiological response is if the client is reporting tension in the back and neck, do some stretching exercises at this point in a trauma chain. By engaging in this, we begin to disrupt the underlying, *cognitive programming*, which disrupts the dysfunctional *trance*, and automatically a *trance* shift occurs.

6.   Building a Congruent and Functional Present Time Trance

Building a congruent and functional present time *trance* based on the elements of *sensory mapping* and the sequencing of the elements within the trauma *trance*, we follow the diagramming sequence noted under "Diagramming Trauma," but in this sequence, we take the picture and sound elements as they were diagrammed initially, and we replace them with pictures and sounds that are occurring in the on-going environment. For instance, if in the face of the stimulus that provokes the trauma *trance* a picture first appeared, then in our newly developed schema we have a picture to appear of something in our current time—a lamp, couch, etc. If next a sound occurred in the diagramming of the trauma *trance*, we have a sound occur and note it in our present-time situation, such as the distant sound of the roadway, the distant sound of a washing machine, etc. If next followed with tightness in the stomach and chest, then in the present time we engage in taking slow, deep breaths as a replacement. In other words, we take the exact diagrammed sequence of *cognitive programming* whose changing leads to a dysfunctional *trance*. We use the diagrammatic elements (pictures, sounds, feelings, etc.), and we use these elements transposed into a present time sense to build a present time *trance* that is aligned with the here and now.

7.   Screen (movie/video) Technique

This technique uses the metaphor of putting the images and sounds out in front of the visual field up on a movie screen.

This has been a technique that in various forms has been utilized by Shaman, hypno-analysts, NLP workers, and other workers in visualization. The client is asked to seat himself comfortably in a chair. Frequently as he is sitting there, we will initiate the technique of *present time sensory alignment,* although this is not mandatory. When we get the okay from the client that he is feeling comfortable, we ask the client to go inside and get in touch with a center or centers that can begin to project a TV screen ten to twelve feet away from the comfortable seating of the client. This can be framed with the client being in the room, or taken a step further, with the client seeing himself in a very comfortable, private, secure movie theater. When we secure the ideomotor signal from the center that it is willing to do this, we ask the center to go ahead and make the appropriate connections and to signal us again when the projection mechanism has been put in place. Upon receiving this designation from the center, we ask the client to go inside and get in touch with the center or centers that are the drivers, projectors, and initiators of the troubling thought, chain of thought, or experiences. When we receive an ideomotor signal from these centers that such contact has been made, we ask the centers if they will be willing to project the thought chain, whether sound or visual, as an experience coming from and around the movie screen. We emphasize to the centers a projection in which the experience is "out there." We then ask the individual to get in touch with other centers that allow the projection to be fast-forwarded, rewound, and allow the sound track to be speeded up or slowed down with the expected distortions. Securing this, we then begin to have the individual fast forward the troubling thought or chain of thoughts on the screen, becoming faster, faster, until the visuals turn into blurs and disappear from the screen. Any associated sounds or auditories become higher pitched, faster, and are reduced to high-pitched squealing and then disappear from the screen. We then ask the centers to do a rewind of the event that was projected. Thus, all the events, even to include the sounds, will take on the distortion of moving backward through space and time, accelerating rapidly in speed as they do so, until they become a blur and disappear from the screen. After training with this technique, the individual is asked to engage in the forward and rewind until the centers will no longer project the images on the screen.

For homework, the client is instructed that any time a stimulus triggers the centers firing this chaining or programming, immediately place this on the screen, and engage in the fast forward, and rewinding until the thought/chaining/programming chaining essentially is "burned out."

8.   Identified Programming Errors *(See programming errors pages 79-91)*

9.   Installation/Replacement

    a.   Spoon feeding technique

    b.   Internal replacement of resources with use of and direction by *neural information centers.*   Ideomotor signaling may be utilized. (*Reference to page 280*)

10. Working with Polarized or non-Assimilated Information Centers *(Reference to page 278)*

11. Homeostatic System Check

We are seeking to come to a resolution between *neural information centers* that may be at odds and in conflict, rather than a disturbance of the *homeostatic* system at that point. (*Reference to page 272*) *also see Updating Centers page 276*).

12. Diamond of Awareness (*Reference to figure 4 on page 171*)

Method of *present time sensory alignment* that emphasizes (I Am Here Now).

This discards I am this or that; or I am there, not here; or I am in the past or future, and not now. Everything within the Diamond, such as I AM HERE NOW is seen as the known and experience-able while things on the outside of the Diamond are seen as the unknown, the created, fabricated, or abstracted requiring some alteration of sensory perception.

13. Life on Life's Terms (*Reference to figure 5 on page 183*)

Teaches the use of *present time sensory alignment* to deconstruct *cognitive programming errors*, confabulatory mapping, and completion errors when new experiences trigger pathological, *homeostatic* responses.

14. Use of Any Part of the Model

    (a)   *Homeostasis*

    (b)   *Neural Information Centers*

    (c)   *Sensory Perceptive Alterations*

    (d)   *Cognitive Programming Errors*

(e)   *Sensory Perceptive Holographic Mapping*

(f)   *Persistent patterns of Trance Clusters*

(g)   *Semantic Reversal Mechanisms*
        All elements and aspects of the model can be used separately or in relationships to initiate *trance* deconstruction.

15. Mind/Body Integration Interrogatory

What are you seeing? What are hearing? What are you feeling? Where are you experiencing that? Notice what physical space it is happening in, be it mind/body or somewhere else. This series of questions begins the focusing on the various interpretations that can occur. Dr. Wolinsky often offered many different techniques for working with energy or emotions (Personal Training, Wolinsky 1992). As you notice an emotion, also become aware of its location in the physical space of the mind/body. What is the emotion's size and/or what is the emotion's shape? Step into the space and notice what occurs. Step out of the space and notice what occurs. Notice the label you have given the space (such as anger, sadness, fear, etc.). Then peel back the label and notice what is behind or underneath the label. Keep experiencing and de-labeling the space until nothing else comes up. Then notice the energy, and let the energy do what the energy does. Other things to notice may be to expand and/or contract the space. Allow full experience of the energy and do not prematurely de-label. At any point, you can ask what observer observes that. Turn your attention around and ask, "What, if anything, has created all of that?"

16. Changing the Physical Aspects of the Identity

Changing posture, breathing, eye movements, and body positioning are all alterations of physical outward manifestations of internal experiences. Some disruption techniques of the outward manifestations of internal experience are as follows: So what does this mean? How do you experience this? When you become aware of your posture, breathing or gestures alter them, and notice what changes occur in your thinking and/or feeling. This is a very simple technique. It actually involves the client changing his posture, breathing, tension, and relaxation in his body by any means necessary that does not conform to the posture, stance, or breathing patterns that are witnessed during a period of being distressed.

John is afraid to disagree with anyone. He begins to have flashbacks of his father telling him he is never to speak back to him, and that he is disrespectful whenever he offers his opinion. He then has other flashbacks of college experiences when he was ridiculed for having ideas that were different from his peers. However, this *cognitive programming* is associated with posturing in which he literally slumps forward, crosses his arms across his chest, looks down, and develops a pattern of very shallow upper chest breathing. The client is asked to visualize himself approaching a conflict situation. As he does, the client is asked to take very low, slow, deep breaths, obviously in contrast to the upper chest, shallow breathing. The client is asked to pull his shoulders back until he feels them grounded against a chair or a wall. The client is asked to look up and look ahead, if not directly at the person, then looking to the side slightly. The client is asked to not only visualize this change in stance, but to physically adopt it as he is visualizing, approaching, and moving through the conflict situation. The client and the therapist next discuss the first signs of postural changes associated with this dysfunctional *trance* state. The client is instructed, "At the first indication of this postural change, then adopt the new scenario of postural changes that we have discussed." The client is given this as practice/homework over the next several days. The goal is that when the client begins to note the chaining of physiological responses developing, he disrupts them by engaging in the new chaining of behavior and thus begins to disrupt the old, dysfunctional *trance* in making way for the organism to replace it with a more functional *trance*.

17. "Ramana Maharshi Technique" *or* "Go Back the Way You Came"

There is a story that a person traveled a great distance to see the Hindu Saint, Ramana Maharshi. Because this person thought he did not know who he was, he felt that this caused him to suffer greatly, and he believed the saint could free him. When he arrived at the feet of Ramana, he said, "Tell me who I am" and Maharshi said, "Go back the way you came." The students of the guru were quite upset and questioned him, saying, "How could you be so cruel?" Maharshi responded, "No, you have misunderstood."

Follow the "I" thought back to where it arose. So when applying this type of questioning or enquiry you ask:

> 1. "Prior to this experience, what were the thoughts or feelings that were being

experienced?" What was the state of the consciousness?

2.   Prior to the event.

3.   Prior to the trauma.

4.   Prior to the belief.

5.   Prior to the chaos.

6.   Prior to being overwhelmed.

7.   Prior to the body-mind.

8.   Prior to the concept.

9.   Prior to the identity.

10.   Prior to the association.

11.   Prior to the memory.

18. Neutral Filter

As you notice your focus of attention on some image, some sound, some feeling, some event, etc., ask yourself to become aware of any judgment, preference, or significance that is being associated with the focus of attention, and then remove it. Notice what, if anything, occurs. As you are working with individuals, become aware of any judgment, preference, or significance that comes up for you in relation to the person or his or her world. Remember that the changes and suggestions that occur need to be congruent within that person's universe, not yours, and he or she must live with the effects and impact, not you.

19. Wolinsky's Maneuver

Whatever you are doing _unknowingly, unconsciously, and unintentionally,_ **now,** _do knowingly, intentionally, and consciously._ Often our patterns of thinking, feeling and responding become automatic or fixed. This procedure has us take things off automatic and notice who, what, when, where and how decisions and responses are made. We can then become aware of the steps to making the decision and re-decide whether it is still workable, now.

20.   Schreiber/Hellams Mapping Paradox

Since all maps, concepts, and beliefs are abstractions, and all languages are symbolic representations of abstractions, we are not attempting to develop a rigid structure or suggest that this is the way. According to the Quantum physicists, all location is relative to position. All positions begin with an "I." Notice that whatever you read or contemplate is just a position that is abstracted from some "I." All of the contemplations are adjustments to the "I" concepts. Become aware of what "I" is affected by, the thought, belief, or idea. Without an "I," there is no map. All maps are "I" generated.

21. Wolinsky Step #2

As you allow yourself to step back to observe the identity, belief, etc., ask yourself", what observer is observing that and what, if anything, created all of that?"

22. The One Question

The singular question is who or what are you being or imagining that you are? From this question proceeds all other identity questions and their functions and purposes or goals. Below are a series of questions that can be asked.

Who or what do you imagine/think/feel/believe that you are? By being that, what, if anything, is wanted? What if anything is not wanted? If that were to occur, what would happen? What would not happen? What or who is being or not being resisted? Who or what authority told you to be that, or told you that, that would happen, or what the result or outcome would be?

Trance deconstruction and reconstruction is an ongoing process. It can occur on its own, or be initiated by the person exploring ways to make changes. Any aspect of energy, space-time, or mass can be altered; and sensory data or its perception may be altered to bring about trance deconstruction. Keep in mind that when there is any change in the Sensory Perceptive Holographic Mapping, then homeostasis will challenge the change, even if it is for the good of the organism. All of these shifts in focus may give one the opportunity to observe/experience the transmutation of identities and energy. In addition, the experience may loosen your trances/associations/references and frames of reference. Where you can, step in the experience, then step out of the experience, allow the experience to dissolve, and then remember, remain prior to your creations and experiences. You are there before the experience.

Installation/Replacement
Spoon-Feeding

1. When a client has difficulty deriving suitable thought replacement, therapist suggests possible replacement.

2. Therapist asks client to "go inside and connect with a *neural information center* that will help us."

3. Therapist asks the center to signal when it can hear the therapist. (This is usually a ideomotor signal.)

4. Once signal is received, center is asked, "Will you assist us in replacing _____(the old thought) with _____(the new thought). Lift one finger for "yes" and two fingers for "no."

5. If answer is "yes," use the model for *Homeostatic System Check* to replace thought, like replacing a behavior.

6. If answer is "no," then proceed to <u>Internal Replacement</u>.

Internal Replacement

1. Therapist asks client to "go inside and connect with a n*eural information center*."

2. Therapist asks center to "signal if it can hear therapist."

3. Therapist presents center with thought that is a *cognitive programming error.*
4. Therapist asks, "Please work with any and all necessary centers to find a replacement."

5. Therapist asks center, "Please signal us when this has been accomplished."

6. When signal is received, therapist asks client to reveal new message.

7. Both apply "test" for appropriate programming (Programming Error Test).

8 If test is passed, therapist utilizes *Homeostatic System Check* with client to complete installation.

9. If "test" is not passed, client and therapist discuss implications for system's approval of a programming error.

The Flame and Light of Consciousness

With the combination of elements and the interaction of forces, the consciousness arises. The consciousness is neither the organism nor the environment it interacts with, but of which it is a part. The organism breathes, consumes, and transmutes the chemicals of the environment interacting with, assimilating, and changing them. That which appears infinite, unchangeable, and permanent becomes that which appears finite, changeable, and impermanent. As Buddha has stated Nirvana is Samsara and Samsara is Nirvana, this is, in fact, a description, a concept and an abstracted representation of the one substance.

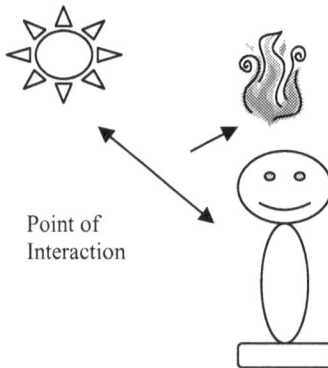

The Flame of Consciousness arises and subsides. It is the Body, it is the Infinite, it is both and neither. It is something in between.

Point of Interaction

The Infinite and the Finite are one. It is an illusion that they are separate.

The body appears to be, and yet it is not. Its appearance creates the illusion of presence and continuance when there is neither. The eight negations of Nagarjuna are an excellent explanation for the consciousness and its illusions.

1. Nothing arises, nothing is created, and nothing is born.
2. Nothing subsides, nothing is eliminated, and nothing dies.
3. Nothing ceases to exist, or can be destroyed.
4. There is no beginning, there is no end.
5. Nothing is the same as anything else, there is no unity.
6. Nothing is different from anything else, no duality.
7. Nothing arises, or comes.
8. Nothing subsides, leaves, departs, or goes.

Sri Nisargadatta Maharaj said to Stephen Wolinsky, "There is no birth, there is no death. There is no person. It is all a concept. It is all an illusion.

The flame of consciousness is a biological process that illuminates and projects images, shapes, and names onto the canvas of the void. It is "Maya" the great illusion of the "I" and its universe. In the Quantum world, the universe and the "I" blink in and out of existence 14 times a second.

I call this capacity for entering other focal points of consciousness-- love; you may give it any name you like. Love says; 'I am everything'. Wisdom says; 'I am nothing'. Between these two, my life flows (I Am That, Sri Nisargadatta Maharaj, 1973).

Is there a world outside of your knowledge? Can you go beyond what you know? You may postulate a world beyond the mind, but it will remain a concept, unproved and unprovable. Your experience is your proof, and it is valid for you only. Who else can have your experience, when the other person is only as real as he appears in your experience? (<u>I Am That</u>, Sri Nisargadatta Maharaj, 1973).

Bibliography

Ackerknecht, Erwin (1968). *A Short History of Psychiatry.* New York, N.Y.: Hafner Publishers

Albrecht, Karl, (1986). *Stress & the Manager.* Englewood, New Jersey: Prentice Hall Inc.

Alexander, Franz Gabriell & Selesnick, Sheldon T. (1966). *The History of Psychiatry.* New York, N.Y.: Harper & Row.

Almaas, A. H. (1986). *The Void.* Berkeley, California: Diamond Books.

----------------(1996). *The Point of Existence.* Berkeley, California: Diamond Books.

----------------(1998). *Essence With The Elixir of Enlightenment.* York Beach, Maine: Samuel Weiser, Inc.

----------------(1987). *Diamond Heart Book One: The Real Man.* Berkeley, California: Diamond Books.

----------------(1987). *Diamond Heart Book Two: The Freedom To Be.* Berkeley, California: Diamond Books.

----------------(1990). *Diamond Heart Book Three: Being And The Meaning Of Life.* Berkeley, California: Diamond Books.

----------------. (1992). *Work on the Super Ego.* Berkeley, California: Diamond Books.

----------------. (1998). *Facets Of Unity: The Enneagram Of Holy Ideas.* Berkeley, California: Diamond Books.

----------------*(1998). The Pearl Beyond Price. Berkeley, California: Diamond Books.*

American Psychiatric Association (1987). *Diagnostic and Statistical Manual of Mental Disorders (Third Edition Revised). Washington, D.C.*

American Psychiatric Association (1994). *Diagnostic and Statistical Manuel of Mental Disorders–TR, (4ᵗʰ Edition). Washington, D.C.: Author.*

Andreas, Connirae; Andreas Steve (1987). *Change Your Mind and Keep the Change. Moab, Utah: Real People Press.*

----------------(1989). *Heart of the Mind. Moab, Utah: Real People Press.*

Andreas, Steve (2006) *Six Blind Elephants Understanding Ourselves and Each Other, Volume I: Fundamental Principles of Scope and Category. Moab Utah: Real People Press.*

----------------(2006) *Six Blind Elephants Understanding Ourselves and Each Other, Volume II. Applications and Explorations of Scope and Category. Moab, Ut: Real People Press.*

Assagioli, Roberto (1965). *Psycho-synthesis, A Collection of Basic Writings. New York, N.Y.: Penguin Group.*

Bandler, Richard & Grinder, John (1975). *Patterns of the Hypnotic Techniques of Milton H. Erickson, MD, Volume I. Scotts Valley, California: Meta Publications.*

----------------(1975). *Patterns of the Hypnotic Techniques of Milton H. Erickson, MD, Volume II. Scotts Valley, California: Meta Publications.*

----------------(1975). *The Structure of Magic, Volume I. Palo Alto, California: Science and Behavior Books.*

----------------(1975). *The Structure of Magic, Volume II. Palo Alto, California: Science and Behavior Books.*

----------------(1979). *Frogs into Princes. Neuro-linguistic Programming. Moab, Utah: Real People Press.*

----------------(1981). *Trance-formations. Moab, Utah: Real People Press.*

----------------(1982). *Reframing – Neuro Linguistic Programming and the Transformation of Meaning. Moab, Utah: Real People Press.*

Bandler, Richard & MacDonald, Will (1988). *An Insider's Guide to Sub-Modalities. Cupertino, California: Meta Publications.*

Bandler, Richard (1985). *Using Your Brain for Change. Moab, Utah: Real People Press*

Bandura , A. (1969). *Principles of Behavior Modification. New York, N. Y.: Holt.*

Barlow, David H., Ph.D. & Rapee, Ronald (1991). *Chronic Anxiety. New York, N. Y.: The Guilford Press.*

Beck, Aaron; Rush, John; Shaw, Brian & Emory, Gary (1979). *Cognitive Therapy of Depression. New York, N.Y.*

Bentov, Itzhak (1977). *Stalking the Wild Pendulum. On the Mechanics of Consciousness. Rochester, Vermont: Destiny Books*

Berg, Insoo Kim (1994). *Family Based Services. New York, NY: W. W. Norton & Company*

Bisbey, Stephen & Bisbey, Lori Beth (1998). *Brief Therapy for Post Traumatic Stress Disorder. West Susix, England: John Wiley & Sons Publishers*

Bloch, James P., (1991). *Assessment and Treatment of Multiple Personality and Dissociative Disorders, Professional Resource Press; Sarasota, Fla.:*

305

Bodenhamer, Bob & Hall, Michael L. (1998). *Adventures with Time Lines*. Capitola, California: Meta Publications.

----------------(1999). *The User's Manual of the Brain, Volume One*. Wales, UK: Crown House.

----------------(1999). *The User's Manual of the Brain, Volume Two*. Wales, UK: Crown House Publishing Limited.

Borrows, George (1976). *Commentaries on the Causes, Forms, Symptoms and Treatment, Moral and Medical, of Insanity*. New York, N.Y.: Arno Press.

Bowlby, J. (1969). *Attachment and Loss: Volume I, Attachment*. New York, N.Y.: Basic Books.

Boyer, Bryce, M.D., & Giovacchinni, Peter L. (1967). *Psycho-Analytic Treatment of Characterological and Schizophrenic Disorders*. New York, N.Y.: Science House, Inc.

Bradshaw, John (1988). *Healing the Shame that Binds You*. Deerfield Beach, Florida: Health Communications, Inc.

Bramwell, J. M. (1903). *Hypnotism, Its History, Practice and Theory*. Philadelphia, Pennsylvania: J. B Lippincott Company.

Brennan, Barbara Ann (1987). *Hands of the Light: A Guide to Healing Through the Human Energy Field*. New York, N.Y.: Bantam Books.

Brennan, Barbara Ann (1993). *Light Emerging, The Journey of Personal Healing*. New York, N.Y: Bantam Books.

Briggs, John & Peat, F. David (1989). *Turbulent Mirror*. New York, N. Y.: Harper & Row Publishers.

Burns, David D., M.D. (1980). *Feeling Good: The New Mood Therapy- Revised and Updated, Avon Books, Harper Collins Publishers*. New York, N.Y.

Byron, T (1992). *The Geo-cubic Matrix Flashing in the Universe and the Cosmos of Energy Matter Caught in its Time Flow Angels Camp, California: T.Bryon G Publishing*

Capra, F. (1976) *The Tao of Physics. New York, N.Y.: Bantam Books.*

Carnes, Patrick J. (1981). *Family Development I, Understanding Us. Minneapolis, Minnesota: Interpersonal Communications Programs, Inc.*

Castaneda Carlos (1991) *Journey to Ixtlan: The Lessons of Don Juan: New York, N. Y.: Washington Square Press.*

-----------------(1991). *The Fire From Within. New York, N. Y.: Washington Square Press.*

----------------(1968). *The Teachings of Don Juan: A Yaqui Way of Knowledge. New York, N. Y.: Washington Square Press.*

----------------(1971). *A Separate Reality. New York, N. Y.: Washington Square Press.*

----------------(1974). *Tales of Power. New York, N. Y.: Washington Square Press.*

----------------(1977). *The Second Ring of Power. New York, N. Y.: Washington Square Press.*

Castaneda, Carlos (1981). *The Eagles Gift. New York, N. Y.: Washington Square Press*

----------------(1987). *The Power of Silence. New York, N. Y.: Washington Square Press.*

----------------(1993). *The Art of Dreaming. New York, N. Y.: Harper Collins Books.*

Cheek, D. B., M.D. & LeCron, L. M. (1968). *Clinical Hypnotherapy. New York, N.Y.: Grune & Stratton Inc.*

Chia, Mantak & Winn, Michael (1984). *Taoist Secrets of Love. Santa Fe, New Mexico: Aurora Press.*

Chia, Mantak (1983). Awaken Healing Energy Through the Tao. Santa Fe, New Mexico: Aurora Press.

Cline, Foster, M.D. & Fay, Jim (1990). Parenting with Love & Logic. Colorado Springs, Colorado: Pinon Press.

Coué', Émile (1923). How to Practice Suggestion & Auto Suggestion. Santa Fe, New Mexico: Sun Publishing.

Csikszentmihalyi, Miahly (1990). Flow the Psychology of Optimal Experience. New York, N. Y.: Harper & Row Publishers.

Damasio, A. (1994). Descarte's Error: Emotion, Reason and the Human Brain. New York, N.Y.: Grosset/Putnam.

----------------(2003). Looking for Spinoza, Joy, Sorrow and the Feeling Brain. New York, N.Y.: Harcourt Books.

Darwin, C. (1884). The expression of emotions in man and animals. Chicago, Illinois: University of Chicago Press.

Davis, Martha Eshelman, Elizabeth Robbins; McKay, Matthew, Ph.D (1981). The Relaxation & Stress Reduction Workbook. Oakland, California: New Harbinger Publications, Inc.

De Nicolas, Antonio (1990). The Bhagavad-Gita. York Beach, Mexico: Nicolas Hays, Inc.

Doane, Benjamin K., Klein, Raymond and Erlbaum, Lawrence (1994). Psychological Concepts and Dissociative Disorders. LEA, Inc., New York, N.Y.

Dolan, Yvonne M. (1991). *Resolving Sexual Abuse, Solution Focused Therapy and Ericksonian Hypnosis for Adult Survivors.* New York, N.Y.: W.W. Norton & Company.

----------------(1985). *A Path with a Heart, Ericksonian Utilization with Resistant and Chronic Clients.* New York, N.Y.: Brunner/Mazel.

Dunn, Jean (Editor) (1982). *Seeds of Consciousness, The Wisdom of Sri Nisargadatta Maharaj.* Durham, N.C.: Acorn Press.

----------------(1985). *Prior to Consciousness, Talks With Sri Nisargadatta Maharaj.* Durham, N.C.: Acorn Press.

----------------(1994). *Consciousness & the Absolute, The Final Talks With Sri Nisargadatta Maharaj.* Durham, N.C.: Acorn Press.

Durlacher, James, M.D. (1994). *Freedom From Fear Forever.* Mesa, Arizona: Van Ness Publishing.

Earle, Pliny (1972) (1886 Reprint Edition). *The Curability of Insanity.* New York, N.Y.: Arno Press.

Ecker, Bruce & Hulley, Laurel (1996). *Depth Oriented Brief Therapy.* San Francisco, California: Jossey-Bass Publishers.

Eleven, Pamela (1988). *Cycles of Powers.* Ukiah, California: Health Communications Inc.

Erickson, Milton H. M.D. Edited by Ernest L Rossi & Margaret O. Ryan (1983). *Healing in Hypnosis Volume I.* New York, N.Y.: Irvington Publishers.

----------------(1985). *Life Reframing in Hypnosis.* New York, N.Y.: Irvington Publishers.

Erickson, Milton H., M.D. & Cooper, Lynn F (1959). *Time Distortion in Hypnosis.* New York, N.Y.: Irvington Publishers.

Erickson, M.H. and Rossi, E.L. (1989). *The February Man, Evolving Consciousness and Facilitating New Identity in Hypnotherapy.* New York, N.Y.: Brunner/Mazel.

Festinger, Leon (1957). *A Theory of Cognitive Dissonance.* Stanford CA: Stanford University Press.

Flint, Garry A Ph.D. (1999). *Emotional Freedom.* Vernon, B. C.: Neo Sol Terric Enterprises.

Foa, Edna B., Ph.D. &R. Reid Wilson, Ph.D. (1991). *STOP Obsessing.* New York, N.Y.: Bantam Books.

Forest, Donna B, Ed.S (2000). *Character Under Construction.* Chapin, SC: Youth Light, Inc.

Fosha, Diana, Ph.D. (2000). *The Transforming Power of Affect.* New York, N. Y.: Basic Books.

Frankl, Viktor E. (1992). *Search for Meaning: An Introduction to Logo Therapy.* Boston, Massachusetts: Beacon Press.

French, Gerald D & Harris, Chrys J (1999). *Traumatic Incident Reduction.* Boca Ratan, Florida: CRC Press.

Freud, Ernest L., Editor (Translated by Tonya & James Stern) (1960). *Letters of Sigmund Freud.* New York, N. Y.: Basic Books.

Freud, Sigmun, Edited by James Strachey (1959). *Collected Papers, Volume I through IV.* New York, N. Y.: Basic Books.

Gallo, Fred P., Ph.D. & Vincenzi, Harry, EdD (2000). *Energy Tapping.* Oakland, California: New Harbinger Publications

Gallo, Fred P., Ph.D. (2000). *Energy Diagnostic and Treatment Methods.* New York, N. Y.: W. W. Norton & Company.

Gawain, Shakti (1978). *Creative Visualization.* New York, N.Y.: MJF Books.

----------------(1986). *Living in the Light*. Mill Valley, California: Nataraj Publishing.

----------------(1993). *The Path of Transformation*. Mill Valley, California: Nataraj Publishing.

Gendlin, Eugene, Ph.D. (1978). *Focusing*. New York, N.Y.: Bantam Book.

Gibson, Eleanor, (1969). *Principals of Perceptual Learning & Development*. Englewood Cliffs, New Jersey: Prentice-Hall, Inc.

Gilligan, Stephen G. (1987). *Therapeutic Trances*. New York, N.Y.: Brunner/Mazel Publishers.

Glasser, William M.D. & Glasser, Carleen (1999). *The Language of Choice Theory*. New York, N. Y.: Harper Collins.

Gleick, James (1987). *Chaos*. New York, N. Y.: Penguin Books.

Golas, Thaddeus (1971). *The Lazy Man's Guide to Enlightenment*. New York. Bantam Books

Goldstein, Allan & Stainback, Berry (1987). *Overcoming Agoraphobia*. New York, N.Y.: Viking Penguin Inc.

Goleman, Daniel (1985). *Vital Lives, Simple Truths*. New York, N. Y.: Simon & Schuste.r

----------------(1995). *Emotional Intelligence*. New York, N. Y.: Bantam Books.

----------------(1988). *The Meditative Mind: The Varieties of Meditative Experience*, New York, N.Y.: Putnam Books.

Gordon, David C. (1978). *Therapeutic Metaphors: Helping Others Through the Looking Glass*. Capitola, California; Meta Publications.

Goulding, M.M. & Goulding, R.L. (1997). *Changing Lives Through Redecision Therapy*. *(Revised Edition)*. New York, N.Y.: Grove.

Grabhorn, Lynn (1992). *Beyond the Twelve Steps: Road Map to a New Life.* York Beach, Maine: Nicolas Hays Inc.

Halevi, Z'ev Ben Shimon (1977). *A Kabbalistic Universe.* York Beach, Maine: Samuel Weiser, Inc.

Haley, Jay (1976). *Problem Solving Therapy.* San Francisco, California. Josey Bass Inc Publishers.

Hanh, Thich Nhat (1975). *The Miracle of Mindfulness.* Boston, Massachusetts: Beacon Press Books.

----------------(1988). *The Heart of Understanding Commentaries on the Prajmaparamita Heart Sutra.* Berkeley, California; Parallax Press.

----------------(1993). *The Blooming of A Lotus.* Boston, Massachusetts: Beacon Press

Hartman, Taylor, (1987). *The Color Code.* New York, N. Y.: Simon & Schuster.

Havens, Ronald A., & Walters, Catherine, M.A. (1989). *Hypnotherapy Scripts.* New York, N.Y.: Brunner/Mazel Publishers.

Hefler, Roy E., M.D. (1978). *Childhood Comes First.* East Lansing, Michigan.

Heller, Steven & Steele, Terry (1978). *Monsters & Magical Sticks: There's No Such Thing As Hypnosis.* Tempe, Arizona: New Falcon Publications.

Helmstetter, Shad (1987). *The Self-Talk Solution.* New York, N. Y.: William Morrow & Company, Inc.

Herbert, N. (1985). *Quantum Reality.* New York, N.Y.: Anchor Press.

Hewitt, Sandra K., (1999). *Assessing Allegations of Sexual Abuse in Preschool Children.* Thousand Oaks, California: Sage Publications.

Horner, Althea J. M.D. (1984). *Object Relations and the Developing Ego in Therapy.* North Vale, N. J.: Jason Aronson, Inc.

Hudson, Patricia O'Hanlon & O'Hanlon, William Hudson (1991). *Rewriting Love Stories.* New York: W. W. Norton & Co

Hunter, Marlene E, M.D. (1988). *Daydreams For Discovery.* West Vancouver, B C: Seawalk Press LTD.

Ivey, Allen & Simek-Downing, Lynn (1980). *Counseling & Psychotherapy Skills, Theories and Practice.* Englewood Cliffs, New Jersey: Prentice-Hall.

Izard, C.E. (1977). *Human Emotions.* New York, N.Y.: Plenum.

James, T. & Woodsmall, W. (1988). *Time Line Therapy and The Basis of Personality.* Capitola, California: Meta Publications, Inc.

Johnson, Stephen M., (1994). *Character Styles.* New York, NY: W. W. Norton & Company.

Jones, Ernest, M.D. (1955). *The Life and Work of Sigmund Freud, Volume One and Two.* New York N. Y.: Basic Books.

Jones, James H (2001). *Are Your Kids Driving You Nuts?* Santa Ana, California: James H Jones Publishing.

Kaku, Michio (1994). *Hyper-Space.* New York: Double Day Anchor Book.

Kaplin, Aryeh (1990). *Sefer Yetzirah. The Book of Creation.* York Beach, Maine: Samuel Weiser, Inc.

Katchadourian, Herant A, M.D. & Lunde, Donald, M.D. (1972). *Fundamentals of Human Sexuality.* New York, N. Y.: Holt, Rinehart and Winston, Inc.

*Korzybski, A. (1993).   Science and Sanity, An
introduction to non-Aristotelian systems and
general semantics (5th Edition). Brooklyn, N.Y.:
Institute of General Semantics.*

*Krishnamurti, J (1996).   Total Freedom.   San
Francisco, California: Harper Publishers.*

*Krishnamaruti,   U.G.   (1982.   The   Mystique   of
Enlightenment: The unrational Ideas of a man
called U.G. India: Dinesh.*

*-----------------(1988).   The Mind is Myth.   Disquieting
Conversations with the Man called U.G.India:
Dinesh Publications.*

*Kroeger, William S. (1977). Clinical and Experimental
Hypnosis, Second Edition.   Philadelphia,
Pennsylvania: J. B. Lippincott Company.*

*Landis, Richard E (1991). Interactive Imageries For
Habit, Feeling & Behavior Changes, Volume
One, Self Re-parenting Guided Imageries.
Laguna Niguel, California: Garrlitea
Professional Publications.*

*Landis, Richard E (1991). Interactive Imageries for
Habit, Feeling & Behavior changes, Volume
Two: Parts-work. Santa Ana, California.
Orange County Society of Ericksonian
Professional Hypnosis Publications.*

*Lankton, Stephen R. & Lankton, Carol H. (1983). The
Answer Within.   New York, N. Y.:
Brunner/Mazel, Inc.*

*Lankton, Stephen, ACSW (1980).   Practical Magic.
Cupertino, California: Meta Publications.*

*LeDoux, Joseph (1996). The Emotional Brain. New
York, N. Y.: Simon & Schuster.*

*LeDoux, Joseph (2002). Synaptic Self. New York,
N.Y.: Viking Penguin.*

*Levi, Eliphas (1984). The Book of Splendours. York
Beach, Maine: Samuel Weiser, Inc.*

Levine, Barbara H. (1991). *Your Body Believes Every Word You Say.* Boulder Creek, California: Asian Publishing Company.

Levine, Peter A., w/Anne Frederick (1997). *Waking the Tiger, Healing Trauma.* Berkeley, California: North Atlantic Books.

Loverne, John D. (1991). *Pathways to Reality.* New York, N. Y.: Brunner/Mazel, Inc.

Maharaj, Nisargadatta, Sri (Translated by Maurice Frydeman) (1973). *I Am That.* Durham, N.C.: Acorn Press.

Mahler, M. (1968) *On the Human Symbiosis and Vicissitudes of Individuation.* New York, N.Y.: International Universe Press.

Maltz, Maxwell, M.D. (1973). *Psycho-Cybernetics.* North Hollywood, California: Wilshore Book Company.

Manfield, Phillip (Editor) (1998). *Extending EMDR.* New York, N.Y.: W. W. Norton & Company Inc.

Markway, Barbara G; Carmin, Cheryl N.; Pollard, Alex C; Flynn, Teresa (Editors) (1992). *Dying of Embarrassment.* Oakland, California: New Harbinger Publishers, Inc.

Maultsby, Maxie C., Jr. (1990). *Rational Behavior Therapy, Howard University-College of Medicine.*

Mascaro', Juan (Translator) (1965). *The Upanishads.* New York, NY. Penguin Books.

McKay, Matthew, Fanning, Patrick (1991). *Prisoners of Belief.* Oakland, California: New Harbinger Publications Inc.

McKay, Matthew, Rogers, Peter; Blade, Joan; Gose, Richard (1984). *The Divorce Book.* Oakland, California: New Harbinger Publications, Inc.

McKay, Matthew, Rogers, Peter, McKay, Judith (1989). *When Anger Hurts.* Oakland, California: New Harbinger Press.

315

Meichenbalm, D. B (1977). *Cognitive Behavior Modification: An Integrative Approach.* New York, N.Y.: Plenam Press.

Miller, Alice (1983). *For Your Own Good.* New York, N. Y.: Farror-Straus Geroux.

Miller, Alice (1997). *The Drama of the Gifted Child.* New York, NY: Basic Books.

Mills, Joyce C. & Crowley, Richard J. (1986). *Therapeutic Metaphors for Children and the Child Within.* New York, N. Y.: Brunner/Mazel Inc.

Gander, Mary J. & Gardiner, Harry W. (1981). *Child and Adolescent Development.* Boston, Massachusetts: Little, Brown and Company.

Morrison, James, M.D. (1995). *DSM-IV Made Easy: The Clinician's Guide to Diagnosis.* New York, N.Y.: Guilford Press.

Myer, Isaac (1888). *Qabbalah.* New York, N. Y.: Samuel Weiser, Inc.

Napier, N. (1996). *Recreating Yourself, Increasing Self Esteem through imaging, and Self Hypnosis.* New York, N. Y.: Norton Publishers

O'Hanlon, William Hudson (1987). *Tap Roots Underlying Principles of Milton Erickson's Therapy & Hypnosis.* New York, N.Y.: W.W. Norton and Company.

O'Hanlon, William Hudson, Martin, Michael (1992) *Solution Oriented Hypnosis.* New York, N. Y.: W. W. Norton & Company

Orstein, Robert & Thompson, Richard F. (1984). *The Amazing Brain.* Boston, Massachusetts: Houghton Mifflin Company.

Osborne, Arthur (Editor) (1972). *The Collected Works of Ramana Maharshi.* York Beach, Maine: Samuel Weiser, Inc.

Ouspensky, P. D. (1997). In Search of the Miraculous. Orlando, Florida: Harcourt Brace &Company.

Overdurf, John and Silverthorn, Julie (1994). Training Trances, Multi Level Communication In Therapy & Training. Portland, Oregon; Metamorphous Press.

Page, Michael, (1988). The Power of Chi. Thorsona, London: Aquarian Press

Palmer, Harry (1994). Resurfacing. Altamonte Springs, Florida: Stars Edge International.

Paulson, Genevieve Lewis (1993). Kundalini and the Chakras. St. Paul, Minnesota: Llewellyn Publications, Inc.

Pavlov, I.P. (1960). Conditioned Reflexes. New York, N.Y.: Dover (Original work published in 1927).

Pearson, Carol S. (1991). Awakening The Heroes Within. New York, NY: Harpers, Collins Publishers.

Perls, Fritz, M.D. (1992). Gestalt Therapy Verbatim.

Perls, Fritz (1942) Ego, Hunger and Aggression. Durban, South Africa.: Knox.

Perls, F. (1969) In and Out of the Garbage Pail. Moab, Utah: Real People Press.

Pert, Candace (1997) Molecules of Emotion. New York, NY: Scribner

Phillips, Maggie (2000). Finding the Energy to Heal. New York, N Y.: W. W. Norton & Company.

Piaget, Jean (2000). The Psychology of the Child. New York, N. Y.: Basic Books.

Pirsig, Robert M. (1974). Zen and the Art of Motorcycle Maintenance. New York, N. Y.: Bantam Books.

Powell, Robert (Editor) (1994). The Ultimate Medicine As Prescribed by Sri Nisargadatta Maharaj. San Diego, California: Blue Dove Press

----------------(1996. *The Experience of Nothingness.
San Diego, California: Blue Dove Press.*
Prince, A. F. & Mou – Jay, Wong (1990). *The
Diamond Sutra, & The Sutra of Hui - Neng.
Boston, Mass: Shambhala Press.*
Putnam, F. W. (1989). *Diagnoses and Treatment of
Multiple Personality Disorder. New York, N.Y.:
Guilford Press.*
Raphael (1993). *Pathway of Fire. York Beach, Maine:
Samuel Weiser, Inc.*
Ratner, Ellen (1990). *The Other Side of the Family.
Deerfield   Beach,   Florida: Health
Communications Inc.*
Resnikoff, Howard L. (1989). *The Illusion of Reality.
New York, N. Y.: Springer-Verlag.*
Riso, Don Richard (1992).   *Discovering Your
Personality Type. New York, N.Y.: Houghton
Mifflin Company.*
Rogers, Carl (1951).   *Client Centered Therapy.
Boston,   Massachusetts: Houghton   Mifflin
Company.*
Ross, C. A. (1989). *Multiple Personality Disorder:
Diagnosis, Clinical Features, Second Treatment.
New York, N.Y.: Wiley Publishing.*
Rossi, E. L (1986) *The Psychobiology of Mind Body
Healing, New Concepts of Therapeutic Hypnosis.
New York: N.Y.: W.W. Norton and Company.*
Roth, Gabrielle (1989). *Maps to Ecstasy. Mill Valley,
California: Nataraj Publishing.*
Rothschild, Babette (2000). *The Body Remembers: The
Psychophysiology of Trauma and Treatment.
New York, N.Y.: W.W. Norton and Company.*
Rutter, Michael, Izard, Carrol, & Read, Peter B (Edited)
(1986).   *Depression in Young People,
Developmental and Clinical Perspectives. New
York, N.Y.: The Gilford Press.*

Schacter, D. (1996). Searching for Memory. New York, N.Y.: Basic Books.

Schore, Allan N (1994). Affect Regulation & the Origin of the Self – The Neurobiology of Emotional Development. Hillsdale, New Jersey; Lawrence Erlbaum Associates Publishers.

Schmidt, Shirley Jean (2002). Developmental Needs Meeting Strategy for EMDR Therapists. San Antonio, Texas.

Schultz, J. (1959). Autogenic Training. New York, N. Y.: Grune & Stratton Publishers.

Schwartz, Richard C. (1995). Internal Family Systems Therapy. New York, N. Y.: Guilford Press.

Selye, Hans (1984) The Stress of Life. New York, N.Y.: McGraw-Hill Publishers.

Shah, Idries (1964). The Sufis. New York, N. Y.: Double Day Publishers.

----------------(1978). Learning How to Learn: Psychology and Spirituality in the Sufis Way. San Francisco, California: Harper & Row.

---------------(1978). A Perfumed Scorpion: The Way to the Way. San Francisco, California: Harper & Row.

Shapiro, Francine, (2001). Eye Movement Desensitization and Reprocessing, Second Edition. New York, N.Y.: Guilford Press.

Shapiro, Francine (1995). Eye Movement Desensitization & Reprocessing. New York, NY: The Guilford Press.

Sherman, Robert & Freeman, Norma. (1986). Handbook & Structured Techniques in Marriage & Family Therapy. New York, N.Y.: Brunner/Mazel Publishers.

Simonton, O. C. (1992). Getting Well Again. New York, N.Y.: Bantam Books.

319

Singh, Jaideva, (1980). *The Divine Creative Pulsation. Delhi, India: Motilal Banarsidass Publishers.*

----------------(1979). *Siva Sutras. The Yoga of Supreme Identity. Delhi, Indiana: Motilal Banarsidass Publisher.*

Small, Jacquelyn (1982). *Transformers. New York, N.Y.: Bantam Books.*

Smalley, Gary. (1988). *Hidden Keys to Loving Relationships. Paoli, Pennsylvania: Relationships Today, Inc.*

Speeth, Kathleen Riordan (1989). *The Gurdjieff Work. New York, N. Y.: G. P. Putnam's Sons.*

Spiegel, D. Editor (1993). *Dissociative Disorders: A Clinical Review. Lutherville, Maryland: Sidran Press.*

Spiegel, Herbert & Spiegel, David (1987). *Trance and Treatment. New York, N.Y.: American Psychiatric Press Inc.*

Starr, Kara (1989). *Merlin's Journal of Time. Solana Beach, California: Raven Starr Publications*

Stevens, John O. (1971). *Awareness, Exploring Experimenting, Experiencing. New York: Bantam Books.*

Stone, Hal & Sidra (1989). *Embracing Ourselves. San Rafael, California: New World Library.*

Stone, Hal & Sidra (1993). *Embracing Your Inner Critic. New York, NY: Harper Collins Publishers.*

Straus, Roger A., (1982). *Strategic Self-Hypnosis. Englewood Cliffs, New Jersey: Prentice Hall, Inc.*

Suares, Carlo (1992). *The Cipher of Genesis. York Beach, Maine: Samuel Weiser, Inc.*

Talbot, Michael (1988). *Beyond the Quantum. New York, N. Y.: Bantam Books.*

----------------(1992). *The Holographic Universe. New York, NY: Harper Perennial.*

Tinker, R H. & Wilson, S. A. (1999). *Through the Eyes of a Child: EMDR with Children. New York, N.Y.: Norton Publishers.*

Tulka, Tarthang (1977). *Time, Space and Knowledge. Berkeley, California: Dharma Publishing.*

Tzu Lao translated by John Chu (1961). *Tao Teh Ching. Boston, Massachusetts: Shambhala Publisher.*

Van der Kolk, B. A., M.D. (1994). *The Body Keeps the Score: Memory and the Evolving Psychobiology of Posttraumatic Stress. Harvard Review of Psychiatry.*

Venkatesananda, Swami (Translator) (1976). *The Supreme Yoga: A New Translation Volume 1, Himalayas, India, Tehri.*

----------------(1976). *The Supreme Yoga: A New Translation Volume 2. Himalayas, India, Tehri.*

Watzlawick, Paul,; Weakland, John,ChE; and Fisch, Richard, M.D. (1974). *Change Principles of Problem Formation and Problem Resolution. New York, N.Y....: W.W. Norton and Company.*

W. Bill (2001). *4th Edition Big Book: World Services Inc.*

Wilson, R. Reid (1986). *Don't Panic: Taking Control of Anxiety Attacks. New York, NY: Harper & Row Publishers.*

Wolf, Fred Allan (1988). *Parallel Universes. New York, N. Y.: Simon & Schuster.*

Wolinsky, Stephen (1996). *Hearts on Fire, The Tao of Mediation. San Diego, California: Blue Dove Press.*

----------------(1991. *Trances Peoples Live. Las Vega, Nevada: Bramble Books.*

---------------(1993). *Quantum Consciousness. Las Vega, Nevada: Bramble Books.*

---------------(1993). *The Dark Side of the Inner Child. The Next Step. Norfolk, Connecticut: Bramble Books.*

---------------(1994). *The Tao of Chaos. BearsVille, New York: Bramble Books.*

---------------(1999). *The Way of the Human. Volume One. Capitola, California: Quantum Institute Press.*

Wolinsky, Stephen (1999). *The Way of the Human. Volume Three. Capitola, California. Quantum Institute Press.*

---------------(1999). *The Way of the Human. Volume Two. Capitola, California: Quantum Institute Press.*

---------------(2000). *Intimate Relationships. Capitola, California.*

---------------(2000). *I Am That I Am. Capitola, California: Quantum Institute Press.*

---------------(2000). *The Beginners Guide to Quantum Psychology. Capitola, California.*

---------------(2002). *You Are Not: Beyond the Three Veils of Consciousness. Capitola, California.*

---------------(2003). *Walden III: In Search of A Utopian Nirvana. Capitola, California: Quantum Institute Press.*

---------------(2005). *The Nirvana Sutras and Advaita-Vedanta. Capitola, California: Quantum Institute Press.*

Woolfolk, Robert L. & Lehrer, Paul M., Editors (1984). *Principals and Practice of Stress Management. New York, N. Y.* *

Young, Jeffrey,; Klosko, Janet, (1993). *Reinventing Your Life, New York, N.Y.: A Dutton Book.*

Zukav, Gary (1989). *The Seat of the Soul. New York, NY: Simon & Schuster.*

Video, DVD and Audio Material

Andreas, Steve & Connirae (1986). *The Swish Pattern. DVD, Evergreen, Colorado: NLP Comprehensive.*

Araoz, Daniel L. ED.D. (1984). *Self-Transformation Through the New Hypnosis. Audio Cassette Series. New York, N.Y.: BMA Audio Cassette Publications.*

Arntz, William (2004). *What the Bleep Do We Know!? Twentieth Century Fox.*

Cameron-Bandler, Leslie and Michael LeBeau (1984). *NLP Video Tape, Home Study Program: Demonstrations of Patterns, 109 minute. Boulder, Colorado: Future Pace, Inc.*

Hendricks, Gay (1989). *The Art of Breathing and Centering: A Workbook and Audio Cassette. New York, N.Y.: St. Martin's Press.*

Klein, Ron (2000). *Eye Movement Integration. Video Cassette: American Hypnosis Training Academy.*

Kubrick, Stanley (1968). *2001. A Space Odyssey. Borgham, England: MGM-British Studios.*

Levine, Peter A. (1999). *Healing Trauma, Restoring the Wisdom of Your Body. 9 Hour Audio Cassette Series. Boulder, Colorado: Sounds True.*

Orange County Society for Ericksonian Psychotherapy and Hypnosis (1978). *Now You Wanted A Trance Demonstrated Today. Milton H. Erickson, M.D., Garden Grove, California: InfoMedix.*

Wolinsky, Stephen (2004). *I Am That I Am. DVD.* *www.netinetifilms.com*

Wolinsky, Stephen (2006). *Nirvana Means Extinction, I Am That I Am Part Two. DVD.* *www.netinetifilms.com*

Wolinsky, Stephen (2007). I Am That I Am part III, Prior to Self Consciousness. DVD. www.netinetifilms.com

Wolinsky, Stephen (2002). Awakening From the Trance of Self, An Experiential Course on Developing Multidimensional Awareness. 9-hour audiocassette series. Boulder, Colorado: Sounds True. www.soundstrue.com

Yu, Ronny (2006). Fearless: Rogue Pictures.

www.ingramcontent.com/pod-product-compliance
Lightning Source LLC
Chambersburg PA
CBHW020655270326
41928CB00005B/129